Prolog
Programming
for Students

With Expert Systems and
Artificial Intelligence Topics

David Callear

Senior Lecturer in Information Science,
University of Portsmouth

DP Publications Ltd
Aldine Place
London W12 8AW

1994

A CIP catalogue record for this book is available from the British Library.

ISBN 1 85805 093 6

Typeset by Jordan & Jordan, Fareham, Hampshire

Printed in Great Britain by Ashford Colour Press, Gosport, Hampshire

Preface

Aim

This book covers all that is needed in an introductory Prolog course lasting one year, introducing such Artificial Intelligence topics as are suitable for students coming new to Prolog. It is aimed at average first or second year degree students, and it assumes that such students have access to a suitable good Prolog interpreter, such as LPA Prolog. (Though Public Domain Prolog, a less elaborate free version, can be used.) It also assumes that good students with an aptitude for research will follow it up with more advanced study, perhaps as a third or fourth year option, using a more detailed text.

The book is suitable for use as a textbook or reference book to accompany a taught course, or for use by students learning the language by themselves through private study.

The need for this book

Prolog is a programming language based on logic. It is considerably different from other languages and students often find it difficult. There are two reasons for this. First, Prolog requires a different way of thinking which students take time to adapt to.

Second, Prolog is associated with the research field of Artificial Intelligence (AI), and AI topics and techniques often form part of a Prolog course. This is unfortunate in one sense as such topics and techniques are conceptually difficult in themselves, and would be so in any language. The novel aspects of Prolog, coming along with the mind-bending problems of AI, cause problems for the average and below average student.

Approach

This book tries to introduce Prolog to students as simply and painlessly as possible. Where AI topics are introduced, they are the easier ones and are treated simply. Prolog is presented as an everyday language for programming, rather than an exotic language for high-powered researchers. The book is *Prolog Programming for Students*, with examples from AI, not a book on AI via Prolog.

To this end the chapters are organised so that easier topics are introduced first. The basics are introduced slowly, in the hope that they will be fully understood before going on to the harder topics. The topics that students find difficult, recursion and lists, are held back until about halfway through the book. Generally, Chapters 2 to 9 are basics, Chapters 10 to 18 are the essentials of the subject, and Chapters 19 to 22 are harder topics.

If used to accompany a taught course, approximately the material of one **chapter** can be covered each week. Each chapter has an introduction which sets the subject matter of the chapter in context where necessary, and introduces basic concepts. Each chapter also has a summary at the end.

The general format is that a topic is introduced as in a lecture, and backed up by **examples** and **questions**. Answers to the questions are given at the end of the chapter. The questions tend to be short, and are intended to encourage the student to check whether he or she is keeping up with the thread of the argument. Where questions are more substantial to answer, they are flagged as 'long questions'.

There are exercises intended as **programming practice** at the end of each chapter, to be done sitting at the computer. Solutions to the programming practice are given at the end of the book. The programming exercises are more practical, such that they can be solved eventually by the student by trial and error at the keyboard. In a taught course they would usually be done in a computer lab with tutor help available.

Also included are some **tests**, with answers at the end of the book, for students to test themselves. One such test is for students to try after the basics have been covered, between Chapters 9 and 10, and the other is to try after the essentials have been covered, between Chapters 18 and 19. The remaining chapters are on AI topics and the more unusual Prolog predicates. (These are harder topics which some lecturers may prefer not to cover with some groups.) Two of the self-tests take the form of **projects,** on which students will need to spend a more substantial amount of time. Answers to these are not given. They are open-ended so that some students can produce more detailed work than others. At the end of the book are some examples of longer **questions**, appropriate to the level reached after a one year course, with suggestions for the answers.

Programs on disc

The longer programs contained in the book as examples, and as answers to questions and programming exercises, are available free on disc to lecturers adopting the book as a course text (please apply in writing to the publishers on college-headed paper). Some of them are quite long. Lecturers making use of this material might want to make the longer databases available to students on a network, for example, so that the students can then try the exercises on them without having to type them in, and they might want to make the solutions available at a later stage.

David Callear
September 1994

Contents

1 About Prolog

1.1 Introduction

This chapter gives a little background to the language and tries to put Prolog in perspective. If you want to get straight on with learning to program, you can miss it out. Or you might find it more useful to come back and read it at some point later on.

Prolog means **pro**gramming in **log**ic. It is a computer programming language which is used to direct computers to do various tasks.

Logic has long been established as a branch of mathematics. Many people were involved in deriving a computer programming language from the discipline of logic, notably Robert Kowalski at Edinburgh University. Prolog was first implemented on a computer by Alain Colmerauer and his team at Marseilles University in the early 70s.

We will not attempt to give the logical background to Prolog in this book, or dwell on the relationship of Prolog to logic, but will treat Prolog as a practical programming language, particularly useful in certain ways.

1.2 Why learn Prolog?

Prolog is taught in more British universities than any other programming language. Why is this?

The growth of Prolog has coincided with the growth of Knowledge Based Systems (KBS), that is, computer systems handling large amounts of knowledge in a database by applying rules. A subset of KBS are Expert Systems (ES), which attempt to encapsulate the knowledge of a human expert. As Prolog consists of a database of rules (and little else apart from a mechanism for searching the database) it is ideally suited to building KBSs and ESs.

It has been found that Prolog also lends itself to a number of other programming techniques pioneered under the umbrella of Artificial Intelligence (AI), such as semantic nets, problem solving involving searches, and natural language, covered in simple form in this book. Prolog has earned for itself the title of 'the language of AI'.

Thus if you are a computer scientist, and could find yourself at some time in the future either building expert systems or doing AI research, Prolog could be an invaluable tool for you. Certainly it will be useful to have it available as a programming option.

Apart from these research reasons, learning Prolog is considered because of the connection with logic to have intrinsic value as an intellectual exercise. We will try to keep this book simple, but you will probably find some of the techniques tricky, and trying to solve some of the more difficult problems of AI using advanced Prolog is as intellectually demanding as logical exercises come.

As well as these reasons for learning Prolog, as we will show later Prolog is becoming more and more widely used as an applications language for building commercial programs. It lends itself readily to structured programming and modularisation. Because it is an interpreted language and has no type declarations, it is very good for prototyping, that is, developing quick experimental programs. Most computing students who really succeed in mastering it come to like it and appreciate its good qualities. There is reason to think that as procedural languages come and go, Prolog will remain. It has already grown steadily in popularity while some other languages have peaked and begun to decline.

Perhaps the best reason for learning Prolog, then, is that it is a good language to program in.

Question 1.1 *(answer on p.5)*

What sort of program would you say Prolog can be used to write, and which would you say it is best at?

1.3   Ideas behind Prolog

Instead of writing programs in a way modelled on how the computer works, programs are designed according to principles of logical problem solving. The notation used has similarities to logic notation, though it is not the same.

Programming in Prolog is declarative. That is, the facts and data relating to a problem are all declared statically in a database. Rules are then designed to draw out information from the database as required. Compare this with more conventional procedural programming, in which the computer is given a list of instructions or tasks to work through, or a procedure to follow. In Prolog, the problem is approached from the point of view of the data rather than the procedure.

Because Prolog always operates on a database, there is a mechanism built into it for searching the database. This is not the case with procedural languages, where any searching process has to be programmed in. Thus programming can often be made shorter and simpler in Prolog. The language does a lot of the work behind the scenes.

It is a matter of debate among students as to whether it is actually easier to solve a problem using logical principles or using good old bottom-up hacking. It depends partly on the problem. But the fact remains that Prolog is a language intended to solve problems from the point of view of the human user, not from the point of view of the procedural computer itself. It tries to be convenient for the programmer, not the computer.

To some extent Prolog attempts to work like a human brain. The way the brain does work, of course, is highly complex and is by no means fully understood, but a simple, naive way of looking at it is as follows. In response to a problem, we look into our memories for facts and techniques which might help to solve the problem. In a similar way Prolog searches through its database for facts and rules that can help to solve a problem. It is thus possible to represent a field of declared knowledge in Prolog, then solve various different problems by asking different questions. Compare this with the way a program is written in a procedural language like BASIC, Pascal or C to carry out a rigid, predefined task.

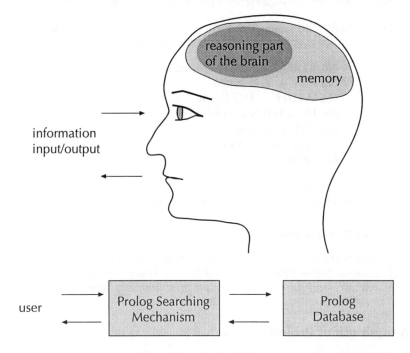

Because it is programmer-oriented rather than computer-oriented, the syntax of Prolog is chosen to make it look like English text as far as possible, and it can be written along the line in words and 'sentences' with fullstops and commas. However, many programmers still like to set it out in list form, as in a procedural program.

Question 1.2 (answer on p.6)

Apart from its merits, could there be any other reason why Prolog is so widely taught?

1.4   Is Prolog really so different?

One thing students soon find out is that Prolog is genuinely very different from other languages. It is common for Computing students to have learned several languages already by the time they come to Prolog, perhaps a selection from Basic, Pascal, Cobol, Fortran, Ada, Modula 2, C and several others. These are all procedural languages.

If you have already done some programming, you need to realise that learning Prolog involves going back to the beginning, and learning to program again, in a different way. Above all, if you are following a course in Prolog at university, don't think it is just another procedural language and you can swot it up in the week before the exam. Keep up with the course. If you fall behind, it will be hard to catch up.

This means there is good news for those who have not done programming before, or have found procedural programming difficult. They will be starting on a level with the experienced procedural programmers.

Just to make the point that Prolog is different, if you've done programming before consider which languages you know that have none of the following:

No REPEAT ... UNTIL loops
No FOR ... DO loops
No WHILE ... DO loops
No IF ... THEN conditions
No GOTO jumps
No type declarations
No arrays

Prolog has none of these, and in fact no rigid control constructs. There are of course other ways of doing the same things.

Question 1.3 *(answer on p.6)*

Can you think of a way of obtaining repetition without any built-in looping constructions? (You will probably only know the answer to this if you have encountered the method in other programming languages.)

1.5   A myth about Prolog

There is a notion still around that Prolog is a restricted language, used only for certain exotic programming tasks by a handful of enthusiasts. This is not true. The notion arose in the early days of Prolog while the language was being developed, and has persisted.

Modern versions of Prolog today are versatile and well-equipped and can be used for any programming task. Where another language is more convenient to use, such as in some cases C, sections of code written in the other language can usually be linked in. LPA Prolog, probably the most widely used version in the UK, has built-in predicates which allow programming of windows, colours and other features, and it can be and is used for professional, commercial applications. LPA Prolog has developed in several directions, including Prolog for Windows, Object Oriented Prolog and a version which links Prolog to the relational database Oracle. Work is currently being carried out at the National Physical Laboratory on a Prolog standard.

Prolog has been used for some time for commercial Expert System applications. It was chosen by Bacon and Woodrow for a knowledge based system for actuaries, and by IBiS for a decision support system to advise on legislative systems. But it is now being used more and more for other real-life commercial applications. It has been chosen for the gene mapping database in the international Human Genome Project. It was chosen by ICL for an update of their personnel system, and by the ICCARUS project for programming a multimedia interactive training system for firemen. It was used successfully by the Chessington Computer Centre for a large mainframe data processing system dealing with government pay, superannuation, attendance, and other personnel matters. The Association for Logic Programming (ALP) who are aiming to popularise Prolog further can supply other commercial examples. (If you are interested in joining ALP, the address is at the end of this book.)

It is worth making this point. Prolog is not just an exotic language but also an everyday useful one.

Question 1.4 *(answer on p.6)*

Prolog is widely taught, but is it a widely used language?

1.6 Summary

Prolog is a computer programming language, based on principles of logic, hence the name. It is a good language to learn because it is widely used in research, specifically 'artificial intelligence' research, and in expert systems. It is also good to learn as an intellectual exercise. It is being used increasingly in commercial applications.

Prolog consists of a static, declarative database rather than a list of instructions for the computer to work through. Problems are solved by asking carefully phrased questions, and Prolog searches for the answer using a built-in searching mechanism. Prolog is thus called a declarative language, rather than a procedural language like most others.

When learning Prolog you will find that it is quite different from other, procedural languages, and if you have done programming before you will need to learn again how to program almost from scratch. However, something to bear in mind is that contrary to common belief there is nothing mystical or exotic or elitist about it – it follows a set of rules like any other language.

Answers to questions

Answer 1.1

Prolog can be used to write any type of program. It is a full computer programming language as complete as any other.

As it consists basically of operations on a database, it is at its best with problems which involve large amounts of data held in databases, in particular the type of program known as a Knowledge Based System (KBS).

Answer 1.2

Prolog is reputed to be the most widely taught language in British universities. This could be because it is taught to some extent in nearly all universities, and so are procedural languages, but there are more procedural languages to choose from, and different universities concentrate on different ones.

Answer 1.3

It can be done by a technique called recursion, which involves a procedure (in most languages) calling itself so as to repeat. In Prolog a rule is the equivalent of a procedure. Recursion will be dealt with at length in Chapters 11 and 12.

Answer 1.4

It is widely used in higher education and research, but not so widely at present in commercial programming, where procedural languages like Fortran, Cobol and lately C have a stranglehold.

2 Basics

2.1 Introduction

Since Prolog is a programming language, most students will want to get started straight away and do some actual programming on the computer. In this chapter we will look at how you use Prolog in a simple way to make the computer do things.

The Prolog language itself is contained in a computer program called an interpreter. Let us look first at how you can run the interpreter to enter the language, and exit from it when you want to.

2.2 Getting started

In most systems, including LPA Prolog, you will enter the language by simply typing the word **prolog** followed by pressing the ENTER key. (If you are using Public Domain Prolog, see the next section.)

You will usually find that a banner appears on the screen, and underneath a prompt of the form:

?-

You can now type and enter things at the prompt to make things happen.

Perhaps the first thing to try is how to leave the Prolog interpreter if you want to. Type:

?-halt. <ENTER>

Note that the word **halt** has a small **h**. Capital letters have a special significance in Prolog, so for the moment let us use just small letters.

The word also has a fullstop after it. Everything entered in Prolog has to have this fullstop, and you need to remember to put it in. This is a nuisance at first, and everybody forgets a fullstop at some time, but eventually you get used to it.

Pressing the ENTER key after typing this will take you out of the Prolog interpreter. Type 'prolog' again to get back in.

2.3 Different implementations of Prolog

At this point we should mention that Prolog interpreters are slightly different depending on whose version you are using. The instructions above are for LPA Prolog, probably the commonest version in use in the UK.

There is a basic, minimum version of the language which was developed at Edinburgh University and is sometimes called the Edinburgh standard. This is described in the book by Clocksin and Mellish, and is also sometimes referred to as the Clocksin and Mellish standard. Most versions of Prolog have additions which go beyond this standard.

In this book, as we cannot cover all versions of Prolog which exist in the world, we will mention relevant points as they arise relating to the two most common versions in the UK, LPA Prolog and Public Domain or PD Prolog.

LPA Prolog is sold by Logic Programming Associates Ltd (address at the end of this book), and is an excellent and popular version used not only in universities but also for many commercial applications.

Public Domain or PD Prolog is used by many students because it is free, and is quite good enough to use while learning Prolog. It can be obtained from sources in most universities, or from companies distributing shareware and free programs who advertise in computer magazines. It was provided on a free disc with Personal Computer magazine in August 1993. As a last resort you can send off for it from Automata & Design Associates, whose address is at the end of this book.

Here we need to point out that if you are using PD Prolog you will need to type **pdprolog** to enter the interpreter, and **exitsys** (then fullstop, then ENTER) to exit from it.

Question 2.1 *(answer on p.14)*

What does everyone forget at first?

2.4 Interpreted Prolog

This is a slightly technical section, which you can leave until later if you want to get on with starting to program. You can miss it out altogether if you do not want to be bothered with technicalities, but it is here to help you understand how Prolog operates.

Prolog is an interpreted language, which means that everything you type and enter is immediately interpreted into computer-understandable form and acted upon. BASIC is another language which is interpreted and which you may have used, but beware of thinking Prolog and BASIC are similar!

Compiled and interpreted languages are fundamentally different in operation. The computer requires everything to be translated into binary numbers called **machine code** so that it can deal with it. A program in a compiled language is typed in an editor as text or **source code**, then the whole of it has to be

compiled into a machine code version, called an **executable program**, before the computer will run it. A program in an interpreted language is not compiled into a whole program of executable machine code but is kept in its source code version, then translated into machine code one instruction at a time as it is being run, by a program called an **interpreter**.

Question 2.2 *(answer on p.14)*

What do you think are the advantages and disadvantages of compiled and interpreted languages respectively? (Try this if you are technically minded.)

The diagrams below are to summarise the differences between interpreted and compiled languages, and show that in general compiled languages are sometimes troublesome while programming, but better when in use, whereas interpreted languages are easier while programming but sometimes troublesome in use.

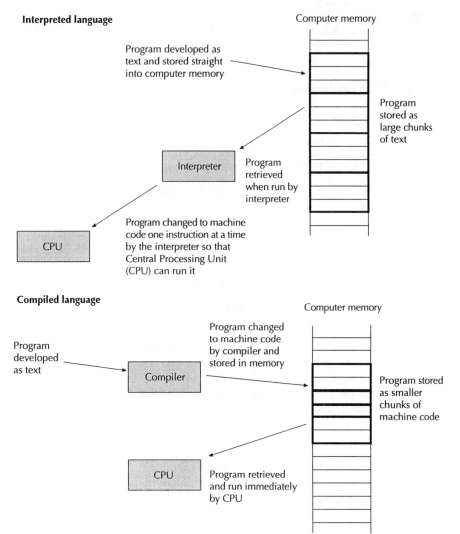

Prolog does not consist of instructions making up a program but of clauses, which are facts and rules, making up a database. They are acted on by the interpreter in response to goals you give it. You can still write conventional-type programs in Prolog, of course, which you set going and which then perform operations of various kinds. We will get round to facts, rules, programs and many other things in due course.

If you are familiar with compiled languages like Pascal and ADA, you may be interested to know that in some versions of Prolog (like LPA) you can compile programs after you have written them. This converts them into efficient executable code which can be run from outside the interpreter, and which other people cannot play about with. This is useful for final versions of commercial programs, but while developing a program (prototyping) the interpreter facility is quick and useful. As you will see later, it means you can automatically test each part of a Prolog program separately.

Question 2.3 *(answer on p.14)*

What does Prolog have in common with BASIC or Pascal? Is it really similar to either?

2.5   A bit of arithmetic

Try typing

        ?-2=2.   **<ENTER>**

Don't forget to put in the fullstop and press the ENTER key.

You will see that Prolog will simply answer 'yes' to this, because it is true that 2 = 2.

Try:

        ?-apple=apple.   **<ENTER>**

Don't forget to put in the fullstop and press the ENTER key.

Again Prolog will answer **yes** because it is also fairly obviously true that the word **apple** is the same as another word **apple** repeated.

Here **apple** is what is called in Prolog an **atom**, or group of alphabetical characters. An atom in Prolog is similar to what in other languages is called a string.

What happens in Prolog is that the interpreter tests everything entered at the prompt to see if it is true. If it is, it comes back with the answer **yes**.

Now try:

        ?-4=2+2.   **<ENTER>**

Don't forget to put in the fullstop and press the ENTER key.

This time, Prolog rather surprisingly answers no. This is because the = sign in Prolog is used to test whether two things are identically the same, and as 4 is a number and 2+2 is an expression, the test fails here.

Try entering:

?-4 is 2+2.   **<ENTER>**

Don't forget to put in the fullstop and press the ENTER key.

This time the response is **yes**, because **is** is used to evaluate expressions, and 2+2 correctly evaluates to 4.

From now on we will stop mentioning the fullstop, and we will omit mention of pressing the ENTER key, assuming that you know you have to do this with all items entered at the prompt.

Question 2.4 *(answer on p.15)*

What will Prolog reply to the following?

> **?- 100=100.**
> **?- 100=1000/10.**
> **?- 100 is 1000/10.**
> **?- 1000 is 100*10.**
> **?- 2 is (5+7)/6.**
> **?- 74 is (5+7)*6.**

2.6   Writing things on the screen

Now try typing

?-write(jane).

You will find this entry has the effect of writing **jane** on the screen. You will also see that there is a yes immediately after **jane**, so that what you see is:

?-write(jane).
janeyes

This seems a bit strange. What has happened is that as **write** is not a number or expression, Prolog looks for it in its database. Now **write** is a special word in Prolog, called a **predicate**, which is always in the database and which succeeds by writing its **argument**, in brackets after it, on the screen. If a predicate is found in the database, and if it succeeds in doing what it is meant to do, Prolog's test succeeds. In this case the argument, which is the atom **jane**, is written on the screen.

Because **write** has now succeeded, Prolog also answers **yes**.

It looks a bit untidy to have the **yes** immediately after the atom, so try entering:

?-write(jane),nl.

This time the response will appear as:

> **?-write(jane),nl.**
> jane
> yes

This looks tidier. **nl** is another standard predicate in Prolog, meaning 'new line', which is always in the database and which succeeds by simply moving the cursor at which things are written on the screen to the next line.

There are two important extra points to note here. One is that by using a comma we have strung together two things for Prolog to test in the same entry. The comma reads as 'and'.

The other important point is that both items have to test as true for Prolog to answer **yes**. *Here both* **write** *and* **nl** *succeed or test as true, and the answer comes back as* **yes**.

Test this by entering a deliberate mistake:

> **?-write(jane),nx.**

nx will not be found in the database and will fail. The answer will come back from Prolog as **no** or **predicate (nx) not defined**, although **write** still succeeds and the **jane** is written.

There is another way to use **write**. If the argument is enclosed in single quotes, whatever is between the quotes is written out. This means you can write out not just atoms but also strings containing spaces and capital letters. Try this with:

> **?-write('Jane Smith'),nl.**

Also for comparison try entering:

> **?-write(Jane Smith),nl.**

If **Jane Smith** is not in quotes, the capital at the start and the space in the middle mean it is not a valid atom, and Prolog gives an error message.

Question 2.5 *(answer on p.15)*

What will Prolog reply to the following?

> **?- write(hello).**
> **?- write(Hello).**
> **?- write('Hello!').**
> **?- write('Hello!'),nl.**

2.7 Entering items in the database

Let us try putting some girls' names in the database. First try entering:

> **?-girl(jane).**

The answer will be **no** or **predicate (girl) not defined**, meaning that the item **girl(jane)** has been searched for in the database and cannot be found. So, let's put it there.

Type the following one after another:

> **?-assert(girl(jane)).**
> **?-assert(girl(sarah)).**
> **?-assert(girl(norma)).**

Note that if youare using PD Prolog, there is no **assert** predicate and you will have to use **assertz** instead.

The predicate **assert** (or **assertz**) is another standard one in the database and succeeds by entering or 'asserting' its argument, in this case **girl(jane)** and the others, into the database as new items there. Note the two pairs of brackets which must be typed correctly or a syntax error will be flagged.

We now have girls in the database. Enter again:

> **?-girl(jane).**

The answer is now **yes** indicating that **girl(jane)** has been found in the database and the entry is effectively 'true', or the search has succeeded. Try also **girl(sarah).** and **girl(norma).** and they will also succeed. If you enter a girl you did not put in the database, like **girl(heidi)**, this will fail, answering no as the predicate **girl** is now defined.

You can look at what is currently in the database by entering:

> **?-listing.**

This is another standard predicate in Prolog which succeeds by writing out the whole of the current database on the screen. It does not write out the standard entries in the database like **write**, **nl** and **assert**, which are always there, just the extras you have entered.

You can specify the items you want **listing** to write out, by entering **listing(girl)**. This will give the same result at present, as we only have **girl** items in the database. The difference is that if other types of item were there as well, **listing** on its own would write them out as well.

Two further points. One is that when you exit from Prolog all items entered in this way are cleared from the database. The other is that to remove one such as **sarah** you can use:

> **?-retract(girl(sarah)).**

retract will succeed by removing **girl(sarah)** from the database. If it is told to remove an item that is not there, **retract** will fail.

2.8 Summary

Prolog consists of an interpreter which takes entries at the prompt and operates on a database. Entries at the prompt can be regarded either as expressions which Prolog tests for truth or falsity, or as goals given to Prolog to search for and find or not find, or as tasks given to Prolog in which it either succeeds or not. Prolog always comes back with an answer of 'yes' or 'no', offering to find more solutions if appropriate.

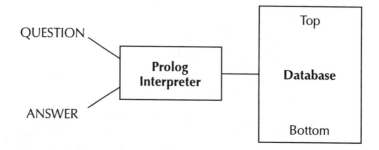

Arriving at the answer to a query involves a search through the database. If Prolog finds the item (or items) given to it, and if the item succeeds according to how it is designed, then the answer is 'yes'. Some standard predicates are always there in the database, and you can also enter your own.

Answers to questions

Answer 2.1

The fullstop when entering queries.

Answer 2.2

Compiled languages are long-winded to develop, as you have to keep compiling them to see if they work, but they are fast in operation, and usually error free, as most of the errors become apparent during compiling. **Interpreted** languages are quick and easy to develop, because you can test small sections without a lengthy compiling process (we say they are good for prototyping), but they are slower in operation, as the source code is being translated into machine code while the program is running, and they give errors while running which have not been sorted out by a compiler. The source code of an interpreted language also takes up more space in the computer memory than the executable machine code of a compiled language.

Answer 2.3

Prolog is interpreted, like BASIC. However, it is very different from BASIC and Pascal in other ways.

Answer 2.4

```
?- 100=100
yes
?- 100=1000/10.
no
?- 100 is 1000/10.
yes
?- 1000 is 100*10.
yes
?- 2 is (5+7)/6.
yes
?- 74 is (5+7)*6.
no
```

Answer 2.5

```
?- write(hello).
helloyes
?- write(Hello).
_23     (or similar)
?- write('Hello!').
Helloyes
?- write('Hello!'),nl.
Hello
yes
```

Programming practice: Basics

1. Test the examples and exercises in the chapter above in Prolog.

2. Type a set of entries at the prompt to put the following animals into the database, labelling them as animals:

   lion, tiger, cow.

3. Enter a query to test whether there is such a thing as a tiger.

4. Enter a query to test simultaneously whether there are such things as a cow and a lion.

5. Now put entries into the database to record two of the animals as carnivores: lion and tiger.

6. Formulate and test queries to see whether a lion is an animal and also a carnivore, and whether a cow is an animal and also a carnivore.

3 Variables

3.1 Introduction

A variable in any computer language, and in mathematics, is a quantity that can take any value. For example, in algebra **X** is often used to stand for an unknown quantity in an equation, and we can write things like

X = 10

The significance of a variable in computer programming is that a variable occupies a particular location or block of locations in the computer memory. It is often compared to a labelled 'pigeon hole' for correspondence, papers or other stored items. Different things can be put into the pigeon hole, but the label of the pigeon hole stays the same. In the same way a variable keeps its name, but can have any contents or value.

3.2 Variables in Prolog

Variables in Prolog are introduced as strings of characters starting with a first letter which is a CAPITAL LETTER. A string without an initial capital is interpreted as a constant or atom.

This is very important in Prolog and cannot be over-emphasised! The first capital letter is what distinguishes a variable from an atom. Beginners in Prolog get into trouble because they forget this.

As in most high level languages, you can invent your own names or identifiers for both variables and atoms, using strings of characters as in written English. What you introduce as a variable or an atom is up to you, and depends on what you are trying to convey or do.

For example:

animal   is an atom (it could be used for a particular animal or the group animal)

Animal   is a variable (it could be used for any individual animal)

john   is an atom (could be used as a name or for a particular john)

John   is a variable (it will behave as any person – not a very useful identifier unless there are several johns and this variable will be used to stand for any one of them)

X   is a variable, x is an atom

3.3   Instantiation

Instantiation is the process in Prolog of making a variable equal to a constant, or giving it a value.

For example:

> **?- X is 2+2.**

This introduces **X** as a variable, and **X** is instantiated to the value of the expression **2+2**. The reply from Prolog is:

> **X = 4**

Prolog then asks if more solutions should be searched for. In LPA Prolog the message is: **spacebar = next solution**. On requesting more solutions by pressing the spacebar, the reply is **no**, as there are no more solutions to this particular expression.

In this example we are in effect telling Prolog to make **X** equal to 4, and it is like an 'assignment' in other high level languages. However, there are other cases where Prolog will automatically give a variable a value without being told to, and will search for a value when one is required, so instantiation is not by any means the same as assignment, and should not be confused with it. The differences will become more apparent as we go on.

Another example:

> **?- X=apple,Y=X.**
> **X=apple**
> **Y=apple**

Here the variable **X** is instantiated to the atom **apple**. **Y**, another variable, is instantiated to the same value as **X**, ie. **apple**.

3.4   Algebra with Prolog

Prolog can cope with queries like the following:

> **?- X=2,Y=3,Z is X+Y.**
> **X=2**
> **Y=3**
> **Z=5**

Notice that at each stage, each variable has been instantiated with a value. The following will be rejected:

> **?- X=Y-2,Y=2X.**

Here we have two 'simultaneous equations'. Logically, Prolog should be able to come back with the answer to this as **X=2, Y=4**. However, this would involve a Prolog interpreter containing algorithms for solving simultaneous equations, and also any other mathematical problems that might arise, and such an interpreter would be impractically complex. A problem such as this could be solved in Prolog, but it would require the programming of a simultaneous equation algorithm.

Question 3.1 *(answer on p.21)*

Can you predict what Prolog will reply to the following?

> ?- **Product is 20*30/60.**
> ?- **A=(20+4)/6,B is (A*A)+4.**
> ?- **X=2+3,Y=8/4,Z=X*Y.**
> ?- **X=2+3,Y=8/4,Z is X*Y.**
> ?- **X is 2+3,Y is 8/4, Z is X*Y.**

Try these examples in your Prolog interpreter to check them.

3.5 Using variables in the database

Instantiation of variables can be used to extract information from the database. For example, look at the following sequence:

> ?- **assert(car(ford)).**
> yes
>
> ?- **car(Car).**
> Car=ford

Here we put **car(ford)** into the database. We then ask if there is a car in the database, using the variable **Car**. Prolog searches the database for a solution.

To find a solution to the query **?- car(Car)**, Prolog first takes the query predicate **car** and compares it with predicate names in the database. It finds that there is a **car** predicate there which is the same, by a simple process of **pattern matching**, checking for two strings of characters that are the same.

Prolog now takes the query argument **Car**, a variable, and checks whether it matches with the argument of the **car** predicate in the database, which is **ford**. As **Car** is a variable, it can be instantiated to any value, and can be given the value **ford** to make it match. Thus a match can be arranged, as it were, and a solution found for the query, by giving the variable the appropriate value. This is carried out and the value of **ford** is returned for the variable **Car**.

Prolog now asks if any more solutions are to be searched for. If the reply is affirmative, it searches, but there are no more entries in the database and the search now fails, giving **no**.

This process of finding a solution by instantiating a variable to achieve a match is similar to the process which is called **unification** in logic.

Question 3.2 *(answer on p.21)*

Have you remembered the syntactical difference in Prolog between variables and atoms, which beginners often forget?

3.6 How Prolog operates

Let us try to formulate what is going on as Prolog replies to a query or searches to achieve a goal.

1. Prolog consists of a database and a mechanism for searching the database.

2. When given a query or goal to test, Prolog searches the database FROM TOP TO BOTTOM and matches the goal with items in the database.

3. Variables can be instantiated to have the value of a constant so as to make the matching process succeed.

4. If a match is found, the search succeeds, or the goal is true, and the values of any variables which have been found are given.

5. Prolog keeps a pointer to the database where a search succeeded, and it is possible to ask for further solutions. Prolog continues searching and the pointer moves down to the next solution. When Prolog can find no more solutions, it says 'no' and the search ends.

3.7 A more detailed example

Suppose we assert the following into the database:

> **boy(ted).**
> **boy(bill).**
> **boy(joe).**

Note that the names cannot start with capitals.

A query **?- boy(john).** ... will fail, as PROLOG will not find this in the database. It will answer no.

A query **?- boy(bill).** ... will succeed. Prolog first finds **boy(ted)**, and tries to match **boy(bill)** with **boy(ted)**, which fails. It searches on and finds **boy(bill)**, which now matches, so it answers yes.

Now we can try a variable. Suppose we query:

> **?- boy(Boy).**

Prolog searches down the database trying to find a match for this expression. It finds **boy(ted)**, and this can be made to succeed by instantiating **Boy** to **ted**. The response is

> **Boy = ted.**

The effect of asking for more is to reject this solution and make it fail. Prolog is obliged to keep searching, continuing down the database from the point reached. The search now produces **boy(bill)**, which can succeed by instantiating **Boy** to **bill**. A new response is given, **Boy = bill**.

On asking for more again, the solution is rejected again, the search moves on, another solution is found, there is a new instantiation, and another response is given, **Boy = joe**.

Asking for more again causes the search to continue, but there are no more boys in the database. The search finally fails, and produces the response **no**.

Question 3.3 *(answer on p.22)*

What is the difference between instantiation and assignment in procedural languages?

3.8   and, not, or

There are some extra points we can make with the little database above. One is that as before we can string things together with **and** conjunctions.

>?- boy(bill),boy(ted).
> yes

>?- boy(ted),boy(jason).
> no

We can introduce here another standard predicate, **not**. This reverses anything given as its argument, so that we get:

>?- not(boy(ted)).
> no

>?- not(boy(jason)).
> yes

Notice that the closing brackets have to match the opening brackets. In fact **not** is an operator as well as being a predicate, which means that we can use it without brackets like the arithmetic operators **+**, **-**, *****, **/**, and **=**. It is clearer to use **not** in this way, followed by a space:

>?- not boy(ted).
> no

>?- not boy(jason).
> yes

We can also introduce **or**, written in Prolog as a semicolon, **;** , although we will avoid using it a great deal as it tends to make expressions complicated, and there are usually other ways of writing them. This is a logic operator, but its use is just the same as in English, and can be seen in the following examples:

>?- (boy(bill) ; boy(ted)).
> yes

>?- (boy(ted) ; boy(jason)).
> yes

Question 3.4 *(answer on p.22)*

What two main parts does Prolog consist of?

3.9 The anonymous variable

Sometimes we want to put a variable into an expression, but are not concerned about its value. For example, in the above database of boys, we might want to ask if there are any boys in the database, without being given their names. In this case we could use the underline symbol, _ , which is called the *anonymous variable*.

The anonymous variable, the underline, is treated in Prolog as a variable but is not instantiated.

> ?- boy(_).
> yes

Prolog will search for a value for the anonymous variable, and will find one, making the query succeed, but it will not report its value.

This tells us that there are boys in the database, but does not trouble us with their names. Notice that queries of **boy()** or just **boy** would give error messages.

3.10 Summary

Variables are quantities that can have any value, and are written in Prolog as strings of characters starting with a capital letter. Variables can be given a value by a process known as 'instantiation'. This is not the same as 'assignment' in procedural languages.

Variables can be used in queries, and as Prolog carries out its search the variables are instantiated by a process of matching them to values in the database. When the search succeeds the values variables have been given are reported.

The underline symbol is used as an 'anonymous variable' which behaves like any other variable, but whose value is not required and is not reported back.

Answers to questions

Answer 3.1

?- **Product is 20*30/60.**	Product = 10	yes
?- **A=(20+4)/6,B is (A*A)+4.**	A=(20+4)/6 B=20	yes
?- **X=2+3,Y=8/4,Z=X*Y.**	X=2+3 Y=8/4 Z=(2+3)*(8/4)	yes
?- **X=2+3,Y=8/4,Z is X*Y.**	X=2+3 Y=8/4 Z=10	yes
?- **X is 2+3,Y is 8/4, Z is X*Y.**	X=5 Y=2 Z=10	yes

Answer 3.2

Variable names start with a capital letter, while atom (constant) names start with a lowercase letter.

Programming practice: Aeroplanes

1. Assert the following examples of aeroplanes into the database.

    aeroplane(spitfire)
    aeroplane(dakota)
    aeroplane(lancaster)
    aeroplane(hurricane)
    aeroplane(comet)

    Test this with the following and explain what happens:

    ?- aeroplane(hurricane).
    ?- aeroplane(jumbo).
    ?- aeroplane(_).
    ?- aeroplane(Plane).

2. Now assert an additional entry into the database:

    aeroplane(Plane)

    Test the database again with all the above queries. Make sure you can explain what is happening!

4 Facts

4.1 Introduction

Facts are the simplest items of data in a Prolog database. We have used them already but have not referred to them as such.

*A fact consists of a **predicate** and zero, one or more **arguments**.*

e.g.

        animal(mammal). [Note fullstop.]

This is a fact with one argument. Note that a predicate name must be an atom.

        animal is the predicate.
        mammal is the argument.

e.g.

        mammal(tiger,mouse,man).

This is a fact with three arguments.

        mammal is the predicate.
        tiger, **mouse**, and **man** are the arguments.

All these arguments are atoms, similar to 'strings'.

One way of looking at a fact in Prolog is that its presence in the database indicates a statement that is **true**. Its absence indicates a statement that is not true.

For example, suppose we assert **animal(mammal)** into the database, on its own, with no other **animal** facts. Suppose we now query

        ?-animal(mammal).

The response will be **yes**, because **animal(mammal)** will be found in the database and will effectively be true. Suppose we query

        ?- animal(reptile).

Now the response will be **no**, because **animal(reptile)** cannot be found and this fact is not true as far as Prolog is concerned.

4.2 Types of argument

Predicate names must be atoms, but arguments can consist of a variety of types of object. Prolog recognises different data types without your having to declare them at the top of the program as in most other languages.

The champions of some other languages make a virtue of rigid type declarations, saying that they discourage careless programming. What this means is that the programmer is made to work extra hard to avoid giving the computer something it doesn't like. Remember, Prolog is intended to be easy on the programmer, not the computer.

The commonest types which Prolog recognises are:

INTEGERS –   consist entirely of digits.

REALS –   also consist entirely of digits and a decimal point.

ATOMS –   start with a lower case letter. Can contain numbers, capitals, underlines, but not spaces.

STRINGS –   any grouping of characters enclosed in single quotes, including spaces, fullstops, initial capitals, etc.

VARIABLES –   start with an upper case letter or capital. Can assume different values as in algebra or other languages.

What the Prolog interpreter does is to look at the keyboard characters which have been entered at the query prompt, and divide them up into groups between limiting characters such as opening bracket, closing bracket, quote, space, and comma. If a group begins with a lower case letter, it is recognised as a constant atom, either predicate or argument depending on its position. If it begins with an upper case letter, it is a variable. If it consists entirely of digits, it is an integer. If it consists of digits with an embedded decimal point, it is a real number.

It is worth mentioning here that arguments of facts can also be facts themselves, and even more complicated objects. Here we are getting into what are referred to as **structures**, dealt with later in Chapter 20.

Question 4.1 *(answer on p.29)*

Does the absence of type declarations mean that Prolog is more prone to programming errors than other languages?

4.3 A database of facts

Let us look at what can be done with information declared as a database of facts in Prolog. Suppose we enter the following facts into the database, asserting them one at a time. Note that although this is a fairly small database, it is becoming rather tedious to construct such a database using **assert**, and there is a better way of doing it, which we will come to in a minute.

```
furniture(sink,kitchen,1).
furniture(chair,lounge,4).
furniture(bed,bedroom,1).
furniture(cooker,kitchen,1).
furniture(chair,kitchen,4).
furniture(wardrobe,bedroom,2).
furniture(sofa,lounge,1).
furniture(chair,bedroom,1).
```

The one type of fact making up this database consists of a predicate which is the atom **furniture** and three arguments, the first two atoms and the third an integer.

This is all Prolog sees, but clearly to our eyes the database describes the items of furniture in the rooms of a house, with the number of each in the room.

If we want to know how many of each item there are in the lounge, for example, we can ask

?- furniture(Item,lounge,Number).

Prolog will supply the answers

Item = chair
Number = 4

Item = sofa
Number = 1

No   **(meaning no more solutions)**

If you can see how these responses are produced, well and good, but if not, here is an explanation.

When given the query **furniture(Item,lounge,Number)** Prolog goes to the database and searches it from the top down, trying to find something to match it with to prove it 'true'. It finds first **furniture(sink,kitchen,1)**. The predicate **furniture** matches, and the first argument **sink** can be made to match by instantiating the variable **Item** to **sink**. But the second argument **kitchen** cannot match with **lounge** because both are constants. This fact therefore fails, and Prolog moves on down the database. It finds **furniture(chair,lounge,4)** and this can be made to match completely by instantiating **Item** to **chair** and **Number** to **4**. Prolog returns this solution as a reply. If told to continue searching, it moves on down the database and finds another match with **Item** instantiated to **sofa** and **Number** instantiated to **1**.

4.4 Using the anonymous variable

When searching for information among facts with several arguments, the anonymous variable (the underscore, _ , remember) is used frequently to 'blank out' arguments we are not interested in.

For example, suppose we want to list all the rooms, without recording the furniture or numbers. We can ask

> **?- furniture(_,Room,_).**

Prolog will reply

> **Room = kitchen**
> **Room = lounge**
> **Room = bedroom**
> **Room = kitchen   … and so on.**

If we wanted each item in the kitchen but not its number, we could use

> **?- furniture(Item,kitchen,_).**

Question 4.2 *(answer on p.29)*

1. *What query would we type in to find out how many chairs are in each room?*

2. *What would we ask if we want to know which rooms have 4 chairs?*

3. *What could we ask to find out which rooms have chairs in, irrespective of the number?*

4. *What would we ask to find out which room has 4 chairs and 1 cooker?*

4.5   Consulting databases

As we mentioned above, asserting large numbers of facts into the database one at a time is tedious. Also, when we exit from Prolog we lose all the data we have typed in so laboriously. In fact constructing a database in this way is clumsy and impractical.

The way we deal with larger databases is to type them out in an editor or word processor, save them as a file, then go into Prolog and read the file into the database.

For example, suppose we want to work with the following database.

```
/* SOLAR SYSTEM DATABASE */

body(mercury,36,small,none,none).
body(venus,67,small,atmosphere,none).
body(earth,93,small,atmosphere,none).
body(moon,93,small,none,none).
body(mars,141,small,atmosphere,none).
body(jupiter,489,large,atmosphere,rings).
body(saturn,886,large,atmosphere,rings).
body(uranus,1782,large,atmosphere,rings).
body(neptune,2793,large,atmosphere,rings).
body(pluto,3670,small,atmosphere,none).

/* END */
```

Before going into Prolog (or after exiting from it using **halt**), we go into an editor such as EDIT, which is supplied with the MSDOS operating system. If you have never used an editor before, you may have to read this up in the operating system manual, but it is very easy to use. In the editor, we type out the database exactly as above.

Note that there is no mention of **assert**, but also note that the fullstops are there. Another point to note is that we can put in a title, or comments if we wish, using the /* … */ symbols. The interpreter ignores anything between /* and */ when reading a file into the database.

When this is typed, before exiting from the editor we save it as a file on the hard disc of the computer (or on a floppy disc). If you use a wordprocessor such as WordPerfect, you need to make sure you save the file as an ASCII format file. An editor like EDIT does this automatically. Give the file a name which is different from any of the names used in the text, or the Prolog interpreter may confuse two 'identifiers' that are the same. For example, you might call the file by a filename **MYFILE.DEC**. If you are using LPA Prolog, you should use an extension **.DEC** for the file. Other Prolog interpreters, such as PD Prolog, may require different extensions such as **.PRO**.

Now exit from the editor and go into Prolog. Files typed out in an editor and saved in ASCII format can be consulted into Prolog using the standard predicate **consult**. They must of course use correct Prolog syntax, or you will see error messages.

For example, suppose you are using LPA Prolog and you have created a file with the name **MYFILE.DEC**. You can read it into the Prolog database by entering at the query prompt

> **?- consult(myfile).**

Note that the DEC extension has not been typed, and note that **myfile** is in lowercase to represent an atom. An alternative quick way to consult in a file in LPA Prolog is to say

> **?- [myfile].**

If you have given the file a different extension, like **.TXT** for example, you will have to consult it in using quotes, because a fullstop symbol is not acceptable syntax as part of an atom:

> **?- consult('myfile.txt').**

If it is on a floppy disc in drive A, you can consult it in by using something of the form:

> **?- consult('a:myfile.txt').**

These details differ slightly for different versions of Prolog, and remember that the above refers to LPA Prolog.

Question 4.3 *(answer on p.30)*

For the database above showing details of the bodies in the Solar System, devise queries to find:

(a) all the bodies with no atmosphere

(b) any bodies which are small and have rings

(c) all the bodies which are more than 100 million miles from the Sun

(d) any bodies which are less than 100 million miles from the Sun and have neither atmosphere nor rings.

4.6 A simple medical expert system

Already, with the basic knowledge of Prolog gained so far, we can devise and use a very simple medical expert system which simulates, albeit crudely, the expertise of a doctor. We start by setting out facts relating to a few diseases and their symptoms.

```
/* MEDICAL EXPERT SYSTEM */

symptom(cold,sneezing).
symptom(cold,headache).
symptom(cold,runny_nose).
symptom(flu,headache).
symptom(flu,shivery).
symptom(flu,temperature).
symptom(brain_tumour,headache).

/* END */
```

What happens if a patient is ill and goes to the doctor? He or she tells the doctor the symptoms of the illness, and the doctor consults his or her medical knowledge and comes up with the disease the patient may be suffering from. We can tell Prolog the symptoms, and it will consult the medical facts we have given it and come up with the disease that fits them.

For example, suppose we say

```
?- symptom(X,sneezing),symptom(X,runny_nose).
```

We are asking here: Is there a disease **X** which has a symptom **sneezing** and also a symptom **runny_nose**?

Prolog will search through the database of facts and reply:

```
X = cold
```

You can see that this very small number of facts could be extended to a large number, and that the simple query might be replaced by a more complex one when we have more skill with Prolog. This elementary program could soon become a powerful tool which might actually help a doctor in his or her job.

We have admitted that this is a simple version of an expert system, but in another language it would probably be a much more substantial and complex program even to do this much. Try programming a program to do this in Pascal or Ada, and you will realise how efficient Prolog is for certain types of knowledge-based system.

Question 4.4 *(answer on p.30)*

1. *Devise a query which will list all the diseases in the medical database, without their symptoms.*

2. *Devise a query which will pick out all the symptoms of flu.*

3. *Devise a query which will pick out the diseases with a symptom of headache.*

4.7 Summary

Facts are simple items of data in the Prolog database, consisting of a predicate name followed by zero, one or more arguments in brackets. Arguments can be integers, reals, atoms, strings or variables.

Information can be drawn from a database of facts using variables and the anonymous variable. Databases can be typed in an editor then 'consulted' into Prolog. Quite useful programs can be constructed using simple databases of facts queried from the interpreter prompt, including a simple medical expert system.

Answers to questions

Answer 4.1

Opinions would probably differ, but it doesn't necessarily mean this. Rigid type declarations simply impose rigid programming onto the programmer. Certainly the absence of declarations makes programming in Prolog more fun, and means you can get on with solving problems without spending an inordinate amount of time on syntax.

Prolog does still recognise data types, of course, although they are not declared in the program. If a variable is treated as an integer in a program, you have to make sure that it cannot be read in as an atom. If it is, an error will be given at the point where it is treated as an integer.

Answer 4.2

1. **?- furniture(chair,Room,Number).**

2. **?- furniture(chair,Room,4).**

3. **?- furniture(chair,Room,_).**

4. **?- furniture(chair,Room,4),furniture(cooker,Room,1).**

Answer 4.3

    (a) **?- body(Body,_,_,none,_).**

    (b) **?- body(Body,_,small,_,rings).**

    (c) **?- body(Body,Dist,_,_,_),Dist>100.**

    (d) **?- body(Body,Dist,_,none,none),Dist<100.**

Answer 4.4

    1. **?- symptom(Disease,_).**

    2. **?- symptom(flu,Symptom).**

    3. **?- symptom(Disease,headache).**

Programming practice: Animals

1. Go into your editor and type out the **furniture** database used in the chapter. Save it, using a filename that is not in your program. (Remember never to do this.) Now exit from the editor and go into Prolog. Consult your program into Prolog and test the examples in the lecture.

2. Now type out the **solar system** database in the chapter in the editor, and try the exercises you did. (Try using the COPY facility which most editors have to make things much easier.)

3. Type the following database in the editor then consult it into Prolog.

```
/* ANIMALS DATABASE */
animal(mammal,tiger,carnivore,stripes).
animal(bird,eagle,carnivore,large).
animal(mammal,hyena,carnivore,ugly).
animal(bird,sparrow,scavenger,small).
animal(mammal,lion,carnivore,mane).
animal(reptile,snake,carnivore,long).
animal(mammal,zebra,herbivore,stripes).
animal(reptile,lizard,scavenger,small).
```

Now devise and test queries to find (a) all the mammals, (b) all the carnivores which are mammals, (c) all the mammals with stripes, and (d) whether there is a reptile which has a mane.

5 Semantic nets

5.1 Introduction

A semantic net is a way of representing information in graphical or diagrammatic form, showing words and their meanings, or semantics.

*A semantic net is a diagram showing a set of labelled **nodes** connected to each other by labelled **links**, which represent relationships between the nodes.*

Semantic nets are useful for representing the data for certain types of problem, where the data is varied and there are many different connections between items. If you are faced with a problem that appears to have no obvious pattern to it, just a lot of data with certain information relating the items, it can help to try to draw a semantic net, simply putting into a diagram all the semantics involved, ie. words with their meanings.

5.2 An example – objects in a room

Suppose we require a representation of a room, maybe the room you are sitting in. There is no obvious and simple way to organise all the different objects in the room, and in fact there are so many possible ways of trying to organise them that we would not know where to start. We can tackle the problem by drawing a semantic net.

The objects and concepts to represent in relation to the room might be:

you,person,chair,furniture,leather,my_chair,brown,seat

These could be represented, putting in their relationships, as follows:

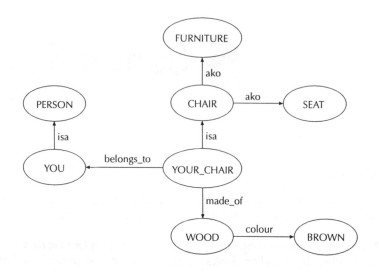

In this diagram **isa** stands for 'is a', a common relationship indicating that something is a named example of something else. Also, **ako** stands for 'a kind of', meaning that something is one of several kinds of something else. These are such common relationships that these two links, **isa** and **ako**, have become standard in drawing semantic nets. (It is sometimes difficult to distinguish between them.) We cannot use these standard links for the other relationships in this example, and others have been invented.

There is a difference between a semantic net and a net used in diagrams in other contexts. A 'net' representation usually has just one type of link between nodes. A semantic net differs in that it can have different links between the nodes.

Semantic nets are very subjective. Any two people will usually represent the same data by drawing two completely different semantic nets. However, one will probably turn out to be a more efficient way of doing it.

Diagrams are usually capable of further refinement. When tackling a problem in this way, it is best to draw a rough diagram first, then re-draw it in a more orderly way, organising nodes with the same links to be close to each other.

The semantic net approach will the recognised as a simple 'artificial intelligence' approach, an attempt to represent data in a way similar to the way it is held in the memory.

5.3 **Prolog and semantic nets**

There is a simple and close connection between Prolog and semantic nets, which means that any problem that can be represented by such a net can very easily be represented also in Prolog.

We can convert a semantic net into a Prolog database by substituting predicates for links, and arguments for nodes.

It's as easy as that. In the example above, we have a database as follows:

ako(chair,furniture).
ako(chair,seat).
isa(your_chair,chair).
isa(you,person).
made_of(mychair,wood).
colour(wood,brown).
belongs_to(your_chair,you).

Suppose we now want, for example, to find out what colour your chair is. The database does not give us the colour of chairs directly, but it does give us the colour of what things are made of. If we first find what your chair is made of, by saying:

made_of(your_chair,X)

… we can then find its colour by adding

colour(X,Colour)

So with a complete query as follows we can find the colour of the chair:

?- made_of(your_chair,X),colour(X,Colour).
X = wood
Colour = brown

Question 5.1 *(answer on p.35)*

See if you can compose a query to determine (a) whether your chair is a seat, and (b) whether it belongs to a person.

5.4 A problem-solving example: carnivores and herbivores

Read the following passage, and express the information it contains in a semantic net. Convert the net to a Prolog database and use it to test (a) whether herbivores ever hunt and (b) whether all herbivores are hunted.

In the animal world, carnivores such as lions and leopards hunt and eat herbivores such as zebras and wildebeeste. Thus some animals are hunters and some are hunted, and generally speaking, carnivores hunt herbivores. However, there are many exceptions to this rule. Elephants, which are herbivores, are rarely hunted because of their size. Nor are bears, which are not normally meat eaters and therefore basically herbivores. Bears will catch and eat other animals when the opportunity arises.

We can draw a semantic net thus:

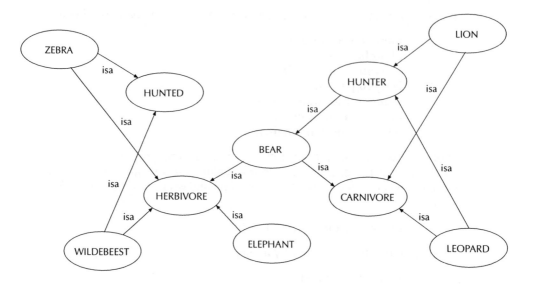

This gives the following database:

isa(carnivore,lion).
isa(carnivore,leopard).
isa(carnivore,bear).
isa(hunter,lion).
isa(hunter,leopard).
isa(hunter,bear).
isa(herbivore,elephant).
isa(herbivore,zebra).
isa(herbivore,wildebeeste).
isa(herbivore,bear).
isa(hunted,zebra).
isa(hunted,wildebeeste).

We can now answer the questions.

(a) Asking whether herbivores ever hunt is the same as saying, is there an example of a herbivore which ever hunts? If we can find such an example in the database, then this is true.
Re-phrasing the question again, we want to ask of the database: Is there an animal in the database which is a herbivore, such that this animal also hunts? This gives the query:

?- isa(herbivore,Animal),isa(hunter,Animal).

(b) Asking whether all herbivores are hunted is like saying: Is there an animal in the database which is a herbivore, but which at the same time is not a hunted animal? We can put this as:

?- isa(herbivore,Animal),not isa(hunted,Animal).

5.5 A schools exercise

Suppose we have the problem of representing the following data relating to schools, so as to answer complex questions on the data.

Parents in the UK are faced with a variety of schools. There are primary schools for young children and secondary schools for older children. Younger children can go to state primary schools or fee-paying prep schools. Older ones mostly go to comprehensive schools, but there are also grammar schools for clever pupils, city technology colleges for very clever ones, and fee-paying public schools. Grammar and public schools offer a more academic education.

See if you can deal with this problem as a student exercise.

LONG question 5.2 (answer on p.36)

Draw a semantic net for the above data.

Convert your semantic net to Prolog facts, and use it to find the choice of schools available to (a) the parents of a young child and (b) parents of an older child who cannot pay fees.

5.6 Summary

A semantic net is a way of representing data by organising it as a diagram of nodes and links representing relationships between the nodes. Having constructed a semantic net to represent the data, it is straightforward to convert the net to a Prolog database by writing each link as a predicate, and the nodes at either end of the link as arguments. Problems can then be solved by devising suitable queries to draw information from the database.

Answers to questions

Answer 5.1

(a) ?-isa(your_chair,X),ako(X,seat).

(b) ?-belongs_to(your_chair,X),isa(X,person).

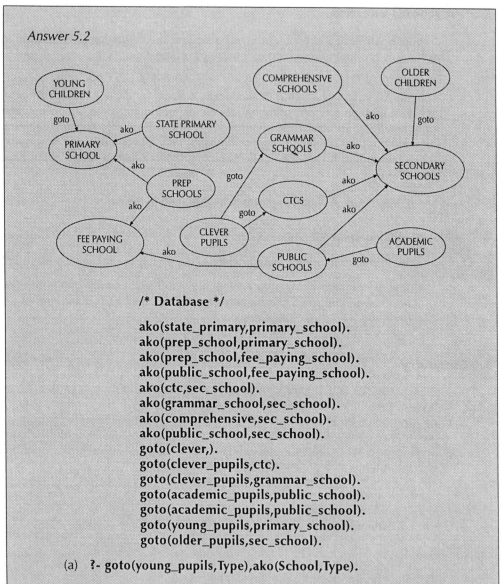

Answer 5.2

/* Database */

```
ako(state_primary,primary_school).
ako(prep_school,primary_school).
ako(prep_school,fee_paying_school).
ako(public_school,fee_paying_school).
ako(ctc,sec_school).
ako(grammar_school,sec_school).
ako(comprehensive,sec_school).
ako(public_school,sec_school).
goto(clever,).
goto(clever_pupils,ctc).
goto(clever_pupils,grammar_school).
goto(academic_pupils,public_school).
goto(academic_pupils,public_school).
goto(young_pupils,primary_school).
goto(older_pupils,sec_school).
```

(a) **?- goto(young_pupils,Type),ako(School,Type).**

(b) **?- goto(older_pupils,Type),ako(School,Type),not ako(School,fee_
paying_school).**

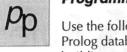

Programming practice: **Dieting semantic net**

Use the following information to construct a semantic net and convert it to a Prolog database, then devise a rule to pick out (a) who eats protein for body-building and (b) the reasons why sugar is eaten.

'Diet is related to people's priorities. Elderly people concerned about their blood-pressure often avoid fats. Athletes, who are concerned with energy and body-building, eat sugar and proteins. For similar reasons, growing children are given these foods. Overweight people who want to lose weight avoid sugar and fats.'

6 Rules

6.1 Introduction

A rule in Prolog is an extension of a fact, with added subgoals that also have to be satisfied for it to be true.

Rules and facts are really different versions of the same thing, collectively called **clauses**.

A rule consists of a **head** and a **body**. The head is like a fact, consisting of a predicate with arguments. The body consists of sub-goals which are usually other clauses, either facts or rules, which must all succeed or be true for the rule itself to succeed or be true. The head and body are separated by **:-** , a special Prolog operator.

eg.   **fault(electrical):-**
        car_will_not_start,
        no_lights.

It can also be written along the line thus:

fault(electrical):-car_will_not_start,no_lights.

This is a rule with two subgoals. **fault(electrical)** is only true if **car_will_not_start** and **no_lights** are also both true. We could read this rule as:

The fault is electrical if the car will not start and has no lights.

At this stage we can point out a few things. Note that a fact is a rule with no body. Conversely a rule is a fact with a body added.

A Prolog database consists of just facts and rules, which as we have said are called **clauses**, and it can be seen that they are really two forms of the same thing. So the database actually consists of just one kind of data.

We can begin to appreciate the amazing simplicity of Prolog. A 'program' in Prolog consists of just a database, and the database consists of just one kind of entry.

This does not mean, of course, that Prolog is necessarily simple to handle. (As you will also be starting to appreciate!) Solving a problem in Prolog can be comparable to building a ship with just a few tools, rather than all the facilities of a shipyard. But as with ships, the end result can be better!

Question 6.1 *(answer on p.45)*

What is a **clause** in Prolog?

6.2 Interpreting rules into English

The operator **:-** simply separates the head of a rule from its body, and is sometimes called the 'neck' operator, sometimes the 'if' operator. The following may help:

1. You can usually read :- as IF, sometimes as THEN.

2. You can usually read commas as AND, sometimes BUT or THEN.

3. You read semicolons as OR.

e.g.

fault(electrical):-car_will_not_start,no_lights.
The fault is electrical IF the car will not start AND has no lights.

Sometimes a rule reads better inverted as follows:

IF the fault is electrical THEN the car will not start AND has no lights.

There is a difference between these interpretations in the English, as we are inverting cause and effect. We are implying that the car will not start and has no lights BECAUSE the fault is electrical, rather than the fault is electrical BECAUSE it will not start and has no lights. We need to use caution in using the first interpretation. The second is closer to what the Prolog represents. The head can only succeed if the body succeeds – the head cannot succeed and therefore make the body succeed!

Question 6.2 *(answer on p.45)*

What is the condition for a rule to succeed?

6.3 How Prolog deals with rules

We can give just the head of a rule as a goal for the Prolog interpreter.

Prolog then works down the database from top to bottom looking for the rule, as with facts, and takes the first one in which all the subgoals succeed or are true.

All the subgoals in the rule have to succeed for the rule to succeed. If one fails, the whole rule fails.

The order of rules with the same predicate name is important. Prolog works through them from the top down, and takes the first one to succeed.

6.4 Example of a weather database with rules

We can make up a database of weather facts on a particular day, and add some rules for describing the weather and forecasting it tomorrow.

```
/* WEATHER DATABASE */

/* Weather facts */

temp(high).
barometer(low).
humidity(wet).
sky(overcast).

/* Rules for weather */

weather(good):-temp(high),
     humidity(dry),
     sky(sunny).
weather(bad):-humidity(wet).
weather(bad):-temp(low).
weather(bad):-sky(overcast).
weather(uncertain).

/* Rules for forecast */

forecast(good):-barometer(high).
forecast(bad):-barometer(low).
forecast(uncertain).

/* END */
```

We can now test it with the following:

```
?-weather(Weather).
```

Prolog will look for the predicate **weather** either as a fact or as the head of a rule. Working down the database from top to bottom, it will first find **weather(good)**, and try to match **weather(Weather)** with **weather(good)**. It can do this by instantiating **Weather** to **good**. This is the head of a rule, so it has to continue and test the subgoals. It finds the first subgoal **temp(high)** and searches the database for **temp**. There is only one **temp, temp(high)**, which matches, so it moves to the next subgoal, **humidity(dry)**. It searches the database from the top looking for **humidity**, and finds **humidity(wet)**, which does not match. There are no more instances of **humidity**, so this subgoal fails. It is thus impossible for this weather rule to succeed, and it duly fails.

Prolog moves on to the next **weather** rule. It finds **weather(bad)**, and instantiates **Weather** to bad. There is one subgoal, **humidity(wet)**, and Prolog looks for this in the database. There it is, and this rule succeeds. Prolog returns to the interpreter with **Weather = bad** and a **yes**.

If asked for more solutions, Prolog moves on to the next **weather** rule, which does not succeed as **temp(low)** does not match with **temp(high)**. It moves on automatically to the next, which succeeds as **sky(overcast)** finds a match in the database. Prolog returns again with **Weather = bad** and **yes**, though for a different reason.

If asked for yet another solution, Prolog will return **Weather = uncertain** and **yes**, which always succeeds at the end of a continued query, as it has no subgoals. There are no more solutions after this.

You should be able to predict what the weather forecast will be in response to the following query:

> **?-forecast(Forecast).**

This weather forecasting system does not make any claim to be meteorologically accurate, of course! If you disagree with any of the conditions, try modifying the rules to improve them.

Question 6.3 *(answer on p.45)*

Write a rule for **forecast(storm)** *and consider where to place it in the database.*

6.5 Tracing Prolog executions

The trace predicate is included in most versions of Prolog so that you can watch what happens while Prolog is carrying out a search or trying to satisfy a goal. It is useful when you have a bug or when the program is not behaving as intended.

Operation of the trace facility varies from one Prolog to another, but typically, as in LPA Prolog, entering the goal '**trace.**' will show on the screen every goal and subgoal that is used subsequently. Entering **notrace.** will switch off the tracing facility. (Note that PD Prolog does not have a trace facility.)

Try this on the weather program above, while searching for the goals **weather(Weather)** and **forecast(Forecast)**.

The goal '**spy**' can be entered to spy on part of a rule or program during a goal execution, used in LPA Prolog as follows:

eg.   **?- spy weather.**
        ?- spy weather/1.

The first will spy on this predicate whenever it is used.

The second will spy on the predicate **weather** with one argument, if there are others with 0,2,3 etc. arguments. Note that no brackets are needed for the argument of **spy**, as it is defined as an operator. Note also the / for the optional argument specification.

Trace is useful at times for debugging, but it is slow, and with a big program it can be so time consuming that it becomes impractical. The operation of **spy** can become complicated and time consuming also. It can be quicker to put **write** messages in the program at strategic points, and see whether the execution reaches them. However, as with all programming, sometimes there is a persistent logical fault which can only be tracked down in Prolog using **trace**, and with a lot of trouble!

6.6   An example using days and months

Suppose we want rules to test an integer to see whether it is valid as a day (from 1 to 31) or as a month (from 1 to 12).

We can define a rule 'valid' as follows:

```
valid(day,Day):-
     Day > 0,
     Day < 32.
valid(month,Month):-
     Month > 0,
     Month < 13.
```

These can be used to test an integer used in the date to see whether it is valid.

eg.

?- valid(day,20).	yes
?- valid(month,20).	no
?- valid(month,3).	yes

Question 6.4 *(answer on p.46)*

*Write an additional **valid** rule which tests a year to see whether it is between 1900 and 2000.*

6.7 Use of the semi-colon (or)

We have already introduced the semi-colon, **;** , which is used in Prolog to mean 'or', and is usually read as 'or'. With this, we can construct complex subgoals within a rule, eg.

fault(electrical):-(car_will_not_start ; has_no_lights).

This would read:

The fault is electrical IF the car will not start OR has no lights.

Note the brackets. If you use **;**, make sure you put in brackets as indicated to make it clear to the interpreter what is intended. Several subgoals can be grouped together, eg.

> **fault(electrical):-((car_will_not_start,has_no_lights) ;**
>   **battery_flat).**

> **The fault is electrical IF the car will not start and has no lights OR the battery is flat.**

The number of opening brackets must, of course, be the same as the number of closing brackets.

The **;** is nearly always replaceable with another construction. The rule above can be re-written, for example, as two alternative rules:

> **fault(electrical):-car_will_not_start,has_no_lights.**
> **fault(electrical):-battery_flat.**

It is also possible to put several conditions together with repeated **;**s, eg.

> **fault(electrical):-(car_will_not_start ; has_no_lights ;**
>   **battery_flat).**

> **The fault is electrical IF the car will not start OR has no lights OR the battery is flat.**

This can be re-written:

> **fault(electrical):-car_will_not_start.**
> **fault(electrical):-has_no_lights.**
> **fault(electrical):-battery_flat.**

In a simple example like this the use of **;** may be a shorter and better way of writing the rule. However, with longer and more complex rules the logic can start to get very involved. Some Prolog interpreters do not seem to cope too well with complex **;** constructions. It is best only to use **;** in short rules where the logic is clear.

In general, the frequent use of **;** makes Prolog more difficult to follow. It is probably best not to get into a habit of using **;** but to get into the habit of using repeated rules instead. We will take the approach in this book that it is best to avoid the use of **;** where there is an alternative construction. Where its use makes Prolog code simpler to understand, however, or appreciably shorter, we will make use of it.

6.8 A dating agency exercise

Look at the following database of facts and rules, which contains data on a number of people or persons, and see if you can work out the purpose of the rules.

```
/* A DATING AGENCY DATABASE */

/* Facts */
person(bill,male,24).
person(carol,female,15).
person(george,male,17).
person(margaret,female,52).
person(alfred,male,15).
person(jane,female,23).

/* Rules */

male(Male):-person(Male,male,_).
female(Female):-person(Female,female,_).

man(Man):-person(Man,male,Age), Age > 17.
boy(Boy):-person(Boy,male,Age), Age < 18.

/* END */
```

This database can be used as the basis for a dating agency 'program' which matches people together. We will look at this as an exercise for you to do.

LONG Question 6.5 *(answer on p.46)*

Extend the database above with rules to define a woman and girl as well. What will happen with the following:

```
?- person(Male,male,_).
?- person(Person,_,15).
?- man(bill).
?- girl(Anybody).
?- man(George).
?- boy(X).
```

Now design

(a) a rule **match** which matches any male with any female, using the **person** facts

(b) a rule **match** which matches any man with any woman, using the man and **woman** rules

(c) another rule **match** which matches any man in his twenties with any woman in her twenties, using the **person** facts.

(d) What will the order of the **match** rules need to be in the database?

6.9 Setting out Prolog

It is an almost universal convention to indent the body of a rule, but not the head, using the TAB key. Notice how this is done in the example programs above.

It is usual (though not essential in most versions of Prolog) to group all occurrences of the same rule together. Most people put above this group of rules an explanation of what the rule is for and what it does, using /* ... */ which causes a comment to be ignored by the Prolog interpreter.

It is up to you whether you type the subgoals of a rule along the line or list them vertically. Listing vertically is really a habit from procedural programming, but where a subgoal is cut in two at the end of a line, it is better to put it all on the new line, in the interests of clarity. Some people like to use capitals for the whole of a variable, not just the first letter, as an aid to clarity. (Another habit from procedural programming.) Some try to make Prolog look as much like ordinary English as possible, hence they type along the line and use capitals for just the first letters of variables.

6.10 Summary

A rule has a head which is like a fact, with a predicate followed by arguments, and a body of subgoals. The subgoals are usually other clauses (facts or rules) in the database. The 'neck' operator connecting the head and the body of a rule can usually be read as 'if'.

All the subgoals of a rule have to succeed for the rule to succeed.

When forming a query, just the head of a rule is given for Prolog to search for. During a search Prolog works down the database from the top, and where there are several instances of a rule it will try them in order.

There is a very useful predicate in most Prolog versions called **trace**, which can be used to show how the subgoals of a rule are searched for.

Answers to questions

Answer 6.1

A clause is a fact or a rule, an item in the database.

Answer 6.2

All its subgoals must succeed.

Answer 6.3

Something along the lines of:

> **forecast(storm):-barometer(high),**
> **humidity(wet),**
> **sky(overcast).**

This needs to go above the other forecast rules, as it is a more complex one (more subgoals) and we want it to be tested before the others, otherwise if we asked **forecast(Forecast)**, we would get **Forecast = good** before being told a storm was on the way.

Answer 6.4

> **valid(year,Year):- Year > 1899, Year < 2001.**

Answer 6.5

Add the rules:

> **woman(Woman):-person(Woman,female,Age),Age > 17.**
> **boy(Girl):-person(Girl,male,Age),Age < 18.**

Answers to queries:

> **?- person(Male,male,_).**
> **Male = bill**
> **Male = george**
> **Male = alfred**
> **no**

> **?- person(Person,_,15).**
> **Person = carol**
> **Person = alfred**

> **?- man(bill).**
> **yes**

> **?- girl(Anybody).**
> **Anybody = carol**

> **?- man(George).**
> **George = bill**

> **?- boy(X).**
> **X = george**
> **X = alfred**

(a) match(X,Y):-person(X,male,_),person(Y,female,_).
     match(X,Y):-person(Y,male,_),person(X,female,_).

(b) match(X,Y):-man(X),woman(Y).
     match(X,Y):-man(Y),woman(X).

(c) match(X,Y):-person(X,male,AgeM),person(Y,female,AgeW),
         AgeM>19,AgeM<30,AgeW>19,AgeW<30.

     match(X,Y):-person(Y,male,AgeM),person(X,female,AgeW),
         AgeM>19,AgeM<30,AgeW>19,AgeW<30.

(d) The order needs to be rules (c), rules (b) then rules (a), so that the more
     demanding rules are tested first. This would give the best solutions
     first. Otherwise rules (a) would always succeed first, and the others
     would only be tested as extra solutions.

Programming practice: a royal family database

1. Type in the weather database, the valid rules, and the dating agency database given in the chapter and test them.

2. The database below declares facts about the Windsor family. Type this in (or cut it down to fewer members of the family and then type it in) then see if you can make up and test successful rules for:

   (a) grandmother_of(Grandmother,X)

   (b) brother_of(Brother,X)

   (c) uncle_of(Uncle,X)

   ### /* DATABASE OF THE WINDSORS */

   female(alexandra).
   female(louisa).
   female(victoria).
   female(maud).
   female(mary_of_teck).
   female(mary).
   female(elizabeth_qm).
   female(elizabeth).
   female(margaret).
   female(anne).
   female(zara).
   female(diana).
   female(sarah).
   female(beatrice).
   female(eugenie).
   male(edward7).
   male(albert).
   male(george5).
   male(alexander).
   male(edward8).
   male(george6).
   male(henry).
   male(george).
   male(john).
   male(philip).
   male(charles).
   male(andrew).
   male(edward).
   male(anthony).
   male(mark).
   male(peter).
   male(william).
   male(harry).

```
father_of(edward7,albert).
father_of(edward7,george5).
father_of(edward7,louisa).
father_of(edward7,victoria).
father_of(edward7,maud).
father_of(edward7,alexander).
father_of(george5,edward8).
father_of(george5,george6).
father_of(george5,mary).
father_of(george5,henry).
father_of(george5,george).
father_of(george5,john).
father_of(george6,elizabeth).
father_of(george6,margaret).
father_of(philip,charles).
father_of(philip,anne).
father_of(philip,andrew).
father_of(philip,edward).
father_of(mark,peter).
father_of(mark,zara).
father_of(charles,william).
father_of(charles,harry).
father_of(andrew,beatrice).
father_of(andrew,eugenie).

mother_of(alexandra,albert).
mother_of(alexandra,george5).
mother_of(alexandra,louisa).
mother_of(alexandra,victoria).
mother_of(alexandra,maud).
mother_of(alexandra,alexander).
mother_of(mary_of_teck,edward8).
mother_of(mary_of_teck,george6).
mother_of(mary_of_teck,mary).
mother_of(mary_of_teck,henry).
mother_of(mary_of_teck,george).
mother_of(mary_of_teck,john).
mother_of(elizabeth_qm,elizabeth).
mother_of(elizabeth_qm,margaret).
mother_of(elizabeth,charles).
mother_of(elizabeth,anne).mother_of(elizabeth,andrew).
mother_of(elizabeth,edward).
mother_of(anne,peter).
mother_of(anne,zara).
mother_of(diana,william).
mother_of(diana,harry).
mother_of(sarah,beatrice).
mother_of(sarah,eugenie).

/* END */
```

7 Using rules to write programs

7.1 Introduction

Remember we have said that Prolog is a declarative language, in which we start to tackle a problem by declaring the data (the facts and rules) relating to the problem. This is a different approach to that of procedural languages like Pascal and Ada, in which we start by thinking of what we need to tell the computer to do, and devising a procedure for it to follow.

However, although the Prolog approach is a good one while solving problems, we will reach a point where the problem has been solved and we simply want to run a program to carry out a job on the database.

This is easily accomplished in Prolog. We just write a rule to carry out the job, which runs as a program might run in a procedural language. Although it is declarative, Prolog works very well as a procedural language.

7.2 Example of a program

Suppose we put the following little rule into the Prolog database, by typing it in an editor, saving it as a file then consulting it into Prolog.

```
go:-write('What is your name? '),
    read(Yourname),
    write('Hello, '),
    write(Yourname),nl.
```

We now enter the following in the interpreter:

```
?- go.
```

This is the first time we have used the predicate **read**. It behaves as you might expect from this example. It succeeds by reading in a value from the keyboard, storing it in the variable **Yourname**. You are expected to enter something like the atom **john** as the variable here, but the **read** predicate will in fact read in an atom, an integer, a real number or a string enclosed in quotes.

*Note that with **read** you have to enter things the same way as at the prompt, with a fullstop and <ENTER> at the end.*

49

Prolog finds the rule **go** in the database, and works through the subgoals of the rule. As they are all standard predicates used correctly there will be no problem about any of them failing, so this rule will execute just like a procedural program. Remember, however, that these are not instructions but subgoals that need to succeed.

If a subgoal fails, the 'program' will come to a stop or do unpredictable things such as 'crash' or 'hang up'. The art of programming in Prolog is thus to make everything keep succeeding, or failing in a controlled way, as we will explain in due course.

Question 7.1 *(answer on p.57)*

Make up a rule **banner** *which puts a box on the screen with your name and other details in it, which you could put at the top of future programs, something like this:*

```
* * * * * * * * * * * * * * * * * * * * * * * * * * * * * * * * * * * *
*                        Mickey Mouse                              *
*                                                                  *
*                        Disneyland                                *
* * * * * * * * * * * * * * * * * * * * * * * * * * * * * * * * * * * *
```

7.3   A trick to start programs

If you include the following at the end of the file containing your program, the interpreter will find it during consulting in the file, and execute it like a query entered at the prompt:

:-go.

This will cause it to consult in the file, then immediately look for **go** as a goal, ie. run the program. This is why it has to be placed at the end, so it is encountered after **go** has been consulted in. This makes it unnecessary to type **go** at the prompt to start the program. However, it is not always a good idea with a large program, as you might want to consult in the file and test part of it before running the whole program.

Question 7.2 *(answer on p.57)*

Can you see a way to make the little program started by **go** *above repeat, using recursion?*

7.4 Branching: a months of the year program

Prolog comes into its own with programs that have a branching structure. There is no need for the complicated 'if' constructions or 'case' constructions used in other languages. Consider the following rules, designed to form a program:

```
/* MONTH CONVERSION */

go:-write('INTEGERS TO NAMES OF MONTHS'),nl,nl,
     write('Enter the month as an integer: '),
     read(Month),
     write('The month is '),
     month(Month),nl.

month(1):-write('January.').
month(2):-write('February.').
...
month(12):-write('December.').
month(_):-write('... ? Incorrect entry.').
```

You should by now be able to work out what this program does and how it does it. Notice the catch-all at the bottom, which comes into operation if none of the other alternatives succeeds, and how easy it is to put in this sort of feature.

In these more procedural rules we have set out the subgoals vertically, after the fashion of a procedural program in other languages. You can do this or write rules like sentences, along the line.

Question 7.3 *(answer on p.58)*

*Write a program **go** which asks the user for a name and says whether it is a girl's name or a boy's name, after consulting a database of names of the following form:*

```
boy(jason).
boy(alfred).
boy(joshua).
girl(fiona).
girl(ruth).
girl(blodwen).
```

*Hint: After reading in the name as **Name**, go to a rule **check(Name)**.*
Put in a catch-all for names that are not known.

7.5 Menus: an arithmetic program

Menus are particularly easy in Prolog. Consider the following simple program, started with **run** just to make a change from go:

```
/* ARITHMETIC PROGRAM */

run:- write('Enter a number: '),read(Num1),
      write('Enter another number: '),read(Num2),nl,
      write('What would you like to do?'),nl,nl,
      write(' a. Add.'),nl,
      write(' s. Subtract.'),nl,
      write(' m. Multiply.'),nl,
      write(' d. Divide.'),nl,
      write(' e. Exit.'),nl,nl,
      write('Answer a, b, c, d or e: '),read(Choice),nl,
      choice(Choice,Num1,Num2),nl,nl.

choice(a,N1,N2):-X is N1+N2,write('Answer = '),write(X).
choice(s,N1,N2):-X is N1-N2,write('Answer = '),write(X).
choice(m,N1,N2):-X is N1*N2,write('Answer = '),write(X).
choice(d,N1,N2):-X is N1/N2,write('Answer = '),write(X).
choice(e,_,_).
choice(_,_,_):-write('Wrong letter.').
```

The longest part of writing a program like this is reading in the two numbers and writing out the menu instructions. The process of making the choices is straightforward in Prolog. The user's choice is read in as **Choice**, then the subgoal **choice** starts a search for the rule **choice**. **Choice** is passed to the rule **choice** as an argument. The two numbers are passed as arguments as well. The appropriate version of **choice** is chosen by Prolog according to the value of the first argument. The second and third arguments are then used to do the arithmetic.

There are a lot of things to notice about this little program, which can be used in modified form in any number of other programs. One is that the choice of **e** does nothing, but just succeeds and ends the program. Another thing to notice is that there is a catch-all, which signals an incorrect letter (or number or atom) whatever it might be. In this case the values of the choice and the numbers do not matter, so underscores are used for all arguments.

There is another very important point to be made from this example, which requires a section to itself.

7.6   A variable name only has meaning within one rule

Notice the way the variables in the example above have to be passed from **go** to **choice** as arguments. This is because **Choice**, **Num1** and **Num2** only have a meaning as variables in rule **go**. The words **Choice**, **Num1** and **Num2** will not have the same meaning in rule **choice**. Their values can, however, be passed to **choice** as arguments.

When the values arrive at **choice**, they are just the first, second and third arguments, identified by their position. Where we have to give them variable names, these could be the same as before, but they can equally well be different names. In the example, **Num1** has been re-christened **N1**, and **Num2** has been re-christened **N2**. The variable that was **Choice** does not need a name now, as we are testing for actual values (**a, s, m, d** or **e**) in the position of the first argument. In the last rule the value does not matter, and we use underscore.

Technically we say that the scope of a variable is only the rule it occurs in. There are no 'global' variables in Prolog.

Question 7.4 *(answer on p.58)*

*Go back to your dating agency database program and write a short program consisting of a rule **go** which reads in a name and finds a partner for him or her, using the **match** rules.*

7.7   Values have to be passed between rules as arguments

This means that to pass variables from one rule to another we have to use arguments. In the program in Section 5 above, the following would not have worked:

> ... **read(Choice),nl,choice,nl,nl.**
>
> **choice:-Choice=a,X is Num1+Num2,write('Ans='),write(X).**
> **choice:-Choice=s,X is Num1-Num2,write('Ans='),write(X). etc.**

This solution assumes that **Choice**, **Num1** and **Num2** are global variables with the same values in **choice** as in **go**, which they are not. There are no global variables in Prolog.

Question 7.5 *(answer on p.58)*

What is the scope of a variable in Prolog, or the area in which its name is valid?

7.8   Rules and procedures

Note the strong similarity between rules with arguments in Prolog and procedures with parameters in Pascal or Ada. In one sense Prolog is like a language written entirely in procedures, each rule being made up of procedure-type calls to other rules. (And facts – a fact is just a rule with no body.)

This is a useful concept at times, but do not forget that rules in Prolog are completely different in operation from procedures in other languages.

Question 7.6 *(answer on p.58)*

Write a short menu-type program which asks the following multiple choice question: Which of the following answers is the capital of Australia? It replies as follows:

a	*Adelaide*	*if this answer, say:*	*No*
b.	*Canberra*	*...*	*Yes, good*
c.	*Sydney*	*...*	*No, but good try*
d.	*Singapore*	*...*	*Nowhere near*
e.	*Melbourne*	*...*	*No, but good try*

Put in a catch-all which says 'Incorrect response.'

7.9 A variable can only have one value within a rule

While on the subject of variables in rules, we can point out the following, the importance of which cannot be overstressed:

Any one variable can only have one value in its rule.

This is unlike procedural languages, where a variable can be re-assigned different values at different times.

The following will not be accepted by Prolog:

```
go:-Total = 0,
    write('Enter a number: '),read(Num),
    Total is Total+Num,
    write('Enter another: '),read(Num),
    Total is Total+Num,
    write('Total is '),write(Total),nl.
```

Here the programmer is trying to use assignments as they would be used in Pascal or Ada, re-assigning new values to **Total** and **Num**. The programmer is using the techniques of procedural languages in declarative Prolog.

Each rule has to be a static, declared entity, in which everything has a constant value. It has to be possible for Prolog to be able to prove all of the rule true at the same time.

Calling something a variable does not mean it can vary within the rule. It simply means that its value is something not apparent before the rule is called up from the database, because it has yet to be instantiated.

Remember that Prolog is testing each subgoal as true or false. If you think about it, an expression like **Total is Total + Num** cannot be true, as Total cannot equal itself plus something else.

The program above would have to be written, for example:

```
go:- Total = 0,
     write('Enter a number: '),read(Num1),
     Total1 is Total+Num1,
     write('Enter another: '),read(Num2),
     Total2 is Total1+Num2,
     write('Total is '),write(Total2),nl.
```

A new variable has to be introduced to hold each different new value. When Prolog has worked through the rule, the whole of it is true at the same time. Each variable has its own value.

This is a major difference, perhaps the main practical difference, between declarative and procedural programming. It is something that programmers coming to Prolog from other languages, which means procedural languages, find hard to adapt to.

Question 7.7 *(answer on p.59)*

How are values of variables normally passed from one rule to another in Prolog? If this method is not used, can you think of any other way at all of doing it?

7.10 Saving and retrieving programs to and from files

When you exit from the Prolog interpreter, everything in the database is destroyed, whether it is what you have entered using **assert**, or something you have consulted in from a file.

If you want to save a program or database from one session in the interpreter to the next, it has to be saved as a file on a floppy disc or on the computer's hard disc. There are three very useful predicates which handle this, one of which is the one you have used already for bringing in files you have edited. They are as follows:

consult(File)   Inputs a named file in correct database syntax, giving error messages if the syntax is wrong. If the file does not exist it fails.

reconsult(File)   Inputs a named file of clauses, and replaces existing clauses with the same predicate names with those from the file

save(File)   Outputs the whole Prolog database to a file of the name specified, creating the file or overwriting it as required.

When specifying a filename with all these predicates, you can give it as an atom, eg. **save(thisfile)**, or if it contains a '.' or if you wish to specify a drive name, you can give it as a string using quotes, eg. **save('a:thisfile.pro')**.

These predicates can be used at the interpreter prompt, or inside a rule or program. Using just these predicates, we can read in a file created with an editor and stored on disc (as we have been doing), then we can modify it in the interpreter, and when we have finished with it we can save the whole database back to the file. Any clauses asserted into the database will now be in the file, and any retracted will have been removed.

We will return to the subject of files in Chapter 9.

7.11 A shopping list example

The following program, when saved in a file called **07–shops.prg,** will reconsult the file each time it is run, will allow an alteration to the shopping list to be made, then will automatically save the amended shopping list in a file with the same name.

```
/* SHOPPING LIST PROGRAM */

go:-reconsult('07–shops.prg'),
    write('a. See list'),nl,
    write('b. Add to list'),nl,
    write('c. Delete from list'),nl,
    read(Choice),
    choice(Choice),
    save('07–shops.prg').

choice(a) :-listing(item),nl.
choice(b) :-write('Enter an item: '),
    read(Item),
    assertz(item(Item)).
choice(c) :-write('Item to delete: '),
    read(Item),
    retract(item(Item)).
choice(_) :-write('Incorrect entry.'),nl.

item(potatoes).
item(bread).
item(coffee).

    /* END */
```

7.12 Summary

Prolog can be used to write procedural-type programs by using a rule specifically for the main program (eg. called 'go' or 'run'). Subgoals are then executed rather like instructions in a procedural language. However, remember that they are not instructions but goals which are tested and either succeed or fail.

There are a number of things to remember about the use of variables in rules. A variable only keeps its meaning within one rule. It can have only one final value when the rule succeeds. Variables cannot be 're-assigned' new values within a rule, like variables in a program in a procedural language. Variables which will be needed in a subgoal have to be passed as arguments.

Prolog programs or a Prolog database can be saved to disc, and consulted back in, using the built-in predicates **save, consult** and **reconsult**.

There is a superficial resemblance between rules with arguments in Prolog, and procedures with parameters in procedural languages. Students who have programmed in other languages may find this useful, but the analogy should not be taken too far, as they behave quite differently.

Answers to questions

Answer 7.1

```
banner:-   write('*********************************'),nl,
           write('*                               *'),nl,
           write('*        Mickey Mouse           *'),nl,
           write('*          Disneyland           *'),nl,
           write('*                               *'),nl,
           write('*********************************'),nl,nl.
```

Answer 7.2

To repeat the program, we simply make the rule call itself again from the end, using recursion:

```
go:- write('What is your name? '),
     read(Yourname),
     write('Hello, '),
     write(Yourname),nl,
     go.
```

The trouble is, this will be impossible to end. We will have to put in a condition, as follows:

```
go:- write('What is your name? '),
     read(Yourname),
     write('Hello, '),
     write(Yourname),nl,
     (Yourname=end ; go).
```

The program will now test first whether the variable **Yourname** has been entered as the value end. If so, this test will succeed and the program will **end**. If not, the other half of the 'or' condition will succeed, calling **go** again and repeating.

You can use this simple technique in your subsequent programs whenever you want to make programs repeat, but we will not deal with recursion in detail until Chapter 11.

Answer 7.3

```
go:- write('Enter a name: '),read(Name),
     check(Name).

check(Name):-boy(Name),write('This is a boy.'),nl.
check(Name):-girl(Name),write('This is a girl.'),nl.
check(_):-write('Name not known.'),nl.
boy(jason).
boy(alfred).
boy(joshua).
girl(fiona).
girl(ruth).
girl(blodwen).
```

Answer 7.4

```
go:- write('Enter a name: '),read(Name),
     match(Name,Match),
     write('A match for this person is '),
     write(Match),nl.
go:- write('Sorry, no match found.'),nl.
```

Answer 7.5

The rule it occurs in.

Answer 7.6

```
go:- write('Which is the capital of Australia?'),nl,
     write('a. Adelaide'),nl,
     write('b. Canberra'),nl,
     write('c. Sydney'),nl,
     write('d. Singapore'),nl,
     write('e. Melbourne'),nl,nl,
     read(Choice),choice(Choice).
choice(a):-write('No'),nl.
choice(b):-write('Yes, good'),nl.
choice(c):-write('No, but good try'),nl.
choice(d):-write('Nowhere near'),nl.
choice(e):-write('No, but good try'),nl.
choice(_):-write('Incorrect response'),nl.
```

Answer 7.7

Variables are normally passed as arguments.

If they are not, the other way to transfer values from one rule to another is by asserting a value as a fact in the database. It is then there until it is retracted or until the interpreter session ends, and can be accessed by any rule, like a global variable. This is a clumsy method compared with direct passing of values as arguments, but where a value will be kept for a long time and will be accessed by several rules, asserting a 'flag' value into the database is sometimes useful.

Programming practice: a French translation database

3. Type the following database in the editor:

```
/* TRANSLATION DATABASE */

tran(you,vous).
tran(window,fenetre).
tran(the,le).
tran(pen,plume).
tran(hello,bonjour).
tran(i,je).

/* END */
```

Now add a rule **run** to the database which reads in an English word and translates it into French, as follows:

What is your word? pen
The French is plume

How could you put in a 'catch-all' to do the following?

What is your word? pencil
The French is not known

Test yourself
A Prolog address book project

Produce your own electronic book for names, addresses, birthdays and telephone numbers. The program should read in, look up, change and delete any of the above, allowing the user a choice of these (and perhaps other) options from a menu.

It should store the data in suitably designed facts, retrieving it as required and adding or deleting new facts using **assert** and **retract**. Give some care to deciding how to store the data. It is probably best to enter most data, such as people's names, as strings using quotes, so that they can be saved and written out again with capitals at the beginning.

The program can be started using a rule **go**, and it should save the database into a file at the end of each usage of the program using **save**, and automatically consult it in at the start of the next run using **reconsult**.

Add as many useful features as you wish. For example, there could be an option to enter a month and have all the people with a birthday in that month listed out. If you decide to do things like this, the form of your data is important. The month part of the date will have to be stored as a separate argument. The human computer interface should be as friendly as you can make it. Aim to make this a program you might actually use yourself for your own addresses and telephone numbers.

8 Backtracking

8.1 Introduction

When Prolog carries out a search to try to satisfy a goal, it is actually much more thorough than we have indicated so far.

If Prolog is working through the subgoals of a rule, and one fails, Prolog does not give up immediately and make the rule fail. It will backtrack to previous subgoals and try other instances of them in the database, then move forward again and see whether this will cause the failed subgoal to succeed.

This process is called backtracking, and the end result of it is that Prolog tries all possible solutions for a goal before it finally fails. If you think about it, some mechanism of this kind is essential. We could not have Prolog failing because the first set of subgoal solutions it found did not succeed, when there were other solutions waiting lower down in the database which would enable the rule to succeed.

Question 8.1 *(answer on p.70)*

What takes place when Prolog answers a query entered at the ?-prompt? (See if you can answer in one sentence.)

8.2 Backtracking

Let us just reiterate what we have said about backtracking, then look at an example to try to make it clear.

*As Prolog works through the subgoals of a rule, it does not give up trying to make the rule succeed the first time a subgoal fails. Instead, Prolog **backtracks** to previous subgoals, tries to find another solution to them, then tries the failed subgoal again.*

As an example of what happens during a search, let us look at how Prolog searches the following database representing an office hierarchy to find the supervisor of **brown**.

/* OFFICE DATABASE */

clerk(jones).
clerk(smith).

typist(brown).

>   manager(patel).
>   manager(lee).
>
>   supervises(X,Y):-manager(X),clerk(Y).
>   supervises(X,Y):-clerk(X),typist(Y).
>   supervises(X,Y):-manager(X),typist(Y).
>
>   /* END */

Suppose we try the following query:

>   ?- supervises(Supervisor,brown).

We will follow the search through in detail. Try to follow it at each point. If you have difficulty, type in the database and follow the search through using **trace** (provided your implementation has the trace predicate).

Prolog finds the first rule for **supervises(X,Y)**, and instantiates Y to **brown** to make the head match the query. It moves on to the subgoals of the rule and tries **manager(X)**. A new search to match **manager(X)** produces **manager(patel)**. Prolog now tries to find **clerk(brown)**, and fails.

This is where backtracking begins. Prolog does not give up on this first **supervises** rule, but now backtracks to **manager(X)**, which it has marked to keep its place in the database. It moves on from **manager(patel)** to **manager(lee)**. It tries again to find **clerk(brown)** and again fails. The first **supervises(X,Y)** now fails, as all its subgoals have failed.

Prolog backtracks to where it marked **supervises** in the database, and moves on to the second one, with the head again as **supervises(X,brown)**. It tries **clerk(X)** and finds **clerk(jones)**. **X** is instantiated to **jones**, and this succeeds. Prolog tries **typist(brown)**, finds it and this also succeeds. The second rule for supervises thus succeeds, and Prolog replies **yes** and **Supervisor = jones**.

Prolog now asks if we want more solutions, and if we say **yes**, this rejects the solution already given and effectively makes it fail. Prolog carries on from the markers it has left to keep its place in the database.

There is a marker at **clerk(jones)**, and Prolog moves on to **clerk(smith)**. This succeeds with **X** instantiated to **smith**, and Prolog moves forward again to **typist(brown)** which again succeeds. This solution is presented as **Supervisor = smith**.

If this solution is rejected or 'failed' by asking for more solutions, Prolog backtracks again to **clerk(smith)** where there is a marker, and tries to search further. There are no more **clerks**, so the second **supervises** rule fails. Prolog now goes on to the third **supervises** rule, instantiates **Y** to **brown** and tries to match the goals. To cut a long story short, this rule now yields two more solutions, **Supervisor = patel** and **Supervisor = lee**. Check that you can see how these are obtained.

8.3 Depth first search

Backtracking is essential to the working of Prolog. In the example above, if the interpreter simply took the first **manager**, then moved on to the **clerks** without ever returning to it, it would only ever deal with the top **manager** in the data-base and the others would not be tested.

Prolog thus goes through a process that tries all possible combinations of solu-tions, and finds all successful ones, before it finally reports that a rule has failed.

The backtracking process is a method that has to be used on a sequential computer, which can only do one thing at a time and has to work through all the possibilities systematically. In the subject of logic, all the subgoals of a rule are taken to be true or not true all at the same time. In Prolog, implemented on a real computer, they have to be worked through until those that are true have been found.

Prolog thus has this procedural aspect, where the order of subgoals is signifi-cant, and they are worked through in much the same way that a procedural language works through instructions, but with backtracking as required when subgoals fail. Pure logic would be purely declarative, and a procedural language is purely procedural.

The exhaustive search method Prolog uses is called a depth first search method.

If we draw out the database in the form of a hierarchical tree structure, we can see how this works.

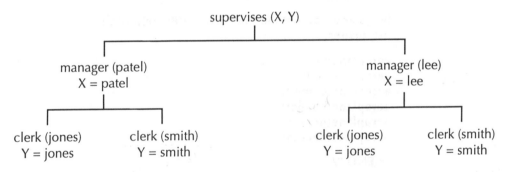

The tree shows the possible solutions for just the first **supervises** rule. Prolog finds **manager(patel)** first, and explores all possibilities of the **clerk** predicate before moving on to **manager(lee)**. It then explores all possibilities of **clerk** again. The execution thus goes as deep as possible down the roots of the tree at each stage.

You can see this in operation by testing the above database with

?- supervises(X,Y).

It is useful to have the **trace** facility 'switched on' while doing this.

Question 8.2 (answer on p.70)

Is Prolog a true implementation of logic programming?

8.4 Rules that succeed once

If there is only one occurrence of a rule in the database, it will succeed once, then fail if encountered again during backtracking, as Prolog will try to move its marker on down the database and fail to find more rules.

This happens with most standard predicates such as **write**, **read**, **nl** and others, which succeed once only. Backtracking passes over them. This is best as it avoids things being written out several times, during backtracking as well as during forward execution.

8.5 Use of 'fail'

fail *is a standard predicate which always fails when encountered, and thus forces backtracking.*

Using fail, we can make a program backtrack when we want it to, and control and make use of backtracking.

The main use of fail is to list out data from a number of facts. As an example, we can list out all the aeroplanes in the following database, using

```
?- listplanes.

/* AEROPLANE DATABASE */

list_planes:-aeroplane(Plane),write(Plane),nl,fail.
list_planes.

aeroplane(hurricane).
aeroplane(spitfire).
aeroplane(comet).
aeroplane(harrier).
aeroplane(jumbo).
aeroplane(dakota).

/* END */
```

What happens here is that **list_planes** is found, and the subgoal **aeroplane(plane)** first succeeds by finding **aeroplane(hurricane)**. **Plane** is instantiated to **hurricane**, and the next subgoal, **write(Plane)** writes out **hurricane**. The next subgoal **nl** succeeds by going to a new line. The subgoal **fail** then fails, causing backtracking.

nl fails on backtracking, so does **write**, and Prolog gets back to **aeroplane** where it has left a marker at **hurricane**. This now moves on, and finds **aeroplane(spitfire)**, which succeeds. **Plane** is instantiated to **spitfire**. Prolog now moves forward again, and encounters **write** again. This time, moving forward, a fresh search is initiated for **write**, so that it is found and succeeds, this time by writing out **spitfire**. **nl** similarly succeeds again in response to a new search.

fail now causes backtracking again, and the process is repeated. All the aeroplanes are listed out, and the listing finally ends when no more **aeroplane** facts can be found.

Note that when the first **list_planes** fails, having listed out all the aeroplanes, there is another **list_planes** which succeeds. It is usual to put in a 'fail-safe rule' in this way, so that if **list_planes** was used in a program, it would succeed and execution would continue.

Remember that when running a Prolog 'program' procedurally, every subgoal has to succeed in the end, or the program will stop or misbehave.

Question 8.3 *(answer on p.70)*

Look at the following animals database:

/* ANIMALS DATABASE */

```
animal(mammal,tiger,carnivore,stripes).
animal(bird,eagle,carnivore,large).
animal(mammal,hyena,carnivore,ugly).
animal(bird,sparrow,scavenger,small).
animal(mammal,lion,carnivore,mane).
animal(reptile,snake,carnivore,long).
animal(mammal,zebra,herbivore,stripes).
animal(reptile,lizard,scavenger,small).
```

/* END */

For this database, add a simple rule in each case which

(a) writes a list of all the animals' names

(b) writes a list of animals and their characteristics

(c) writes a list of those which are mammals.

8.6   True and repeat

These are two more standard predicates. **true** succeeds once, as though it occurs only once in the database. **repeat** always succeeds, even on backtracking, as though there were an infinite number of **repeats** in the database.

true is not often used, except as an aid to readability in programs. For example, if we wanted, in the last example above, to stress that the second **list_planes** must succeed, we could write it as follows:

list_planes:- true.

repeat on the other hand is often used.

*We use **repeat** to stop backtracking and send the Prolog execution forward again.*

This can be seen in the following example:

```
words:-  write('Which word stops this program?'),nl,
         repeat,
         write('Enter a word: '),read(Word),
         Word=stop,
         write('Stop is correct.'),nl.
```

The first message is written out once, then repeat is passed, and the second message is written out. The user enters a word, and if this is anything other than the atom **stop**, the expression **Word=stop** fails. The program backtracks, passes over **read** and **write** which can only succeed once, then encounters **repeat** which succeeds and sends it forward again. The second message gets written out again, another word is entered, and the process is repeated, until **stop** is entered, when **Word=stop** succeeds and the rule ends with all its subgoals met.

Question 8.4 *(answer on p.70)*

What will happen with the following?

(a) **t_test:-true,**
     write('Hello.'),nl,
     fail.
     t_test.

(b) **r_test:-repeat,**
     write('Hello.'),nl,'
     fail.
     r_test.

8.7 A murder mystery example

This program, which appeared in the magazine PC World as part of a series on Prolog, borders on Artificial Intelligence, using Prolog to do the reasoning to solve a murder mystery. It can be looked on as an expert system to simulate the expertise of a detective, or as a prototype mystery type of game.

It is a superb example of how a problem that at first sight appears quite incapable of solution by a computer turns out to be short and concise when tackled in Prolog. Just try to program this in C or Pascal!

Notice the declarative approach. We represent the information of the passage in a database of facts, write rules to relate them to each other, and it becomes clear how to construct a main rule **whodunnit** to find the murderer. To see who it is, we just need to enter **?-whodunnit(Murderer)** at the prompt.

/* MURDER AT THE MANSION *

At ten o'clock at the mansion house, the maid discovered Celia, the vicar's wife, lying in a pool of blood on the Colonel's tigerskin rug. She had been horribly bludgeoned to death with a blunt instrument.

The maid, a frail, deaf old lady in her nineties, had been in service all her life with the Colonel's family. She said she had gone to bed at 9.40, five minutes after the Colonel had set off for his regular game of dominoes with the vicar. She had forgotten to put the cat out, and when she got up to do so she discovered the body. She phoned the police immediately.

Detective Pierre O'Log arrived at the scene of the crime at 10.10 and immediately took the corpse's temperature, to determine the earliest possible time of death. He also did a thorough check for fingerprints. He then went straight to the vicarage to impart the terrible news to the vicar.

The vicar was in the middle of a game of dominoes with the Colonel, which they had been playing since 9.55. In spite of his grief, he gave a lucid account of his activities that evening. His unfortunate wife had left at 9.25, saying she was going to visit some parishioners. Neither he nor the Colonel knew why she had ended up at the Colonel's mansion. The Colonel had arrived at 9.50, and before he had even taken his coat off, Nigel, the local cad and lecher, had called at the door, asking for help because his flashy sports car had broken down. The vicar had charitably told him the local garage's opening time, and gone back inside to start his dominoes. The Colonel confirmed the vicar's story but had not seen who had been at the door.

O'Log then went immediately to the cottage where Nigel lived with his wife, Cynthia. Nigel remembered saying goodbye to Cynthia at the cottage at 9.30. He had been 'intending to go and have a few beers with his chums', but his car had broken down. He had called for help at the vicarage, but when none was forthcoming he had been forced to walk home. He arrived back at about 10.30, just as his wife was going to bed.

Cynthia, a rather robust lady, said that she had stayed at home all evening, mixing cement for a garden wall she was building. She confirmed that Nigel had been out between 9.30 and 10.30.

The fingerprint tests revealed that the prints of the Colonel, the maid, Celia and Nigel were all present in the mansion.

Armed with this information, Detective O'Log only needed to carefully measure the fastest possible journey times between the mansion, the vicarage and the cottage before he knew the murderer's identity. */

/* FACTS */

/* Knowledge base, containing the data relating

   to the problem */

```
/* Victim is Celia */
body_discovered_at(60,mansion).

/* Death caused by bludgeoning */
cause_of_death(bludgeoning).

/* Body temperature at 10:10 was 96.4F */
body_temp_at(70,96.4).

/* Specify the suspects */
suspect(maid).
suspect(colonel).
suspect(vicar).
suspect(nigel).
suspect(cynthia).

/* Everybody's physical strength rating:
     1 = bed-ridden, 10 = strong as an ox */
physical_strength(vicar,7).
physical_strength(colonel,4).
physical_strength(maid,2).
physical_strength(nigel,8).
physical_strength(cynthia,5).

/* Where everybody lives */
lives_at(celia,vicarage).
lives_at(ronald,vicarage).
lives_at(maid,mansion).
lives_at(colonel,mansion).
lives_at(nigel,cottage).
lives_at(cynthia,cottage).

/* Fastest possible travel times between key locations */
time_between(mansion,vicarage,12).
time_between(vicarage,mansion,12).
time_between(cottage,vicarage,18).
time_between(vicarage,cottage,18).
time_between(cottage,mansion,24).
time_between(mansion,cottage,24).
time_between(Anywhere,Anywhere,0).

/* Everybody's whereabouts */
saw(vicar,celia,vicarage,0,20).
saw(vicar,nigel,vicarage,52,52).
saw(nigel,cynthia,cottage,0,30).
saw(nigel,cynthia,cottage,90,99).
saw(colonel,vicar,vicarage,50,99).
saw(cynthia,nigel,cottage,90,99).
saw(vicar,colonel,vicarage,50,99).
saw(maid,colonel,mansion,0,35).
saw(nigel,vicar,vicarage,52,52).
saw(colonel,maid,mansion,0,35).
saw(celia,nigel,cottage,0,30).
```

```
/* Specify whose fingerprints were found */
finger_prints_found(celia).
finger_prints_found(colonel).
finger_prints_found(nigel).
finger_prints_found(cynthia).

/* RULES */

/* This is the reasoning part, the 'inference engine'
    of an expert system simulating a detective */

whodunnit(Person):-suspect(Person),
    unexplained_fingerprints(Person),
    not(has_alibi(Person)).
whodunnit(Person):-suspect(Person),
    strong_enough(Person),not(has_alibi(Person)).

unexplained_fingerprints(Person):-
    finger_prints_found(Person),
    body_discovered_at(_,Scene_of_crime),
    not(lives_at(Person,Scene_of_crime)).

has_alibi(Person):-
    body_discovered_at(Latest,Scene_of_crime),
    earliest_time_of_death(Earliest),
    saw(_,Person,Somewhere,Early_time,Late_time),
    time_between(Scene_of_crime,Somewhere,Travel_time),
    Latest < Late_time + Travel_time,
    Earliest > Early_time - Travel_time.

earliest_time_of_death(Time):-
    body_temp_at(Time_temp_taken,Temp),
    Time is Time_temp_taken - (98.4-Temp)*10.

strong_enough(Person):-cause_of_death(bludgeoning),
    physical_strength(Person,Rating),Rating >= 4.
strong_enough(Person):-cause_of_death(shooting),
    physical_strength(Person,Rating),Rating > 1.
strong_enough(Person):-cause_of_death(poisoning).

/* END */
```

Try to follow through how this program works, at least roughly. The main rules **whodunnit** which find the murderer do so by exploring all possible solutions, employing backtracking. See if you can predict the murderer from studying the text, then by studying the program, and if you are still not sure, type the program in and run it to find out!

It is useful to modify the program so that the cause of death is (a) shooting and (b) poisoning, and see what effect it has on the solutions.

8.8 Summary

Backtracking is the mechanism by which Prolog tries all possible solutions for a goal it is given before finally failing. When a subgoal fails, Prolog backtracks to previous subgoals and tries them again, then moves forward and re-tries the failed subgoal. The process is called depth-first searching.

Backtracking can be controlled using two important predicates, **fail** which always fails and **repeat** which always succeeds. These can be used for specialised repeating constructions. There is also **true** which succeeds once.

Answers to questions

Answer 8.1

Prolog matches the query with clauses in the database, and if it matches with the head of a rule matches all the subgoals as well, instantiating variables as required until a solution is found.

Answer 8.2

It is more accurate to say that Prolog is a programming language based on logic. True logic programming would be purely declarative, and Prolog as it is implemented has definite procedural aspects. It is useful that it does, however. The procedural characteristics of Prolog make it easy to write conventional computer programs in Prolog.

Answer 8.3

(a) **write_names:-animal(_,Name,_,_),write(Name),nl,fail.**
   write_names.

(b) **write_characteristics:-animal(_,Name,_,Char),**
       write(Name),write(' '),write(Char),nl,fail.
   write_characteristics.

(c) **write_mammals:-animal(mammal,Name,_,_),write(Name),nl,fail.**
   write_mammals.

Answer 8.4

(a) This will write **Hello** once, then answer **yes**. On backtracking, **nl**, then **write**, then **true**, then **t_test** will fail. The second **t_test** will then succeed.

(b) This will write **Hello** for ever more. **fail** will cause backtracking, which will pass over **nl** and **write**, then **repeat** will always succeed. The execution will be trapped between **repeat** and **fail**, and will 'bounce' backwards and forwards until interrupted by pressing <CONTROL> <BACKSPACE> or some similar drastic action.

Programming practice: **world cities**

Type the following database.

```
/* CITY DATABASE */

capital(bern).
capital(london).
capital(prague).
capital(bonn).
capital(belgrade).

city_in(prague,czechoslovakia).
city_in(bratislava,czechoslovakia).
city_in(berlin,germany).
city_in(leipzig,germany).
city_in(bonn,germany).
city_in(hamburg,germany).
city_in(belgrade,yugoslavia).
city_in(zagreb,yugoslavia).
city_in(bern,switzerland).
city_in(zurich,switzerland).
city_in(london,united_kingdom).
city_in(edinburgh,united_kingdom).

belongs_to(czechoslovakia,'COMECON').
belongs_to(germany,'EC').
belongs_to(switzerland,'EFTA').
belongs_to(united_kingdom,'EC').

/* END */
```

1. Write rules to

    (a) list all the capital cities in the database

    (b) list all the cities

    (c) list all the countries in the EC.

2. Devise a rule to find the capital of a country, used as follows

    ?- capital_of(City,france).

3. Devise a rule to find capital cities in the EC, used as follows

    ?- capital_in_EC(Capital).

9 Input, output and files

9.1 Introduction

A **file** is a named unit where data can be stored or accessed by a program, external to the program. An example is a block of data or file created on a floppy disc or hard disc.

Input is data that a program takes in from a source like the keyboard or a file. **Output** is data that the program sends out to a destination like the VDU (visual display unit) or a file.

The keyboard and the VDU are called the **default** input and output. The Prolog interpreter looks for input from the keyboard, and sends output to the VDU, unless otherwise specified.

Prolog treats the input from the keyboard as though it were being read from a file called **user**, and it treats the output to the VDU as though it were being written to the same file **user**.

9.2 Files and the database

Do not confuse outputting to a file with asserting facts into the database. Files are stored permanently on hard or floppy disc, while the Prolog database is stored in part of the computer's internal memory. When you exit from the Prolog interpreter, all the clauses in the database are destroyed, and they will not be there when you next go into Prolog.

The only way you can save things from one session at the interpreter to the next is by saving them in a file. Having saved the file, you have to consult it in at the start of the next session before the database is available again. This is why files are essential – to save data from one session to the next.

Before going on to look at file handling, it may be a good idea to spell out all the predicates for asserting clauses into the database, and for retracting them out again.

asserta(Clause)   puts the clause specified into the database at the top.

assertz(Clause)   put the clause specified into the database at the bottom.

assert(Clause)   in versions of Prolog where this is included, **assert** is identical to **assertz**.

retract(Clause)   removes the first occurrence of the clause specified. Fails if there are none.

retractall(head(_)) removes all clauses for predicate **head**. Succeeds when it has done this, or if there are none.

In Prolog versions where **retractall** does not exist, it can be entered into the database as follows:

> **retractall(X):-retract(X),fail.**
> **retractall(_).**
>
> eg. **retractall(person(_,_,_)),...**

This removes all occurrences of **person** from the database.

Question 9.1 *(answer on p.77)*

What is the main difference between putting data into the Prolog database using assert, and putting data into a file?

9.3   Saving and retrieving whole databases to and from files

This is done with the three predicates we have already described, and which you have probably used by now:

> **consult(File)**
>
> **reconsult(File)**
>
> **save(File)**

Refer to Chapter 7 for the use of these predicates.

Question 9.2 *(answer on p.77)*

Suppose you have absent-mindedly consulted in your program file 'myfile.pro' twice, so that you have everything doubled up in the Prolog database, and this is messing up your program. How can you put the database right very simply?

9.4   Input and output predicates

We have met some of these already. They are as follows in standard, basic Prolog. (There will be extra ones in your Prolog implementation.)

read(Var)   This reads an atom, an integer, a string in quotes or a real number into the variable **Var**. There must be no disallowed characters like spaces, and there must be a fullstop at the end, which does not become part of the term read in.

write(Var)   This writes an atom, an integer, a real number, a string in quotes or a term to the output stream, whatever is the value of **Var**.

get0(Char)	Reads in a single character, as its ASCII code, ie. an integer. (Computers deal with numbers, and always convert characters into numbers called ASCII codes.) The ASCII code of the first character encountered is taken, and others are ignored until the next <ENTER>, which is required.
get(Char)	The same as **get0**, except that **get** only accepts printing characters. Less commonly used than **get0**.
put(Char)	The reverse of get0. **put** takes an integer and outputs it as an ASCII code, eg. **put(97)** puts 'a' on the screen, **put(12)** clears the screen, **put(7)** makes a bleeping sound.
nl	Sends a new line signal to the VDU, or records it in a file as an end-of-line.
tab(N)	Writes N space characters to the output, where N is an integer.

Question 9.3 *(answer on p.78)*

Try the following at the interpreter prompt:

```
?- get0(X).
a <ENTER>
?- get0(X).
a. <ENTER>
?- get0(X).
abc <ENTER>
?- get0(X).
<SPACE><ENTER>
?- get(X).
<SPACE><ENTER>
?- put(97).
?- put(12).
?- put(7).
?- tab(20).
```

9.5   File access predicates

Prolog has file predicates which allow more detailed operations on files than simply consulting or saving a whole database.

tell(File)	Opens a named file as the current output stream.
told	Closes the file which is currently being used for the output and reverts to the VDU.
see(File)	Opens the named file as the input stream.
seen	Closes the file which is currently being used for the input and reverts to the keyboard.
eof(File)	This succeeds if the end of the named file has been reached during input, otherwise fails.

Once a file has been opened for input or output, the usual predicates for reading input or writing output can be used, ie. **read**, **write**, **get0** and **put**, just the same as if the input came from the keyboard, or the output was going to the VDU.

In addition there are two more file predicates which are less commonly required.

telling(File)   If **File** is an uninstantiated variable, it will be instantiated to the current output.

seeing(File)   If **File** is an uninstantiated variable, it will be instantiated to the current input.

These two predicates thus provide information about the current files being handled. In most programs this will not be necessary, unless the program is handling files in a complex way.

9.6   Some useful examples

The following rule **savefile** with its subrule **write_db** saves all the **person** facts in the database (with three arguments) to a file **test.pro**, first deleting any old version of the file. If there is no such file, the rules create one.

```
savefile:-tell('test.pro'),write_db,told.

write_db:-person(A,B,C),X=person(A,B,C),
     write(X),write('.'),nl,fail.
write_db.

person(bill,smith,25).
person(fred,bloggs,20).
person(elvis,presley,56).
```

The following rule **readfile** will read in a named file, character by character, and write it out on the screen.

```
readfile(File):-
     see(File),
     repeat,get0(Ch),put(Ch),
     eof(File),seen.
```

Note that when file names are entered, and they have an extension separated by a period, they need to be input as strings with quotes.

Question 9.4 *(answer on p.78)*

Try the following at the interpreter prompt, or see if you can predict what they will give:

1.	?- telling(X).
2.	?- seeing(X).
3.	?- assert(test(fact)).
	?- save('testprog.pro').
4.	?- see('testprog.pro'),seeing(X),seen.
5.	?- see('prog.pro'),seeing(X),seen.

9.7 Extensions to basic Prolog

Most textbooks for Prolog stick to the Edinburgh standard of the language, described in the book Programming in Prolog by Clocksin and Mellish. This is because different implementations differ from this standard and from each other, though usually because they go beyond it rather than deviating greatly from it. (TurboProlog is an exception; it is very non-standard.) This book will do the same – otherwise it would become a manual for one commercial version of Prolog.

Most versions of Prolog now have additional predicates for input and output, and for much else besides, such as putting output into windows, changing the screen colours, and so on. We cannot deal with these in this book, but it is worth mentioning one point in connection with input.

Students become very irritated with the fullstop in Prolog. The command **read** in other high level languages will accept input without the fullstop, and it does seem strange to have an input predicate which requires a fullstop which is then thrown away.

There are ways round this. It will depend on the implementation you are using, but in LPA Prolog the following user defined rule **getstring** will read in a string as an atom, ended by an <ENTER> with no fullstop. (If you put in the fullstop it will become part of the string.) You can put in spaces, capitals and other 'illegal' characters, and the whole string of characters will be entered enclosed in quotes, as a single atom.

```
getstring(String):-
      fr('BUF:',[s(0)],[Inword]),
      stringof(Inword,TempWord),
      concat(String,'~M',TempWord).
```

fr, **stringof** and **concat** are LPA specific string and stream handling predicates. They are not standard Prolog and will not necessarily be found in other versions of Prolog.

In Public Domain (PD) Prolog, the built-in predicate **ratom** does this. If you prefer to use **getstring**, you can enter it into your programs like this:

```
getstring(String):-ratom(String).
```

The fullstop and <ENTER> is particularly annoying when using menus, as most people expect to operate a menu with a single keypress, and even if we use the Prolog **get0** a second press of <ENTER> is needed. Again, in LPA Prolog only, the following two-argument version of **get0** will do the trick:

get0('TRM:',Char), ...

This will take a character as a single keypress, inputting it as its ASCII code. We can include this in a program as **getchar** (which is a common identifier used in other languages -TurboProlog has it built-in) as follows:

getchar(Char):-get0('TRM:',Char).

If you don't have LPA Prolog, see your manual!

9.8 Summary

When you exit from the Prolog interpreter, the Prolog database is destroyed, so that if you want to save it you must output it into a file on disc. Similarly, when you enter Prolog the database is empty, and you have to input things into it, either directly at the prompt or by consulting in a file from disc.

There are standard predicates in Prolog which can be used to open files on disc, and read from them and write to them directly. Prolog also contains standard predicates for inputting from the keyboard and outputting to the Visual Display Unit.

Answers to questions

Answer 9.1

The practical difference is that data put into the Prolog database is only there during one session in the interpreter, as the database is held in the computer's memory. Data put into a file is saved permanently on a backup medium like a hard or floppy disc.

Answer 9.2

The neat way to do this is to bring in the file a third time, but this time using **reconsult**. This will clear out all the doubled up clauses before bringing them in again correctly.

Alternatively, you would have to use **retractall** for all the clauses separately, then consult the file in again, or use one of the methods peculiar to your implementation, such as **kill(all)** in LPA Prolog, which clears the whole database. You would still have to consult again. Another way to put things right, rather drastic, would be to use **halt** to exit from Prolog altogether, then come back in, to an empty database, and consult again.

Answer 9.3

> **a <ENTER> with get0 gives X = 97**
> **a. <ENTER> with get0 gives X = 97**
> **abc <ENTER> with get0 gives X = 97**
> **<SPACE><ENTER> with get0 gives X = 32**
> **SPACE><ENTER> with get will not be accepted**
> **put(97) puts an 'a' on the screen**
> **put(12) clears the screen**
> **put(7) makes a bleep**
> **tab(20) moves the cursor 20 positions across the screen**

Answer 9.4

1. telling(X) will return something like X = 'WND:', the system code for the current output.

2. seeing(X) will return something like X = 'BUF:', the system code for the current input.

3. ?- assert(test(fact)).

   ?- save('testprog.pro').

   The first line will assert a test fact into the database, and the second line will save it into a file.

4. ?- see('testprog.pro'),seeing(X),seen.

   This will return X = 'testprog.pro'. Why?

5. ?- see('prog.pro'),seeing(X),seen.

   This will give 'no' or an error, unless you happen to have a file called 'prog.pro' already saved.

Programming practice: **telephone numbers**

Write a program which reads in names and telephone numbers as **telephone** facts and asserts them into the database. The program should give options of viewing all the telephone numbers, entering a new one, deleting one, or changing one. On leaving the program, the program saves the facts only into a file **'phone.pro'**. At the start of each run it uses reconsult to refresh this file. Test the program.

Test yourself
Prolog basics

1. The name Prolog stands for _____

2. Prolog is unlike the more usual procedural languages in being a _____ language.

3. Prolog consists of two main parts, an _____ where queries are entered and a _____ of clauses.

4. There are two basic types of clause in Prolog, _____ and _____

5. Prolog answers a query entered at the ?- prompt by _____ it with clauses in the database.

6. A fact in Prolog consists of a _____ and one or more _____ in brackets after it.

7. A rule in Prolog consists of a _____ and a _____ connected by a :- operator.

8. For a rule to succeed, all the subgoals must _____

9. The process of giving a variable a value during a search is called _____

10. Names of variables in Prolog are distinguished from atoms by _____

11. The scope of a variable in Prolog, or the area within which its name is valid, is _____

12. Values of variables are normally passed between rules as _____

13. The underscore in Prolog is called the _____ and is used as_____

14. Prolog continues searching for solutions even after a sub-goal fails by a process called _____

15. This results in a searching strategy called _____

16. Say briefly what the following predicates do when used in a Prolog program:

    save(Filename) _____

    tell(Filename) _____

    told _____

    see(Filename) _____

    seen _____

    get0(Ch) _____

17. The function of the predicate 'fail' in Prolog is that it always fails and is used to _____

18. The predicate 'repeat' has a special use in Prolog, which is to _____

19. A semantic net can be converted to facts quite simply by writing the _____ as _____ and writing the _____ as _____

20. For the following database, write rules as follows:

    country(uk,london,europe,english).
    country(zaire,kinshasa,africa,swahili).
    country(kenya,nairobi,africa,swahili).
    country(usa,washington,north_america,english).

    (a) A rule countries (no arguments) which writes out a list of the names only of the **countries** in the database, then succeeds:

    _____

    _____

    (b) A rule **caps** which writes out a list of the cities in Europe where English is spoken, then succeeds:

    _____

    _____

10 Expert systems

10.1 Introduction

An expert system (ES) is a computer program which is designed to carry out tasks associated with a human expert. It is a program which tries to do things which are usually regarded as the province of humans, involving judgements and decision making.

As human experts tend to have a great deal of specialised knowledge in their fields, expert systems are usually knowledge based systems (KBSs) which contain large databases of knowledge information.

Expert systems originated as a branch of Artificial Intelligence.

10.2 Parts of an expert system

As many experts work from a collection of rules, either consciously or otherwise, and Prolog is a rule-based language, Prolog is particularly useful for programming expert systems.

In very simple terms, an expert system is usually said to be made up of three main parts:

A *knowledge base* – consisting of knowledge relating to the field of the expert.

An *'inference engine'* – a system for manipulating the knowledge so as to draw inferences from it.

A *user interface* – making the knowledge of the expert accessible to the non-expert user.

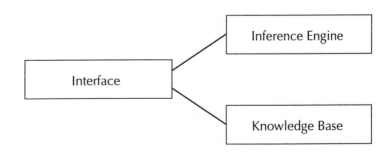

10.3 Knowledge engineering

Making up the knowledge base of the expert system is usually the difficult part, as the programmer does not have this knowledge and has to extract it from an expert in the field in a lengthy 'knowledge engineering' exercise. This knowledge will often be difficult to convey to a non-expert, but apart from this the expert will often be quite inarticulate in explaining it, and may resent the idea of a machine taking over his precious expertise, and may show antagonism to the whole exercise.

As we are concerned here with constructing the expert system in Prolog, we can gloss over the knowledge extraction problem and simply use some knowledge which we can assume has already been correctly put together.

Experts use their knowledge to give answers to questions, or solutions to problems. (This of course is what the Prolog interpreter is designed to do.) One type of expert system, which we will look at first, takes in all the information relating to a problem and returns one of a range of possible solutions as the correct or most likely one.

Question 10.1 *(answer on p.86)*

What are some of the problems encountered in obtaining the knowledge for an expert system knowledge base from an expert?

10.4 A dog spotter expert system

Let us make up a simple expert system to identify dogs – in fact a small selection of well-known dogs from the large number there are. Let us assume that the dogs' features can be summarised in the following table:

Dog	Size	Colour	Length of coat	Used for
alsatian	large	black and tan	thick	guarding
rottweiler	large	black	thick	guarding
bulldog	small	grey	short	guarding
St Bernard	large	golden	thick	finding people
greyhound	large	any	short	racing
terrier	small	grey	wiry	chasing things
golden retriever	average	golden	long	gun-dog
sheepdog	average	black and white	long	herding sheep
dalmation	large	spotted	short	pet
poodle	small	any	fluffy	pet

This table of features represents our expert knowledge.

We can put this into a database of rules as follows.

```
         rule(1,alsatian):-
             size(large),
             colour(black_and_tan),
             coat(thick),
             used_for(guarding).

         rule(2,rottweiler):-
             size(large),
             colour(black),
             coat(thick),
             used_for(guarding).
```

… and so on. In fact we do not need four features for every dog, as a few important features are enough to distinguish each one. We can write the rules concisely as follows.

```
         rule(1,alsatian):-colour(black_and_tan),used_for(guarding).
         rule(2,rottweiler):-colour(black),used_for(guarding).
```

Having made up the rest of the database along these lines, we need a rule to collect features of a particular dog from the user, to go through the rules and find one that fits, then to inform the user which dog it is – in other words, a combined inference engine and interface.

The finished rudimentary expert system could be as follows:

```
/* DOG SPOTTER */

/* Inference engine and interface */

go:- write('** DOG SPOTTER **'),nl,nl,
     write('How big is the dog? Choose from large, average'),nl,
     write('or small: '),read(Size),
     write('What colour is it? Choose from golden, grey,'),nl,
     write('black,black_and_white, black_and_tan, spotted,'),nl,
     write('or any: '),read(Colour),
     write('Describe its coat. Choose from short, long,'),nl,
     write('wiry, thick or fluffy: '),read(Coat),
     write('Describe what it is used for. Choose from '),nl,
     write('racing, chasing, guarding, gun-dog, pet,'),nl,
     write('finding_people, or herding_sheep: '),read(Use),nl,
     assertz(size(Size)),assertz(colour(Colour)),
     assertz(coat(Coat)),assertz(used_for(Use)),
     rule(Rule,Dog),
     write('The dog is: '),write(Dog),nl,nl,
     write('The rule used was Number '),write(Rule),nl,nl,
     retractall(size(_)),retractall(colour(_)),
     retractall(coat(_)),retractall(used_for(_)).

/* Knowledge base */

         rule(1,alsatian):-colour(black_and_tan),used_for(guarding).
         rule(2,rottweiler):-colour(black),used_for(guarding).
         rule(3,bulldog):-size(small),used_for(guarding).
```

```
rule(4,st_bernard):-used_for(finding_people).
rule(5,greyhound):-used_for(racing).
rule(6,terrier):-size(small),coat(wiry),used_for(chasing_things).
rule(7,golden_retriever):-colour(golden),used_for(gun-dog).
rule(8,sheepdog):-used_for(herding_sheep).
rule(9,dalmation):-colour(spotted).
rule(10,poodle):-size(small),coat(fluffy),used_for(pet).
rule(11,'not known.').
```

/* END */

?

Question 10.2 *(answer on p.86)*

Can you think of another another way of storing data on dogs, and identifying them, using a Prolog database?

10.5 Transparency

A point to notice about this program is that we have put in an extra line to say which rule was used to find the answer. This is considered very important in expert systems – making the system try to explain itself, and say how it arrived at its result. It is obviously important to do this where non-experts are being expected to accept the suggestions of a system which they may disagree with. Making an expert system explain itself is known as 'transparency'. In the program above, simply stating the rule used does not explain things very much, but it's a start.

This program, although simple, also shows the difficulty of making rules reliable. The rules shown are designed for this knowledge base only and would need to be much more specific to be extended to other dogs. For example, Rule 7 picks out a golden coloured gun-dog, but might get confused if we added a spaniel to the list.

If the system is to be extendable, it becomes necessary to establish a list of questions that will unambiguously identify any possible dog. If we included in each rule all the features entered, as we did at first above, it would go some way towards this, but clearly many more questions would be needed to make the system infallible.

10.6 An alternative approach

It is worth looking at another way of writing the program for identifying dogs. Using the original data, we can write a dog database as facts as follows.

```
dog(alsatian,large,black_and_tan,thick,guarding).
dog(rottweiler,large,black,thick,guarding).
dog(bulldog,small,grey,short,guarding).
dog(st_bernard,large,golden,thick,finding_people).
dog(greyhound,large,any,short,racing).
dog(terrier,small,grey,wiry,chasing_things).
dog(golden_retriever,average,golden,long,gun-dog).
dog(sheepdog,average,black_and_white,long,herding_sheep).
```

> dog(dalmation,large,spotted,short,pet).
> dog(poodle,small,any,fluffy,pet).

We could then rewrite the main program rule as follows:

> go:- write('** DOG SPOTTER **'),nl,nl,
>   write('How big is the dog? Choose from large, average'),nl,
>   write('or small: '),read(Size),
>   write('What colour is it? Choose from golden, grey,'),nl,
>   write('black,black_and_white, black_and_tan, spotted,'),nl,
>   write('or any: '),read(Colour),
>   write('Describe its coat. Choose from short, long,'),nl,
>   write('wiry, thick or fluffy: '),read(Coat),
>   write('Describe what it is used for. Choose from '),nl,
>   write('racing, chasing, guarding, gun-dog, pet,'),nl,
>   write('finding_people, or herding_sheep: '),read(Use),nl,
>   *dog(Dog,Size,Colour,Coat,Use),*
>   *write('The dog is: '),write(Dog),nl,nl.*

This main rule is the same as before except for the last two lines in italics. This program will work as well as the other under most circumstances. At first sight it may look a shorter and better way of doing it, but the rule-based method has several advantages.

The main one is that it uses logical rules rather than the blunt instrument method of simply matching all the data for a particular dog. This is usually a better method, closer to how experts work. For example, we may not know all the data for a dog, but we may know that it is used for rescuing people. Or we may make a mistake in entering the data, but still get right the crucial feature of rescuing people. In these circumstances the rule-based program will correctly identify the St Bernard, whereas the other program as written would not work. This is how an expert would reach his conclusion. If we told him that the dog rescued people, he would know it was a St Bernard even if we could tell him nothing else.

Another advantage is that the rule-based program will tell us which rule it used, and enable us to check how it arrived at its conclusion. The other program cannot do this without further modification, beyond saying that the data we entered worked or not.

Generally speaking, the more complex the data and the rules become, the more the rule-based approach comes into its own. In complex systems, simple fact matching will not usually work.

?

LONG Question 10.3 *(answer on p.87)*

Devise rules to identify the following ten common fruits, and put them into a GROCER expert system to tell a user what fruit he is looking at.

banana, orange, apple, pear, grape, pineapple, peach, apricot, melon, date

10.7 Summary

An expert system attempts to capture the expertise of an expert in some field into a computer program. Prolog is particularly well suited to building expert systems, as this chapter tries to show.

An expert system usually consists of a knowledge base, an inference engine and a user interface. As the knowledge base contains large amounts of specialised knowledge, ESs are sometimes referred to as knowledge based systems, and as the inference engine usually contains a collection of expert rules they are also referred to as rule based systems.

The collection of the knowledge from the expert is often a difficult and time-consuming task in the building of an ES. An important feature of ESs is transparency, allowing the user to see how they reach their conclusions.

Answers to questions

Answer 10.1

Expert knowledge is usually technical and the knowledge engineer, a non-expert, has difficulty understanding it.

The expert is often poor at explaining it.

There is often antagonism on the part of the expert, who wants to show that he is really indispensable.

Answer 10.2

We could save the data in simple facts, of the type

dog(bulldog,small,grey,short,guarding).

We could then find a dog by reading in the five characteristics for the dog facts, and see if there was a fact with arguments to match. This is an apparently simpler solution to the problem. It is dealt with in more detail in Section 10.6, which also explains why the rule based approach is better.

Answer 10.3

```
/* GROCER */

/* Inference engine and interface */

go:- write('** GROCER **'),nl,nl,
     write('How big is the fruit? Choose from large,'),nl,
     write('average or small: '),read(Size),
     write('What colour is it? Choose from orange, green,'),nl,
     write('yellow, brown, green_or_red, or other: '),
     read(Colour),
     write('Describe its skin. Choose from thick, soft,'),nl,
     write('smooth or segmented: '),read(Skin),
     write('What shape is it? Choose from round, '),nl,
     write('long or pear_shaped: '),read(Shape),nl,
     assertz(size(Size)),assertz(colour(Colour)),
     assertz(skin(Skin)),assertz(shape(Shape)),
     rule(Rule,Fruit),
     write('The fruit is: '),write(Fruit),nl,nl,
     write('The rule used was Number '),write(Rule),nl,nl,
     retractall(size(_)),retractall(colour(_)),
     retractall(skin(_)),retractall(shape(_)).

/* Knowledge base */

rule(1,orange):-colour(orange),skin(thick).
rule(2,peach):-colour(green_or_red),shape(round),skin(soft).
rule(3,banana):-colour(yellow),shape(long).
rule(4,apple):-colour(green_or_red),shape(round).
rule(5,pear):-shape(pear_shaped).
rule(6,grape):-size(small),shape(round).
rule(7,pineapple):-size(large),skin(segmented).
rule(8,apricot):-colour(orange).
rule(9,melon):-colour(green),size(large).
rule(10,date):-size(small),shape(long).
rule(11,'not known.').
```

Programming practice: a dinosaurs expert system

Make up a JURASSIC expert system to identify dinosaurs. Use the following information:

Dinosaur	Eating	Habitat	Size	Neck	Stance	Horns,crests
triceratops	veg	land	large	short	quadruped	three_horns
ichthyosaur	carn	sea	large	none	swimming	none
pterodactyl	carn	air	small	short	flying	beak
brontosaurus	veg	swamp	large	long	quadruped	none
pteranodon	carn	air	large	long	flying	crest
diplodocus	veg	swamp	large	long	quadruped	none
brachiosaurus	veg	swamp	large	long	quadruped	domed_head
tyrannosaurus	carn	land	large	short	biped	none
protoceratops	veg	land	small	short	quadruped	beak
stegosaurus	veg	land	large	short	quadruped	back_plates
iguanodon	veg	land	large	short	biped	none
velociraptor	carn	land	small	short	biped	none
corythosaurus	veg	land	large	short	biped	crest
plesiosaur	carn	sea	large	long	swimming	none

Make the program as efficient as possible. Some of the dinosaurs are very easily identified by one feature. At least two others are impossible to tell apart from the data given. There will be alternative solutions to the problem.

11 Recursion

11.1 Introduction

Readers who have programmed in other languages, which means most people who come to Prolog, will be familiar with constructions such as REPEAT ... UNTIL, WHILE ... DO, FOR ... DO, not to mention GOTO. There are no such constructions in Prolog for making a section of code repeat.

We have seen two methods of causing rather specific actions to be carried out repeatedly in the last chapter – writing things out from the database repeatedly using **fail**, and reading in atoms repeatedly using **repeat** and a condition. Although these are really tricks which use backtracking, they are useful techniques which are frequently used by Prolog programmers. However, they cannot cover all eventualities that arise, and the usual method of achieving repetition in Prolog is to use **recursion**.

11.2 Recursion

Recursion is not by any means unique to Prolog, and it can be and is used in many other high-level languages. In procedural languages recursion simply means a subroutine or procedure or section of program calling itself.

In Prolog recursion means a rule using itself as a subgoal.

Recursion is considered a more respectable, logical way to achieve repetition than ways which make use of backtracking, which is a mechanism that has to be used to implement logic programming on real computers. It is also the neatest and best way to achieve it, in most cases, and in some the only way.

The following is an example of a recursive loop:

loop:-write('This is a loop.'),nl,loop.

When the rule has written out the message and gone to a new line it encounters itself as a subgoal. It searches the database, finds the same rule again, and this process repeats.

There is one thing wrong with this loop. It will never end. (Use CTRL <- to stop it if you try it in LPA Prolog.) The rest of this chapter will deal with how loops can be constructed so as to end neatly and in a controlled way.

Question 11.1 (answer on p.94)

Which is the most 'logical' method of achieving repetition, recursion or using repeat?

11.3 Conditional recursion

Perhaps the simplest way to see how a recursive loop can be ended is to use a ; condition as follows.

> **loop:-write('Type end, to end: '),read(Word),**
> **(Word = end ; loop).**

When the rule has proved the write and read subgoals, it encounters the subgoal which says: Succeed and end the rule if the word is **end**, or look for and repeat the rule **loop**.

This construction is the equivalent of a REPEAT ... UNTIL loop in languages such as Pascal, with the condition tested at the end of the loop. The loop will execute at least once. This loop is similar to the Prolog **repeat** loop given as an example in the last chapter.

This is quite a neat way to construct such a simple rule, but we need to observe the caution made in a previous chapter, that ; can lead to complexity and lack of clarity in more lengthy rules, especially where the rule has a lot of arguments, or where there may be backtracking into the rule.

It is more usual to end a recursive loop by putting the 'boundary condition' or terminating condition in a separate rule before the recursive rule, which Prolog comes to first but passes over until the condition is met.

> **loop(end).**
> **loop(_):-write('Type end, to end: '),**
> **read(Word),loop(Word).**

This repeats the message while **end** has not been typed in. If Word is **end**, the first predicate succeeds and prevents a loop taking place. If **Word** is anything else, the first predicate fails, and Prolog enters the second rule which calls itself so that a loop takes place.

This replaces WHILE ... DO in languages such as Pascal, with the terminating condition tested at the start of the loop. The loop will not execute at all if the condition is met initially.

To start the loop, type the predicate **loop** as a goal at the interpreter prompt with any argument but **end**, or call it from within another rule, in this way:

> **?- loop(anything).**

> OR: **go:-loop(something).**

As a useful aid to seeing how recursion works in the **loop** rule above, you should use the **trace** predicate in Prolog while you run it. This will show you what is happening at every stage. The **trace** facility (introduced in Chapter 6) comes into its own with recursive rules and programs, and you should use it frequently whenever you are in doubt about what is happening. (Note that if you are using PD Prolog, it unfortunately does not include the predicate **trace**.)

Question 11.2 *(answer on p.94)*

Write a program which keeps saying 'Hello!' until you type in **be_quiet**.

11.4 Counted recursion

We often want to specify a loop which is to execute a predetermined number of times. We have to construct a loop with an argument which can be used to count the number of times it has executed.

This can be done again in at least two ways. The first has a simple **;** condition at the end of the loop as a terminator, as follows:

> **loop(N):-write('The value of N is: '),write(N),nl,**
> **M is N-1,(M = 0 ; loop(M)).**

Again there is an alternative form, more usual, which has a boundary rule or condition at the beginning:

> **loop(0).**
> **loop(N):-write('The value of N is: '),write(N),nl,**
> **M is N-1,loop(M).**

These loops will execute in an identical manner as far as the user is concerned, for most values of the argument. Either is started with the number of times the loop is required to execute, for example

> **?- loop(3).**

This loops 3 times and the counter goes down from 3 to 1. These correspond to a FOR … TO loop in other languages, or more exactly to a FOR … DOWNTO loop in languages that have it.

There is a difference between the two loops above in execution. If tested with loop(0), the second will end without doing anything, while the first will get caught in a rather nasty never-ending loop, with N increasing negatively. This can be prevented by putting in another condition as follows:

> **loop(N):-not N=0,**
> **write('The value of N is: '),write(N),nl,**
> **M is N-1,(M = 0 ; loop(M)).**
> **loop(_).**

The extra fail-safe rule at the end is there to make the rule succeed finally rather than fail, which is necessary if it is to be used in a program. This rather detracts from the simplicity of this loop, and for non-negative numbers makes the boundary rule version preferable. To stop either crashing when a negative number is used as the argument, an additional condition **N > -1** is required.

Question 11.3 *(answer on p.95)*

Write a Prolog program **clear** *to clear the screen by using recursion and calling* **nl** *25 times.*

[Note: This will leave the cursor at the bottom of the screen. Another way of clearing the screen which leaves the cursor at the top is simply to use **put(12)***, the ASCII code to 'home' the cursor.]*

11.5 A worked example of recursion

Let us take the boundary rule version of the counting loop above, and follow through what happens during execution of the rule when given the goal

> ?- loop(3).   /* Original query (A) */

Prolog searches the database and finds the loop rule. It passes over the loop(0) boundary condition and instantiates the variables in the second rule successively as follows:

> loop(3):-   /* Second loop rule (B) */
>   write('This loops N times. Counter is '),
>   write(3),nl,2 is 3-1,
>   loop(2).

> loop(2):-   /* Second loop rule again (C) */
>   write('This loops N times. Counter is '),
>   write(2),nl,1 is 2-1,
>   loop(1).

> loop(1):-   /* Second loop rule again (D) */
>   write('This loops N times. Counter is '),
>   write(1),nl,0 is 1-1,
>   loop(0).

> loop(0).   /* First loop rule succeeds (E) */

Rule B cannot succeed completely until rule C has succeeded. Rule C cannot succeed until rule D has succeeded. Rule D cannot succeed until rule E has succeeded. When E succeeds (the boundary rule), D succeeds, then C, then B, then the original goal A at the interpreter prompt.

The recursion thus builds up in successive rules A to E, then 'unwinds' as they succeed from E to A.

The process shown in this section, working through an example of a rule in operation, is sometimes called a 'hand trace'. You can see it in action as mentioned above using the built-in **trace** facility of most Prologs (but not PD Prolog).

Question 11.4 *(answer on p.95)*

*Write a rule **stars** to draw a specified number of stars or asterisks in a horizontal line on the screen, and **trace** it as it draws a small number of about 5 stars.*

11.6 Another example

Another version of a counting rule is as follows, counting up from 0 to a fixed value:

> **loop_up(3).**
> **loop_up(N):-M is N + 1,write('Counter is '),**
> **write(M),nl,loop_up(M).**

This can be started as follows:

> **?- loop_up(0).**

Or with a rule:

> **go:-loop_up(0).**

This will write the message 3 times then end. For the first loop N is 0. N then increases up to 2, and when loop_up(M) becomes loop_up(3), the first predicate succeeds and stops the looping.

This is a better replacement for the FOR...TO...DO loop in Pascal, but it is a less flexible loop than the version given above, as to change the number of times it loops we need to edit the database and change the first rule, eg.

> **loop_up(5).**   **(Loops 5 times.)**

Question 11.5 *(answer on p.95)*

Write a rule block which uses the rule stars in Question 11.3 as a subgoal to draw a block of stars on the screen, 70 wide and 20 deep. Put the two rules into a program started by go, which simply draws the block of stars.

11.7 Recursion and iteration

Generally speaking, recursion is not the same as **iteration**, which is repetition of the same piece of program code over and over again. Recursion involves a rule making a fresh call to itself as a subgoal, and involves a new area of 'program space' each time. Thus the longer a recursive loop goes on, the more computer memory it uses up, which is not the case with iteration.

This can cause problems, which are overcome, when they occur, by use of the **cut**. The cut is not a logical feature of Prolog, but is there to circumvent this and other problems. We will deal with it in Chapter 18.

Although recursion does not usually execute iteratively, modern Prologs contain methods of detecting recursive constructions which can be executed iteratively (not all can) and performing them this way. As it does not then involve continually constructing new reference frames and saving markers for repeated rules, converting recursion to iteration makes the use of computer memory more efficient and also makes programs run faster. However, this happens behind the scenes and need not concern us when programming.

11.8 Summary

Recursion takes place when a rule in Prolog uses itself as a subgoal. It is the usual way in Prolog to achieve repetition.

A recursive loop is usually ended by a boundary rule placed above the recursive rule in the database, but it can also be ended using a **;** condition. Tracing the execution of recursive rules is a useful aid to understanding how recursion operates.

The recursion process sets up a new version of the recursive rule each time it repeats, so that it is not the same as iteration, which is repetition of the same piece of program code. These repeated rules succeed in turn as the recursion 'unwinds' after the boundary rule has succeeded.

Answers to questions

Answer 11.1

Repeat loops use backtracking to achieve repetition, and you will remember we pointed out that backtracking is the mechanism that has to be used on a sequential computer to ensure that every one of the subgoals in a rule is tested. Backtracking is thus not a 'logical' feature of Prolog, but one that we can make use of because it is there.

Recursion involves only the testing of a subgoal of a rule, which happens to be the same as the rule itself, and is quite 'logically respectable'.

Answer 11.2

```
loop(be_quiet).
loop(_):-write('Hello! '),nl,
    read(Word),loop(Word).
```

Answer 11.3

Like this, calling the rule with clear(25):

```
clear(0).
clear(N):-nl,M is N-1,clear(M).
```

Or like this, calling the rule with clear(0):

```
clear(25).
clear(N):-nl,M is N+1,clear(M).
```

Answer 11.4

```
stars(0).
stars(N):-write('*'),M is N-1,stars(M).
```

Answer 11.5

```
go:- lock(20).

block(0).
block(N):-stars(70),nl,M is N-1,block(M).

stars(0).
stars(N):-write('*'),M is N-1,stars(M).
```

Programming practice: share prices

Share prices for a company at the end of each month are saved as facts of the form:

```
share(jan,65).
share(feb,70).
share(mar,55).
share(apr,30).
share(may,25).
```

Write a rule **display** which writes these out in two columns on the screen using **fail**.

Modify this rule to call the rule **stars** you wrote in answer to one of the questions in this chapter, as a subgoal, and draw the share prices as lines of stars on the screen, instead of writing the numbers. They should form a type of horizontal graph of the shares, something like this:

```
jan      *************
feb      ****************
mar      ***********
apr      *********
may      ********
```

12 More recursion

12.1 Introduction

In this chapter we will look at how recursion can be used to make whole programs repeat, rather than single rules; summarise some of the different ways recursion can be achieved and used; then look at some harder examples of repetition loops using recursion.

12.2 A recursive menu structure

Let us go back to the procedural use of Prolog in writing conventional programs. The programs described in Chapter 7 were simple 'linear' programs which executed from start to finish, then ended. However, using recursion, it is easy to make a simple program repeat.

A common structure for programs on all kinds of subject is to offer a menu of options, allow the user to make a choice of activity, provide the means of carrying out the activity, then return to the menu. This type of program can be written in general terms as follows.

```
/* MENU PROGRAM */

go:-start_message,menu.

start_message:-put(12),
       write('This shows how a repeated menu works!').

menu:-nl,nl,write('MENU'),nl,
       write('===='),nl,nl,
       write('a. Activity A'),nl,
       write('b. Activity B'),nl,
       write('c. Activity C'),nl,
       write('d. Activity D'),nl,
       write('e. End'),nl,nl,
       read(Choice),nl,choice(Choice).

choice(a):-write('Activity A chosen'),menu.
choice(b):-write('Activity B chosen'),menu.
choice(c):-write('Activity C chosen'),menu.
choice(d):-write('Activity D chosen'),menu.
choice(e):-write('Goodbye!').
choice(_):-write('Please try again!'),menu.

/* END */
```

This program starts when **go** is entered at the query prompt, and after clearing the screen writes a start-up message contained in the rule **start_message**. (It clears the screen by using the standard predicate **put** to send the ASCII code 12 to the screen, which clears all text and positions the cursor at top left.) The program then goes to the rule **menu**, which writes out the menu of options on the screen. The user chooses an activity by entering **a**, **b**, **c** or **d**, or opts to end the program with **e**. The program then goes to a rule **choice**.

The version of **choice** which is executed is determined by the letter entered. For **a**, **b**, **c** or **d**, an appropriate message is written, then the rule recursively calls **menu** again. The program will continue doing this as long as the user keeps making correct menu choices.

If the user chooses **e**, a message is written then the rule choice simply ends. Execution returns to **menu**, which also ends. This returns execution to **go**, which ends.

Notice that it is very easy to include a catch-all **choice** rule, which traps any incorrect input. If anything other than **a**, **b**, **c**, **d** or **e** has been entered, the rules for these letters will fail and the last **choice** will be executed, which writes an error message and returns to the menu for another try.

There are things wrong with this simple menu structure, but it will work. One undesirable feature is that choices are entered using **read**, which requires a full-stop and <ENTER> each time it is used. With a menu, people expect to press one letter key only. There is no predicate to do this in standard Prolog, but a way round it in LPA Prolog is given in the chapter on input.

Another thing wrong with this structure is that it is actually inadvisable to use recursion for a main program loop. We will return to this later in the chapter on the cut, explain why, and give another way of doing it. For the time being, let us keep using this sort of menu structure when we need to.

12.3 An Olympic Games exercise

The table below shows the final medals for the top 15 countries in the 1992 Barcelona Olympics (out of 64 countries with medals).

Country	G	S	B	Total
CIS	45	38	29	112
United States	37	34	37	108
Germany	33	21	28	82
China	16	22	16	54
Cuba	14	6	11	31
Spain	13	7	2	22
South Korea	12	5	12	29
Hungary	11	12	7	30
France	8	6	15	29
Australia	7	9	11	27
Italy	6	5	8	19
Canada	6	5	7	18
Great Britain	5	3	12	20
Romania	4	6	8	18
Czechoslovakia	4	2	1	7

Let us use this table to illustrate the writing of a menu based program, and approach it as a student exercise.

LONG Question 12.1 *(answer on p.103)*

*Devise a suitable form of fact with predicate name **medals** to contain this medal data, then write a program which provides certain operations on the data, from a menu as follows:*

a.   *A list of names of all available countries*

b.   *Details of medals for a named country*

c.   *Delete a country and medals*

d.   *Exit from the program*

The menu on screen should look as it does above. Put a catch-all in the program to cater for incorrect entries.

12.4 Summary of loops in Prolog

Although this chapter is on recursion, let us recap at this point all the methods we have used to achieve repetition in Prolog.

Use of **fail**

This is used almost exclusively as a method of repeatedly retrieving facts from the database. It can be looked on as a trick which uses the Prolog backtracking mechanism.

```
loop:-person(Name),write(Name),nl,fail.
loop.
```

This will write out all the names of people stored in facts with predicate **person**, in database order.

Use of **repeat**

This method can be used for loops with no arguments, ended by a simple condition. It is easy to grasp, and some programmers like it because of its similarity to the REPEAT ... UNTIL in procedural programming. It is not practical, however, for loops which need to pass arguments from one execution to the next, which is the case when a counter is involved. As it depends on backtracking, it can be unpredictable except in simple cases.

```
loop:-repeat,write('Enter end to end.'),nl,
    read(X),X=end.
```

Several conditions can be included using semicolons:

```
loop:-repeat,write('Enter end to end.'),nl,
    read(X),(X=end;X=0).
```

The use of repeat has the advantage that it is 'iterative', that is, it involves the same section of code being repeated over and over again, whereas recursion involves a new rule being executed afresh each time it is called. This means that methods involving repeat do not use the computer stack (see Section 11.7, and Chapter 18).

Recursion using a boundary condition rule

This is the usual method of using recursion. It is the most versatile construction and the neatest when several arguments and complex terminating conditions are involved.

```
loop(end).
loop(_):-write('Enter end to end.'),nl,
    read(X),loop(X).
```

Recursion using a condition with or (;)

This is easy to follow, and it can be used where the terminating condition is best placed at the end of the loop. But do not try to use it in all cases, as it becomes complicated if the terminating condition should logically go at the beginning, or if the terminating condition is a complex one.

```
loop:-write('Enter end to end.'),nl,
    read(X),
    (X=end;loop).
```

Recursion using a subgoal

This can be used for menu-type constructions, but also for simpler loops as well. It is more long-winded than other constructions, and clumsy where there are several arguments to be passed back into the main rule.

```
loop:-write('Enter end to end.'),nl,
    read(X),test(X).

test(end).
test(_):-loop.
```

Counted recursion using a boundary condition rule

This is usually the best method to use where there are arguments to be passed from one loop to the next, as needs to be the case where a counter is being used. The alternative of using a ; condition becomes harder to follow, and becomes difficult when the loop may need to be prevented from executing at least once. The alternative using a subgoal is longer and requires the introduction of a new rule.

loop(0).
loop(N):-write(N),nl,M is N-1,loop(M).

Summary

The methods described above can be used at a programmer's discretion, though it must be said that the most versatile and most frequently used method of achieving repetition is the boundary rule method. Many Prolog books only mention this, apart from the special cases of fail and repeat.

12.5 Some harder examples of recursion

As an exercise, let us write a rule which will calculate the **factorial** of a number, that is, the product of all numbers counting up to the number.

eg. ?- factorial(4,Factorial).
Factorial = 24

Prolog returns 24 as the factorial of 4. This is because

4 x 3 x 2 x 1 = 24

This can be written in a very short, efficient rule as follows.

factorial(1,1).
factorial(N,Factorial):-M is N-1,
factorial(M,Fact),
Factorial is Fact * N.

This is a new type of construction, which may seem strange, as the recursion takes place from the middle of the rule. You may think, how can we use **factorial** to find the factorial of M, which is N-1, when it has not yet found the factorial of N?

Well, Prolog will quite happily hold M as an uninstantiated variable while it continues recursing. It will keep reducing the number by 1 and trying to find its factorial, until it gets down to the number 1, whose factorial is provided as 1 in the boundary rule. As it then comes out of the recursion, it can instantiate all the uninstantiated variables, and fill in the factorials as the variables multiplied by the next higher number.

Let us try to make that clearer with a worked example, such as you can also observe by running the rule and tracing it:

?- factorial(4,Factorial).

Prolog searches the database to satisfy this goal, and finds the rule **factorial**, which is then used successively as follows. The values of the instantiated variables are shown at each point.

factorial(4,Factorial):-3 is 4 -1,
    factorial(3,Fact),Factorial is Fact * 4.   {A}

factorial(3,Factorial):-2 is 3 – 1,
    factorial(2,Fact),Factorial is Fact * 3.   {B}

factorial(2,Factorial):-1 is 2 -1,
    factorial(1,Fact),Factorial is Fact * 2.   {C}

factorial(1,1).   {D}

This last rule D is fully instantiated, allowing the rule C to be completed. This allows B to complete, and so on, until the variable in the original query is known, as follows:

factorial(1,1).   {D}

factorial(2,2):-1 is 2 -1,
    factorial(1,1),2 is 1 * 2.   {C}

factorial(3,6):-2 is 3 – 1,
    factorial(2,2),6 is 2 * 3.   {B}

factorial(4,24):-3 is 4 -1,
    factorial(3,6),24 is 6 * 4.   {A}

?- factorial(4,Factorial).
Factorial = 24

Thus the part of the work which cannot be done as the recursion is built up is done later as the recursion 'unwinds'.

Question 12.2 (answer on p.104)

*Write a rule **total**, along the lines of the one above, which totals all the numbers up to a particular number, eg.*

?- total(4,Total).
Total = 10

Prolog returns 10 because 4 + 3 + 2 + 1 = 10

Question 12.3 *(answer on p.104)*

Write a similar rule, **series(N,Total)**, *which totals the series*

$$1 + 1/2 + 1/3 + 1/4 + ... + 1/N$$

This should be used as follows:

> ?- series(4,Total).
> Total = 2.08333

This is because 1 + 0.5 + 0.25 + 0.33333 = 2.08333

Question 12.4 *(answer on p.104)*

Write a rule that calculates a power of two, **power(N,Power)**, *as follows:*

> ?- power(4,Power).
> Power = 16

Because 2 x 2 x 2 x 2 = 16

Question 12.5 *(answer on p.104)*

Modify or extend the last example into a rule to find any power of any number, **power(Num,Index,Power)**, *eg.*

> ?- power(3,4,Power).
> Power = 81

Because 3 x 3 x 3 x 3 (4 times) = 81

12.6 Summary

This chapter explains a menu based structure for programs using recursion; summarises some of the ways of achieving recursion; and explains some harder examples of repetition loops using recursion.

Answers to questions

Answer 12.1

Although this program shows again the economy of Prolog in producing quite complex programs in a brief and concise form, it is rather more substantial than previous examples, so notice the conventions observed in setting it out, such as the heading, the indentation, and the brief explanations of each rule. There are no hard and fast rules, of course, but something close to this layout has been found to be clearest and best for Prolog.

```prolog
/* OLYMPICS PROGRAM */

/* Main program and menu */

go:- write('OLYMPICS 1992'),nl,nl,
     write('a. A list of names of all available countries'),nl,
     write('b. Details of medals for a named country'),nl,
     write('c. Delete a country and medals'),nl,
     write('d. Exit from the program'),nl,nl,
     read(Choice),nl,choice(Choice).

/* Option rules – list all countries */

choice(a):-medals(Country,_,_,_,_),write(Country),nl,fail.
choice(a):-go.

/* Details of a country */

choice(b):-write('Which country? '),read(Country),nl,
     medals(Country,G,S,B,T),write(G),nl,write(S),nl,
     write(B),nl,write(T),nl,nl,go.

/* Remove a country */

choice(c):-write('Which country? '),read(Country),nl,
     retract(medals(Country,_,_,_,_)),go.

/* End program */

choice(d):-write('Goodbye!'),nl.

/* Catch-all */

choice(_):-write('Please try again.'),nl,go.

/* Data facts */

medals('CIS',45,38,29,112).
medals('United States',37,34,37,108).
medals('Germany',33,21,28,82).
     ...etc

/* END */
```

Answer 12.2

```
total(1,1).
total(N,Total):-M is N-1,
    total(M,SmallTotal),
    Total is SmallTotal + N.
```

Answer 12.3

```
series(1,1).
series(N,Total):-M is N-1,
    series(M,SmallTotal),
    Total is SmallTotal + 1/N.
```

Answer 12.4

```
power(0,1).
power(N,Power):-M is N-1,
    power(M,SmallPower),
    Power is SmallPower * 2.
```

Answer 12.5

```
power(_,0,1).
power(Num,Index,Power):-SmallIndex is Index-1,
    power(Num,SmallIndex,SmallPower),
    Power is SmallPower*Num.
```

Programming practice: **student marks**

1. Write a program which reads in student percentage marks, prompting the user for each new mark and ending when a negative mark is read in. The program should keep a running total then print out the total mark at the end.

2. Modify this program to print out also the average mark for the student. This involves counting the number of marks entered as well as keeping a running total.

13 Expert system shells

13.1 Introduction

You will probably have realised, in making up the expert systems in the previous expert system chapters, that there were considerable similarities between the expert systems devised on completely different knowledge bases. In Chapter 10, the main rules for the expert systems to identify dogs, fruit and dinosaurs were almost identical.

An important feature of expert systems, which was realised soon after they began to appear, is that the inference engine and interface can be separated to form a **shell**, which can be used to enclose different types of expert knowledge base. This means a single shell can be used to simulate different types of expert.

One of the first shells was EMYCIN, a shell derived from the medical expert system MYCIN. EMYCIN stands for empty MYCIN – the original expert system emptied of its medical knowledge to form a generalised shell.

13.2 A car mechanic expert system

Let us look at a rule-based expert system which is slightly more elaborate than the others we have looked at. For simplicity it is not numerical, but simply rule-based and qualitative. After explaining how this works, we will make some modifications to it to convert it into a shell, then use it with some other knowledge bases.

The program simulates the job of a mechanic in finding out what is wrong with your car when it won't start.

```
/* SIMPLE MECHANIC EXPERT SYSTEM */
/* ============================= */

/* INFERENCE ENGINE */

        /* Collects symptoms via questions, establishes a fault
           then tells the user what it is */

go:- initialise,
     collect_symptoms,
     rule(Number,Fault),
     reply(Fault,Reply),
     write(Reply),nl,
     write('The rule used was number '),write(Number),nl,nl,
     retractall(symptom(_)).
```

```
go:- write('Sorry can''t help')nl,nl,
     retractall(syptom(_)).
```

/* USER INTERFACE */

/* Puts initial messages on the screen */

```
initialise:-put(12),
     write('*** MECHANIC ***'),nl,nl,
     write('It is assumed the car will not start.').
     write('Please answer the following questions').
     write('with y (yes) or n (no).').
```

/* Gets symptoms and questions about them */

```
collect_symptoms:-question(Ques,Sympt),write(Ques),nl,
     getyesno(Yesno),nl,Yesno=y,assertz(symptom(Sympt)),fail.
collect_symptoms.
```

/* Inputs either y or n */

```
getyesno(X):-repeat,write('Please answer y or n: '),
     read(Z),nl,check(Z),X=Z,!.
```

```
check(y). check(n).
```

/* KNOWLEDGE BASE */

/* These facts relate questions to symptoms */

```
question('Do the headlights come on?',lights_work).
question('Does the starter motor turn the engine?',
     engine_turns).
question('Is there a spark at the distributor points?',
     distrib_spark).
question('Is there a spark at the spark plugs?',
     plug_spark).
question('Do the headlights dim when you use the starter?',
     lights_dim).
question('Does the pointer move on the petrol gauge?',
     gauge_reads).
question('Is there petrol in the float chamber?',
     petrol_in_float_chamber).
question('Do the spark plugs look wet?',plugs_wet).
```

/* The rules establish a fault from symptoms reported */

```
rule(1,batt_flat):-not(symptom(lights_work)),
     not(symptom(engine_turns)).
rule(2,low_voltage_fault):-symptom(lights_work),
     not(symptom(distrib_spark)),symptom(engine_turns).
rule(3,high_voltage_fault):-symptom(lights_work),
     symptom(distrib_spark),symptom(engine_turns),
     not(symptom(plug_spark)).
rule(4,starter_motor_fault):-symptom(lights_work),
     not(symptom(engine_turns)),not(symptom(lights_dim)).
rule(5,out_of_petrol):-not(symptom(gauge_reads)),
     not(symptom(petrol_in_float_chamber)).
```

```
rule(6,blocked_jet):-symptom(gauge_reads),
    symptom(petrol_in_float_chamber),not(symptom(plugs_wet))).
rule(7,feed_pipe_blocked):-symptom(gauge_reads),
    not(symptom(petrol_in_float_chamber))).
rule(8,engine_flooded):-symptom(gauge_reads),
    symptom(plugs_wet).
rule(9,engine_seized):-not(symptom(engine_turns)),
    symptom(lights_work),symptom(lights_dim)).
```

/* These facts relate a fault to a message to be output */

```
reply(batt_flat,'The battery is flat.').
reply(low_voltage_fault,
    'There is a fault in the low-voltage ignition circuit.').
reply(high_voltage_fault,
    'Fault in the high voltage ignition circuit.').
reply(starter_motor_fault,
    'The starter motor is jammed or faulty.').
reply(out_of_petrol,'You have run out of petrol.').
    reply(blocked_jet,
    'There is a blocked jet in the carburettor.').
reply(feed_pipe_blocked,
    'Blocked feed pipe from petrol tank to carburettor.').
reply(engine_flooded,'The engine is flooded.').
reply(engine_seized,'The engine seems to be seized up.').
```

/* END */

13.3 How it works

The main rule **go** represents the inference engine of the expert system. It first puts onto the screen an initial title and message via the subrule **initialise**, then collects symptoms from the user via the rule **collect_symptoms**. This rule works its way through a series of **question** facts, each of which has two arguments. The first is the text of a question, which **collect_symptoms** writes out on the screen, and the second is an atom representing a symptom, which is present if the answer to the question is 'yes'. **collect_symptoms** gets the user's input via a rule **getyesno**, which takes in an ASCII code via **get0** and only accepts it if it is y, Y, n or N. In the event of the answer being 'yes', **collect_symptoms** asserts the symptom into the database as the argument of a fact **symptom**.

The rule **collect_symptoms** is better than the methods used for collecting user input in our previous expert systems, as it will ask as many questions as there are **question** facts in the database, and stop when it comes to the end of them, without the number of questions having to be programmed in.

Having collected all the symptoms the car is showing, **go** works through a series of **'rule'** rules which check the **symptom** facts in the database. When the first **rule** succeeds, it returns its argument **Fault**, which represents a car fault corresponding to the symptoms recorded. This is used to locate a **reply** fact, which has a first argument **Fault**, and a second argument which is the text for a reply. This reply **Reply** simply tells the user what the fault is, and it is written out on screen. The number of the rule used is written out as well to explain what is going on. The last thing **go** does is to retract all the **symptom** facts from the database so that the user can run the program again if required without these facts introducing errors.

13.4 Converting this program to a shell

It can be seen that the inference engine and interface of the program are fairly independent of the knowledge base already. The knowledge base consists of the question facts, the rules, and the reply facts, all of which are specific to the subject of car mechanics. It is easy to see that knowledge for a different subject could be used to make up questions, rules and replies, and these could then be fitted into the system.

What we need to do to form a separate shell is

1. Remove anything remaining in the inference engine and interface parts of the system which is subject specific

2. Separate the knowledge base completely so that it can be read in as a separate file.

The subject specific parts in the present car mechanic system are the title and start-up message, contained in **initialise**. This needs to be changed so as to read these in as text from the knowledge base, instead of having them embedded in the program code of the shell. **initialise** can be rewritten so that it calls up the title from a **title** fact, writes it on the screen, then calls a subrule **write_message** which writes out the starting message from **message** facts in the database, as follows:

> **... title(Title),write(Title),nl,nl,write_message,nl.**

> **write_message:-message(Mess),write(Mess),nl,fail.**
> **write_message:-nl.**

Something else which is rather subject specific is the use of the idenfifiers **symptom** and **fault**. We might want to use the expert system shell for a job like identifying dinosaurs, which does not involve things going wrong. This will not affect the functioning of the shell, of course, only the clarity of the code. However, better identifiers in a generalised shell might be **observation** and **reason**.

Separating the knowledge base physically from the rest of the program does not require a major rewrite of the program, but does involve drastically cutting the code in two. The knowledge base is edited into a separate file, and is consulted in by name from the main program, as follows:

> **... write('Enter name of expert file to use: '),**
> **read(File),consult(File), ...**

Something else we now need to do, at the end of the program, is not only to retract the **symptom** or **observation** facts, but to retract all the **title**, **message**, **question** and **reply** facts as well, in fact everything that has been read in from the knowledge base file. We could do this in a rule **finish** as follows:

```
        finish:-retractall(title(_)),retractall(message(_)),
            retractall(question(_,_)),retractall(rule(_)),
            retractall(reply(_,_)),retractall(observation(_)).
            retractall(symptom(_)).
```

This is rather long and untidy. Instead, we can use **reconsult** instead of **consult** to bring in the knowledge file each time. This will automatically clear away all previous instances of these facts before bringing in either new ones, or the same ones again.

13.5 An expert system shell program

We now have a basic shell program which will read in a new and different database each time it is run. It has its limitations, because we have tried to keep it simple, but it works. The full program code is as follows.

```
/* A SIMPLE PROLOG EXPERT SYSTEM SHELL */

/* INFERENCE ENGINE */

/* Reads in a file containing a knowledge base, puts up a
      title and instructions from the database, asserts an
      observation fact via questions, finds a rule which fits
      the observations, replies what the reason is, then
      clears the database for another run. */

go:- initialise,
      collect_observations,
      rule(Number,Reason),
      reply(Reason,Reply),
      write(Reply),nl,
      write('The rule used was '),write(Number)nl,nl,
      retractall(observation(_)).

go:- write('Sorry, can''t help!'),nl,nl,
      retractall(observation(_)).

/* USER INTERFACE */

/* Start-up rule */

initialise:-cls,nl,nl,
      write('* * PROLOG EXPERT SYSTEM SHELL * *'),nl,nl,
      write('Enter name of expert file to use: '),
      read(File),reconsult(File),
      cls,title(Title),write(Title),nl,nl,
      write_message,nl,nl.

/* Writes out a message relating to a particular database */

write_message:-message(Mess),write(Mess),nl,fail.
write_message:-nl.

/* Collects observations according to the questions in the
      database. Adjusts to the number of questions there */
```

```
collect_observations:-question(Ques,Obsn),write(Ques),nl,
    getyesno(Yesno),nl,Yesno=y,assertz(observation(Obsn)),fail.
collect_observations.
```

/* Inputs either y or n (accepting Y or N as well) */

```
getyesno(X):-repeatwrite('Please answer y or n: '),
    read(Z),nl,check(Z),X=Z,!.
```

check(y). check(n).

/* Clears screen */

cls:-put(12).

/* END */

13.6 Databases for the shell

We now have a shell which is an expert on anything which is presented in a knowledge base file of the correct form. The car mechanic database file has been modified to include:

/* CAR MECHANIC KNOWLEDGE BASE */

/* This is saved in a separate file and consulted
   in from the shell */

/* Initial headers */

title('** MECHANIC **').

message('It is assumed the car will not start.').
message('Please answer the following questions').
message('with y (yes) or n (no).').

The rest of the MECHANIC knowledge base is the same, with **symptoms** replaced by **observations**.

We can now use other knowledge bases with the shell, including the knowledge bases from the examples and exercises in Chapter 10, after they have been modified into the correct form. The following is the dog spotter knowledge base in the form of a file for the shell.

/* DOG SPOTTER KNOWLEDGE BASE */

/* This is saved in a separate file and consulted in from
the shell */

/* Initial headers */

title('** DOGS **').

message('Please answer the following questions').
message('with y (yes) or n (no).').

/* Questions */

question('Is the colour black and tan?',black_and_tan).
question('Is the colour all black?',black).
question('Is the dog used as a guard dog?',guarding).
question('Is the dog small?',small).
question('Is it used for finding people?',finding_people).
question('Is it used for racing?',racing).
question('Does it have a wiry coat?',coat_wiry).
question('Is it used for chasing other small animals?',
    chasing_things).
question('Is golden brown in colour?',golden).
question('Is it used as a gun-dog?',gun-dog).
question('Is it used for herding sheep?',herding_sheep).
question('Is the dogs coat spotted?',spotted).
question('Is its coat fluffy?',fluffy).

/* Rules */

rule(1,alsatian):-observation(black_and_tan),
    observation(guarding).
rule(2,rottweiler):-observation(black),observation(guarding).
rule(3,bulldog):-observation(small),observation(guarding).
rule(4,st_bernard):-observation(finding_people).
rule(5,greyhound):-observation(racing).
rule(6,terrier):-size(small),observation(wiry),
    observation(chasing_things).
rule(7,golden_retriever):-observation(golden),
    observation(gun-dog).
rule(8,sheepdog):-observation(herding_sheep).
rule(9,dalmation):-observation(spotted).
rule(10,poodle):-observation(fluffy).

/* Replies */

reply(alsatian,'The dog is an alsatian.').
reply(rottweiler,'This dog is a rottweiler.').
reply(bulldog,'It seems to be a bulldog.').
reply(st_bernard,'It has to be a St. Bernard.').
reply(greyhound,'Must be a greyhound.').
reply(terrier,'This is a terrier.').
reply(golden_retriever,'It must be a golden retriever.').
reply(sheepdog,'That will be a sheepdog.').
reply(dalmation,'It will be a dalmation.').
reply(poodle,'The dog will be a poodle.').

/* END */

13.7 An electronic engineer expert system exercise

Suppose we have the following information for diagnosing what is wrong with a television set, and want to put it into an expert system to simulate an expert electronic engineer.

If there is no indicator light, no sound and the screen is dark, there is a fault in the mains circuit and the fuse is probably blown.

If the indicator light is on but the screen is dark and there is no sound, there could be a fault in the mains transformer.

If there is sound but the screen is dark, the cathode ray tube may have gone.

If the screen lights up but there is no picture and no sound, the fault is probably in the tuner.

If there is a picture and sound but the picture is unsteady, the control circuits are faulty.

If there is a good picture but no sound, the speaker may have a loose connection or be faulty.

LONG Question 13.1 (answer on p.113)

Make up an ELECTRONIC ENGINEER knowledge base file to fit the shell, using the information above. The expert system should then simulate an electronics engineer when he diagnoses a fault in your TV set. (Rather crudely, of course!)

13.8 Commercial expert system shells

It is possible to buy software which allows you to build your own expert system in this way, by putting in rules and data. Some such commercial expert system shells are better than others, and all tend to be expensive, but generally it would be true to say that all such standardised shells have limitations of one sort or another. For example, some are like the shell described above, purely qualitative with no facility for putting numbers in.

In practice, if a company wants to develop an expert system to cover part of its expertise, it is better to program it in a programming language, rather than 'authoring' it into a restrictive commercial shell. The best choice of such a language (depending on the programming expertise available) is usually Prolog.

?

LONG Question 13.2 *(answer on p.114)*

*The shell we have developed is rather basic in the sense that it does not repeat in a program loop, but has to be re-run using go from the interpreter. Each time this is done, the file needs to be read in again. This can become a little tedious, so see if you can modify the code for **go** to make the program keep running more effectively. This will involve a menu with options such as*

a.   *Run the present expert system again*

b.   *Read in a new expert system file*

c.   *Exit the program*

There is more involved here than is at first evident. When the program is first started, option a cannot be used until option b has been used to read in a file. Subsequently, option a needs to clear the observation facts before offering another run, and option b needs to clear all the facts of the old file from the database before reading in a new one.

13.9 Summary

The inference engine and user interface of an expert system can be separated from the knowledge base to form a 'shell'. Different knowledge bases can then be fitted into the shell to form expert systems on different subject domains. A simple version of such an expert system shell is developed in this chapter.

Answers to questions

Answer 13.1

Notice in this example that we can make the rules simpler by expressing some of the observations in negative form, eg. **observation(no_picture)** rather than **observation(picture)**. This makes some of the questions harder to express clearly, but is probably worth the trouble.

We can also make databases simpler by the careful positioning of rules. Look at rules 1, 2 and 3 and consider the effect of changing their order.

/* ELECTRONIC ENGINEER KNOWLEDGE BASE */

**/* This is saved in a separate file and consulted in from
    the shell */**

/* Initial headers */

title(' ELECTRONIC ENGINEER **').**

**message('Please answer the following questions').
message('with y (yes) or n (no).').**

```
          /* These facts relate questions to observations */

          question('Is there NO indicator light? Answer y if none.',
               no_indicator).
          question('Is there NO sound? Answer y if none.',no_sound).
          question('Is the screen dark?',screen_dark).
          question('Is the picture missing? Answer n if screen
               dark or uniformly bright.',no_picture).
          question('Is the picture unsteady? Answer n if the picture
               is steady or if none at all.',picture_unsteady).

          /* The rules establish a reason from observations reported */

          rule(1,mains_circuit):-observation(no_indicator),
               observation(no_sound),observation(screen_dark).
          rule(2,transformer):-observation(no_sound),
               observation(screen_dark).
          rule(3,crt):-observation(screen_dark).
          rule(4,tuner):-observation(no_picture),
               observation(no_sound).
          rule(5,control_circuits):-observation(picture_unsteady).
          rule(6,speaker):-observation(no_sound).

          /* These facts relate a reason to a message to be output */

          reply(mains_circuit,'Fault in mains circuit – check fuse.').
          reply(transformer,'Fault could be in mains transformer.').
          reply(crt,'The cathode ray tube may have gone.').
          reply(tuner,'The fault is probably in the tuner.').
          reply(control_circuits,
               'Probably the control circuits are faulty.').
          reply(speaker,'Speaker or speaker connections faulty.').

          /* END */
```

Answer 13.2

The inference engine part of the program needs to be modified along the following lines. Note that as well as constructing a menu, we have had to assert the current file in use into the database as the argument of a **file_in_use** fact, so as to be able to use **reconsult** to refresh the database as before. All the rest, ie. the interface and the knowledge bases, can stay the same.

```
          /* MENU VERSION OF EXPERT SYSTEM SHELL */
          /* ================================== */

          /* INFERENCE ENGINE */

          go:- cls,nl,nl
               write('* * PROLOG EXPERT SYSTEM SHELL * *'),nl,nl,
```

```
                write(' a.  Run the present expert system'),nl,
                write(' b.  Read in a new expert system file'),nl,
                write(' c.  Exit the program'),nl,nl,
                read(Choice),option(Choice).

        option(a):-file_in_use(File),not File=any,
                reconsult(File),title(Title),cls,write(Title),nl,nl,
                write_message,nl,nl,collect_observations,
                rule(Number,Reason),reply(Reason,Reply),
                write(Reply),nl,
                write('Rule used was: '),write(Number),nl,nl,
                write('Return to continue'),get0(_),
                retractall(observation(_)),
                assertz(observation(anything)),go.

        option(b):-write('Enter name of expert file to use, in quotes'),nl,
                write('if there are any illegal characters: ')
                read(File),retractall(file_in_use)(_)),        .
                assertz(file_in_use(File)),reconsult(File),go.

        option(c):-write('Goodbye!'),nl,nl.

        option(_):-nl,nl,write('Sorry, can''t help.'),nl,nl,
                write('Return to continue'),get0(_),
                retractall(observation(_)),
                assertz(observation(anything)),go.

        file_in_use(any).
```

Programming practice: zoo

Type the expert system shell into a file, in the modified repeating form in Answer 13.2. Type either the mechanic or electronic engineer database into a file and test it with the shell.

Devise a new ZOO knowledge base for the expert system shell which identifies different animals.

- Use the title and message facts to put an appropriate initial message on the screen.

- Next choose a few distinctive animals such as lion, tiger, elephant, mouse, zebra, walrus, eagle, sparrow, shark, goldfish, and make up a rule to identify each, with characteristics or features replacing the symptoms in the expert system.

- Now make up question facts to elicit the characteristics of an animal to be identified, covering all those used in the rules.

- Finally make up reply facts to say what animal it is.

14 Lists in Prolog

14.1 Introduction

A list in Prolog is an ordered sequence of elements, that can have any length. Elements can be any type of Prolog object. They can even be mixed within one list.

We usually use lists in Prolog where we would use arrays in Pascal and other languages. Generally, lists and arrays are used for holding groups of elements or objects or terms, while operations are performed on them. Elements of a list can be constants, integers, reals, atoms, variables, facts, other lists or even rules.

The elements of a list are enclosed in square brackets and separated by commas.

> **e.g. [1,2,3,4,5]**
> **[a,b,c,d]**
> **[peach,pear,plum]**
> **[peach,2,b,[3,4,5]]**

These are all valid lists with correct syntax.

14.2 Handling Lists

Lists are manipulated by separating the head from the tail.

The separator used is a vertical line, | , found at the bottom left of most keyboards.

> **e.g. List = [L | Lt]**

L is the first element or head of list **List** and **Lt** is its tail. The tail of a list is itself a list, e.g.

> **[1 | [2,3,4,5]]**
> **[a | [b,c,d]]**
> **[a | X]**
> **[peach | [pear,plum]]**

These are all valid lists with correct syntax.

We can use this notation to form new lists, eg. Z = [X|Y] adds element X to the front of list Y to form a new list Z.

Or: ?- Z = [5 | [4,3,2,1]].
   Z = [5,4,3,2,1]
   yes

Beware of structures which look rather like lists but are not actually valid lists, perhaps entered by mistake.

For example:

[ford | renault]

... is a structure which is not a list, although the interpreter will accept it, because **renault** is an atom, not a list.

[ford,renault] ... IS a list. It is the same as:

[ford | [renault]]

Note that although the [Head|Tail] form is usually used to separate the head from the tail of a list, it can also be used in the form [First,Second|Tail] to separate the first few elements of the list from the rest. In other words, the | separator does not always have to have a single element on the left of it. It does, however, have to have one or more elements on the left of it, while on the right of it is a list representing the remainder of the original list.

eg.   **[5,4 | [3,2,1]] and [5,4,3 | [2,1]] are correct syntax.**

Question 14.1 *(answer on p.121)*

(a) *Write the following as enumerated lists (i.e. in full, with elements separated by commas):*

bert fred mary
p q r s t
20 15 10 5 0

(b) *Write the above in head/tail form.*

(c) *Are the following valid as lists?*

[l,m,n]
[l | [m,n]]
[l | m,n]
n
N
[y]
[Q]
[lion | elephant]

14.3 Writing out a list

Operations on lists are always carried out by working through the list, successively removing the head, then removing the head from the tail, until the element required is reached or until the list is empty. This is done by recursion.

There is no alternative to this. Lists are sequential structures, and are not 'random access'. There is no way to go straight to a particular numbered element as with an array, though we can write a rule to access a particular element (one is given in the next chapter).

A list is written out very easily by using recursion and successively writing out the head, as follows:

> **writelist([]).**
> **writelist([L | Lt]):-write(L),nl,writelist(Lt).**

This writes out the list vertically.

It is worth going through an example to see how this works. As we have mentioned before, it is very useful to run a rule like this using the **trace** facility (not in PD Prolog), particularly so with recursive list examples. The following explanation is similar to what you will see during a trace, depending on the way the **trace** predicate works in your Prolog implementation.

Suppose we consult **writelist** into the database and then, at the query prompt, tell it to write out a list of integers [5,4,3] as follows:

> **?- writelist([5,4,3]).**

The interpreter searches for **writelist**, passes over **writelist([])** because the list is not empty, and finds the second rule. The list is split up into head and tail form as follows:

> **writelist([5 | [4,3]]):-write(5),nl,writelist([4,3]).**

The 5 is written out, and the rule calls itself again.

> **writelist([4 | [3]]):-write(4),nl,writelist([3]).**

The 4 is written out, and the rule is executed again:

> **writelist([3 | []]):-write(3),nl,writelist([]).**

The 3 is written out, and **writelist** is searched for again, but this time the first **writelist** rule succeeds and stops the recursion.

> **writelist([]).**

The three previous rules can now succeed, and the recursion 'unwinds'. The whole list has been written out vertically on the screen.

Question 14.2 *(answer on p.122)*

Modify the rule writelist so that it writes out a list horizontally along the line rather than vertically.

14.4 Reading in a list from the keyboard

To read elements into a list from the keyboard, and end when the atom **end** is input, we can use the following rule:

getlist([L | Lt]):-read(X),not X=end,L=X,getlist(Lt).
getlist([]).

Again, let us go through a worked example to see what happens. We will put
letters by the successive executions of the rule so that we can keep track as the
recursion unwinds at the end. With **getlist** consulted into the database, we start
off with:

?- getlist(List).

The interpreter will find the first **getlist** in the database and try to prove its first
subgoal, **read**. It will go to the next line on the screen and wait for input.
Suppose we enter an atom **jane**. The first three subgoals of the rule now
succeed as follows.

getlist([jane | Lt]):-
    read(jane),not jane=end,jane=jane,getlist(Lt).   {A}

read succeeds with argument **jane**, **not jane=end** succeeds because **jane** does
not equal **end** so this is true, **jane=jane** succeeds, instantiating **L** to **jane**, and
the execution reaches **getlist(Lt)**. The rule is executed again, reaches **read**, and
again waits for input. Suppose we enter **fred**. We now have:

getlist([fred | Lt]):-
    read(fred),not fred=end,fred=fred,getlist(Lt).   {B}

Again **getlist** is called, and suppose we enter bill. We have:

getlist([bill | Lt]):-
    read(bill),not bill=end,bill=bill,getlist(Lt).   {C}

This time when getlist is called, suppose we enter end. Now we have the
following:

getlist([L | Lt]):-
    read(end),not end=end,L=X,getlist(Lt).

This time the execution does not get past **not end=end**, which is now untrue.
When this fails, the execution backtracks over **read**, which can only succeed
once, and the whole rule fails. The execution moves on to the second **getlist**,
which succeeds with an empty list as its argument.

getlist([]).   {D}

Because D has now succeeded completely, C can now succeed with Lt instantiated to the empty list []. The recursion now unwinds with all variables
becoming instantiated as follows:

getlist([bill | []]):-
    read(bill),not bill=end,bill=bill,getlist([]).   {C}

getlist([fred | bill]):-
    read(fred),not fred=end,fred=fred,
    getlist([bill]).   {B}

getlist([jane | [fred,bill]]):-
    read(jane),not jane=end,jane=jane,
    getlist([fred,bill]).   {A}

The list **[jane,fred,bill]** is returned to the interpreter prompt as the solution to the query:

List = [jane,fred,bill]

14.5 name

This is a standard Prolog predicate with two arguments which converts an atom (first argument) into a list of ASCII codes (second argument), and vice versa.

The ASCII code of a character is the number it is converted to so that the computer can handle it. (It stands for American Standard Code for Information Interchange.)

> **e.g. ?- name(bill,Name).**
> **Name = [98,105,108,108]**
>
> **?- name(X,[105,108,108]).**
> **X = ill**
>
> **?- name(Char,[97]).**
> **Char = a**

Question 14.3 *(answer on p.122)*

Write a program which reads in your name as a list of characters, then writes it out in normal form.

> **e.g. ?- writename(['A',m,y]).**
> **Amy**

14.6 A test for a list

If we work through a list to the end, when we get there we should be left with just the empty brackets, or an empty list.

As we mentioned above, it is possible to enter into a program, perhaps accidentally, structures which look rather like lists but are not, things like **[ford | renault]**. Such a structure cannot be properly processed as a list, as the atom **renault**, its 'tail', cannot be processed itself as a list. The 'list' is incorrectly formed.

We can say that a list is correctly formed if it has an empty list at the end, and we can use this to write a rule which tests a list.

> **islist([]).**
> **islist([_ | X]):-islist(X).**

This rule recursively works through a list given as its argument until it gets to the end, and checks whether there is an empty list there. If not, it fails.

For example:

> **?- islist([ford | [renault]]).**
> **yes**
>
> **?- islist([ford | renault]).**
> **no**

Question 14.4 *(answer on p.122)*

*Use **name** to write a program **asc** which writes out the characters and corresponding ASCII codes from 32 to 126. (If you go outside this range drastic things can happen.)*

14.7 Summary

A list is a collection of Prolog objects enclosed in square brackets and separated by commas. It is used to hold objects while performing operations on them, like an array in a procedural language. Operations are performed on lists using a special head and tail notation.

Operations such as writing out and reading in a list can be performed using user-defined rules like the ones given in the chapter. There are also built-in predicates for certain operations, like **name** which converts an atom into a list of ASCII codes. To understand how list rules work, it is very useful to use the **trace** predicate.

Answers to questions

Answer 14.1

   (a)   Write the following as enumerated lists:

       [bert,fred,mary]
       [p,q,r,s,t]
       [20,15,10,5,0]

   (b)   Write the above in head|tail form.

       [bert | [fred,mary]]
       [p | [q,r,s,t]]
       [20 | [15,10,5,0]]

(c) Are the following valid as lists?

[l,m,n]	**yes**
[l | [m,n]]	**yes**
[l | m,n]	**no**
n	**no**
N	**yes**
[y]	**yes**
[Q]	**yes**
[lion | elephant]	**no**

Answer 14.2

```
writelist2([]).
writelist2([L|Lt]):-write(L),write(' '),writelist2(Lt).
```

Answer 14.3

First solution – this reads in the characters as a list of atoms using read (each one needs a fullstop after it), then writes out the list of atoms using a version of writelist.

```
go:-getlist(Name),nl,nl,writelist(Name),nl.

getlist([L|Lt]):-read(X),not X=end,L=X,getlist(Lt).
getlist([]).

writelist([]).
writelist([L|Lt]):-write(L),writelist(Lt).
```

Second solution – this uses get0 to read in a list of ASCII codes, then converts the list of ASCII codes to an atom using name, then simply writes out the atom using write:

```
go:-getlist(Name),nl,nl,name(Atom,Name),write(Atom),nl.

getlist([L|Lt]):-get0(X),not X=end,L=X,getlist(Lt).
getlist([]).
```

Answer 14.4

The program could be as follows:

```
asc:-ascii(32).

ascii(127).
ascii(ASC):-name(Char,[ASC]),
      write(Char),write(' '),write(ASC),nl,
      Next is ASC+1,ascii(Next).
```

Programming practice: lists

1. Type **writelist**, **getlist** and **islist** into a file and consult them into the database. Test the examples and exercises given above, using **trace** to see how they work.

2. Try the examples given for **name**, and some others.

3. Write a rule **putlist(List)** which asserts the elements of a list into the database in facts of the form **element(Element)**. Try the rule with:

   ?- putlist([peach,pear,plum]).

   Use **listing** after running the rule to test whether it has worked.

4. Use **name** to write a rule **caps** which converts a character entered to upper case, if it is lower case, and otherwise leaves it alone.

   e.g. ?- caps(a,X).
   X = 'A'
   ?- caps(3,X).
   X = 3

Note: Upper case characters have ASCII codes from 65 to 90, and lower case characters have codes 97 to 122.

15 Common list rules

15.1 Introduction

This chapter contains a collection of useful list rules which are frequently used in list processing. These are not part of standard Prolog, but some are built-in predicates in some versions of Prolog.

We will not explain each of these rules in detail, but you should try to satisfy yourself as to how they work. Try going through the examples given as worked examples, in the same way that **writelist** and **getlist** were explained in the last chapter. Also, run the examples given using **trace**.

What is particularly important is to know how to use these common rules for list processing.

15.2 Reversing a list

reverse(L1,L2) reverses list **L1** to give list **L2**. Elements are transfered from the front of the first list to the front of the second list. When the first list becomes empty, the second is the final list.

> **reverse (L1,L2):-rev(L1,[ ],L2).**
> **rev([ ],L,L).**
> **rev([X | L],L2,L3):-rev(L,[X | L2],L3).**
>
> eg. ?- **reverse([3,4,5],List).**
>   **List = [5,4,3]**

Question 15.1 (answer on p.129)

Go through a worked example of the following use of reverse, giving each separate call of the rule and showing which variables are instantiated, first going forward, then unwinding out of the recursion.

> ?- **reverse([p,q,r],List).**
>   **List = [r,q,p]**

15.3 Testing for membership of a list

member(X,L) succeeds if object **X** is a member of list **L**. It fails otherwise.

> **member(X,[X | _]).**
> **member(X,[_ | Lt]):-member(X,Lt).**

eg. ?- member(mouse,[vole,mouse,rat]).
yes

Users of LPA Prolog should note that **member** is a built-in predicate, but has the name **on**.

Question 15.2 (answer on p.130)

*Write a rule **indef_art** which takes an atom as its first argument, and returns the indefinite article, either **a** or **an**, as its second argument, correctly matching the atom, ie. if the atom begins with a vowel, it should be **an**, if it begins with a consonant it should be **a**, as follows:*

?- indef_art(elephant,X).
   X = an
?- indef_art(giraffe,Y).
   Y = a

15.4 Testing for a sublist

sublist(S,L) succeeds if list **S** is a sublist of list **L**, i.e. fits into it with elements consecutively in the same order.

sublist(S,L):-prefix(L,M),!.
sublist(L,[_ | M]):-sublist(L,M).

prefix([],_).
prefix([X | L],[X | M]):-prefix(L,M).

eg. ?-sublist([4,5,6],[1,2,3,4,5,6,7,8]).
yes

15.5 Appending or concatenating one list onto another

append(L1,L2,L3) appends list **L2** onto the end of list **L1** to give list **L3**.

append([],L,L).
append([X | L1],L2,[X | L3]):-append(L1,L2,L3).

eg. ?- append([1,2,3],[4,5,6],List).
List = [1,2,3,4,5,6]

Note that **append** is sometimes called **concat**, and that LPA Prolog has **concat** as a built-in predicate. If you are using LPA Prolog, and if you tried to enter **concat** into the database, you would get an error because the predicate is a reserved word.

Question 15.3 *(answer on p.130)*

Use one of the standard list rules to write a rule **rotate(L1,L2)** *which rotates each element of L1 to the left, moving the first element to the end, and forming* **L2**.

eg. ?- rotate([1,2,3,4,5],X).
    X=[2,3,4,5,1]

15.6 Deleting elements from a list

delete(X,L1,L2) deletes all occurrences of element **X** from list **L1** to give list **L2**.

delete(_,[],[]).
delete(X,[X|L],M):-!,delete(X,L,M).
delete(X,[Y|L1],[Y|L2]):-delete(X,L1,L2).

eg. ?- delete(q,[x,p,q,r,s,q],List).
    List = [x,p,r,s]

15.7 Counting elements in a list

count(List,N) counts the **N** elements of list **List**.

count([],0).
count([_|Lt],N):-count(Lt,M),N is 1+M.

eg. ?- count([p,q,r,s,t],N).
    N = 5

Again, if you are using LPA Prolog, note that LPA has a built-in predicate length which is the same as **count**.

Question 15.4 *(answer on p.130)*

Write a rule **sumlist**, *based on* **count**, *which sums or totals all the integers in a list of integers.*

eg. ?- sumlist([3,4,5],Sum).
    Sum = 12

15.8 Getting a numbered term from a list

getnum(N,List,Term) gets term number **N** from list **List**. It also finds which number in the list a specified term is. If there are more than one of the specified term in the list, it gives the number of the first one.

getnum(N,L,T):-get_term(N,L,T,1).
get_term(N,[L|_],L,N).
get_term(N,[_|Lt],X,M):-Q=M+1,get_term(N,Lt,X,Q).

eg. ?- getnum(3,[a,b,c,d,e],Term).
    Term = c

```
?- getnum(Num,[a,b,c,d,d],d).
   Num = 4
```

15.9 findall

This is a very useful predicate which makes items from the database into a list. (LPA Prolog has it as a built-in predicate.) It takes the form:

findall(Variable,Fact,List)

Variable identifies part of the fact **Fact**, and **findall** then returns a list **List** made up of such parts.

eg. Suppose we have a database of fishes as follows:

```
fish(shark,teeth,big).
fish(goldfish,gold,small).
fish(stickleback,spikes,small).
```

We can make a list of all the names of the fishes as follows:

```
?- findall(F,fish(F,_,_),List).
   List = [shark,goldfish,stickleback]
```

Or a list of all the small fishes as follows:

```
?- findall(S,fish(S,_,small),List2).
   List2 = [goldfish,stickleback]
```

If your version of Prolog does not have **findall** built in (for example if you are using Public Domain or PD Prolog), you can enter it in the database as follows:

```
findall(X,G,_):-asserta(found(mark)),G,
     asserta(found(X)),fail.
findall(_,_,L):-collect_found([],M),!,L=M.

collect_found(S,L):-getnext(X),!,
     collect_found([X|S],L).
collect_found(L,L).

getnext(X):-retract(found(X)),!,not X=mark.
```

This is modified slightly from the Clocksin and Mellish version, and will work in PD Prolog. We will not explain the operation of **findall** here, just how to use it, though you should be able to see roughly how it works. The '**!**' is a 'cut', explained in Chapter 18.

Question 15.5 *(answer on p.130)*

person(charlene,18,'Ramsay Street').
person(sherlock,40,'Baker Street').
person(harold,45,'Ramsay Street').
person(margaret,55,'Downing Street').

*In the above database, use **findall** to make a list of*

1. *All the people in the database.*

2. *All the ages.*

3. *All the people in Ramsay Street.*

15.10 An example to plot lists on a graph

At the end of Chapter 11 we tried as an exercise a recursive program to draw a simple graph, using stars going horizontally along the line. We can now write a rule **plot(List1,List2)**, which plots two lists of integers one against the other on a proper two-dimensional graph.

This can be tested with something like:

?- plot([0,5,10,15,20],[0,15,30,45,60]).

To write a program to do this we need a predicate which can move the cursor around the screen. There is not one in standard Prolog, but all recent implementations have a built-in predicate to do this. Usually they take three arguments, one of which specifies the window the cursor is in. If you are using LPA Prolog, you need to define a predicate **curs** by adding the following in the program:

curs(Y,X):-cursor('&:',Y,X).

Or if you are using Public Domain Prolog, add:

curs(Y,X):-cursor(Y,X,0).

This is a straightforward recursive rule, but requires some experimentation to position the graph suitably on the screen. Note that if you use this in a program, the numbers in the lists must be scaled to be in the right range, or **curs** will fail. The rule will not fail if the lists are not the same length, but will just plot to the length of the shortest.

```
/* PLOTTING LISTS ON A GRAPH */

plot(L1,L2):-put(12),nl,write(' Y-axis'),
     draw_y(21),draw_x(65),plot2(L1,L2),
     curs(22,1).

/* Draws Y axis (range 0 to 20) */

draw_y(0).
draw_y(N):-Y is 22-N,curs(Y,10),
     write('|'),M is N-1,draw_y(M).
```

```
/* Draws X axis (range 0 to 60) */

draw_x(0):-curs(22,60),write('X-axis').
draw_x(N):-write('_'),M is N-1,draw_x(M).

/* Plots graph of List1 (Y) against List2 (X)
    Ends when either list is empty. */

plot2(_,[]).
plot2([],_).
plot2([L|Lt],[M|Mt]):-Y is 21-L,X is M+10,
    curs(Y,X),write('*'),plot2(Lt,Mt).

/* Defines cursor rule for LPA Prolog */

curs(Y,X):-cursor('&:',Y,X).

:-go.

/* END */
```

The rule **plot(L1,L2)** clears the screen with **put(12)**, then draws the Y axis vertically on the screen, via the rule **draw_y** which uses **curs** and writes the | 'pipe' symbol recursively. It then draws the X axis horizontally via **draw_x** which writes the _ underline symbol recursively. The rule **plot2** is then called with the two lists as arguments. This rule takes the heads off the two lists and plots them using **curs**, writing a star * at the point where the cursor is located, then goes on to the next two points recursively, working through the lists. After plotting the lists, **plot2** returns the cursor to the bottom of the graph.

15.11 Summary

There are a number of useful rules for manipulating lists, some built-in and some which you need to consult into your programs as user-defined rules. They include, as well as those given in Chapter 14, **reverse**, **member**, **sublist**, **append**, **delete**, **count**, **getnum**, **findall** and **plot**, all given in this chapter.

Answers to questions

Answer 15.1

```
?- reverse([p,q,r],List).

reverse ([p,q,r],L2):-rev([p,q,r],[],L2).
rev([p|[q,r]],[],L3):-rev([q,r],[p|[]],L3).
rev([q|[r]],[p],L3):-rev([r],[q|[p]],L3).
rev([r|[]],[q,p],L3):-rev([],[r|[q,p]],L3).
rev([],[r,q,p],[r,q,p]).
```

This is the boundary rule which first succeeds.

```
rev([r | []],[q,p],[r,q,p]):-
    rev([],[r | [q,p]],[r,q,p]).
rev([q | [r]],[p],[r,q,p]):-
    rev([r],[q | [p]],[r,q,p]).
rev([p | [q,r]],[],[r,q,p]):-
    rev([q,r],[p | []],[r,q,p]).
reverse([p,q,r],[r,q,p]):-
    rev([p,q,r],[],[r,q,p]).

?- reverse([p,q,r],List).
    List = [r,q,p]
```

Answer 15.2

```
indef_art(Word,an):-
    name(Word,[N | _]),
    name(aeiou,Vowels),
    member(N,Vowels).
indef_art(_,a).
```

Answer 15.3

```
rotate([L | Lt],L2):-concat(Lt,[L],L2).
```

Answer 15.4

```
sumlist([],0).
sumlist([N | Nt],Total):-sumlist(Nt,SubTotal),
    Total is SubTotal + N.
```

Answer 15.5

1. findall(X,person(X,_,_),List).

2. findall(A,person(_,A,_),List2).

3. findall(P,person(P,_,'Ramsay Street'),List3).

Programming practice: **palindromes using lists**

Pp

1. Write a rule **palindrome(List)** which succeeds if **List** is the same backwards as forwards. (A palindrome is a word which is the same backwards as forwards.) Test your rule.

2. Remember that the built-in predicate **name** converts an atom into a list of ASCII codes of its characters.

    eg. ?- name(fred,X).
    X = [102,114,101,100]

    This information should enable you to put **palindrome** into a short program to test a typed in word to see whether it is a palindrome (ie. a word which is the same backwards as forwards) started by a rule **pal**. Test it with palindromes such as 'ada' and 'madam'.

3. Write a rule **convert** which works through a list of integers, takes all those between 64 and 91, and adds 32 to them. In other words, if the list of integers is a list of ASCII codes, it converts all the ASCII codes of upper case characters to the ASCII codes of their corresponding lower case characters.

4. You can now put this into your program **pal**, and test it with the string

    'Able was I ere I saw Elba'

    This famous palindrome was supposedly spoken by Napoleon. (Did he speak English?)

16 Quantitative expert systems

16.1 Introduction

We have developed one type of expert system, and a simple expert system shell, in Chapters 10 and 13. Another type of expert system, instead of suggesting one of a number of solutions to a problem, assesses the numerical likelihood of a single factor being true. In other words, it deals with the problem in a numerical, quantitative way rather than simply qualitatively.

For example, a mining expert system might take as input all the geological information relating to a particular area, and calculate the numerical likelihood of oil being found in that area.

Such expert systems often use fairly complex mathematical techniques to calculate the probability of something of this kind. As this is a book on Prolog, and we do not want to take up a large part of the book in explaining probabilities, we will not use them here, but a simpler points system.

The examples which follow are not necessarily less valid for being less mathematically rigorous, and could be modified to use probabilities. If this subject interests you, several larger textbooks treat the use of Prolog for expert systems in considerably more detail. (See the bibliography.)

Remember that none of the advice provided by the examples of expert systems given here is guaranteed to be accurate – but then, neither is the advice of most experts!

Question 16.1 (answer on p.142)

The way we tackle the next little expert system can be regarded as an exercise in how to write a program in Prolog. How do you think the approach to programming a larger program in Prolog should be different from that in other languages?

16.2 A bank manager expert system

A bank manager has skill and experience in many areas, but very often his or her job will consist of a single task – assessing a customer who comes in to ask for a loan, and deciding whether he or she is suitable for such a loan or not. In other words, the bank manager has to assess the customer's credit rating.

In practice he or she will probably do the job by asking questions, then either consciously or subconsciously apply certain 'rules of thumb' to make the decision. Let's suppose that a researcher has questioned a typical manager, and boiled down the process into the following questionnaire.

The customer scores points for each answer as indicated, then his or her points total determines the credit rating and whether or not he or she gets a loan. After each question, the way the answers are interpreted for awarding points is shown. This is not part of the questionnaire the user sees.

Credit rating questionnaire

1. Are you single, married, widowed, divorced, or separated? (Answer s, m, w, d or p.)

    [s = 2, m = 5, w = 3, d = 1, p = 1]

2. What is your age?

    **[1 if < 25, 5 if 25 to 29, 3 if 30 to 49,
    5 if 50 to 59, 3 if > 59]**

3. Would you describe the area where you live as run-down inner city, average or high class? (Answer r, a or h.)

    [r = 2, a = 5, h = 9]

4. How many years (to the nearest year) have you been at your present address? (Answer 0.5 if six months or less.)

    **[1 if 0.5, 3 if 1 to 3, 4 if 4 to 7,
    6 if 8 to 12, 7 if >12 years]**

5. Is your present address occupied as owner (o), tenant (t), unfurnished or council tenant (u), with parents or relatives (r), free with job (f), or lodger (l) ?

    [o = 9, t = 4, u = 7, r = 1, f = 3, l = 2]

6. Is your job office worker (o), skilled manual (s), part-time (pt), unemployed (u), supervisor (s), manager or director (md),professional (p), or self-employed (se) ?

    [o = 3, s = 3, pt = 2, u = 1, s = 4, md = 7, p = 9, se = 3]

7. Can you supply your employer's name and address? (y/n)

    [y = 4, n = 0]

8. Credit cards: none (n), Access (a), Visa (v), Amex (x), Diners (d).

    [1 if none, 4 if a or v, 5 if x or d]

9. How many loans do you have outstanding?

    [4 for 0, 6 for 1, 2 for 2, 1 for > 2]

10. Have you had previous credit with this bank? (Answer n for none, one for one successful loan, two for two or more successful loans, or term for a loan that was terminated.)

> **[4 if n; if y, 7 for one good loan, 10 for two good loans, and -20 for a bad history of debt]**

Credit rating for purposes of loan

Over 35:	**Get loan**
25 to 35:	**Maybe**
Under 25:	**No chance**

We now have to express this expertise in the form of an expert system, a computer program.

Constructing a knowledge base

The questionnaire above contains knowledge of which factors are important in assessing credit rating, which questions to ask, and how to weigh the answers given. The questions, the answers and the points allocation comprise the knowledge base of this expert system.

The text for the questions can be stored in the database in text facts as follows, stored with the number of the question as the first argument and the text as the second:

> **text(1,'1. Are you single, married, widowed, divorced,').**
> **text(1,' or separated? (Answer s, m, w, d or p.)').**
>
> **text(2,'2. What is your age?').**
>
> **text(3,'3. Would you describe the area where you live as').**
> **text(3,' run-down inner city, average or high class?').**
> **text(3,' (Answer r, a or h.)').**

… and so on.

We need to do the following with each possible answer to each question in the questionnaire:

> **FOR q1, answer s, award 2 points**
> **FOR q1, answer m, award 5 points**
> **FOR q1, answer w, award 3 points**
> **… etc, etc**

This can be expressed in data facts thus:

> **data(1,s,2).**
> **data(1,m,5).**
> **data(1,w,3).**
> **… etc, etc**

This ties the answer given (the second argument) to the points associated with it (the third argument) and the question the answer belongs to (the first argument). As we have several possible answers for each question, each question has several facts.

When we have added up the total of all the points for all the answers, the criteria for awarding the loan can be expressed in some short rules **decide**. These are the bank manager's 'rules of thumb', and in our little system the rules take the points total and write a reply, as follows:

```
decide(Total):- Total > 35,
     write('You get your loan.'),nl.
decide(Total):- Total < 25,
     write('Sorry, no loan.'),nl.
decide(_):-write('You might get a loan.'),nl.
```

The interface

This expert system is so simple that there is very little to the interface apart from writing out the questions for the user, and reading in the answers.

A rule **write_question** which writes out the text for a specified question number is given below.

```
write_question(Q):-text(Q,Text),write(Text),nl,fail.
write_question(_):-nl.
```

The inference engine

We now have all the data for the questions to ask, and the points to give for each possible answer. It remains to write a program rule to ask the user the questions, collect the answers, totalling the points for them, arrive at a decision and tell the user the decision. This will have to do something along the following lines, written in pseudo-code:

```
start the program
ask the questions using a loop:
     get a question
     ask it
     get the answer
     get the points for the answer
     add these to the total
     repeat, until last question number
after all questions, get the decision
output the decision
```

The program might be:

```
go:-    write('BANK MANAGER'),nl,nl,
        ask_questions(0,Total),
        decide(Total).
```

We have included here a rule **ask_questions** which has to do the job of the loop in the pseudo-code above. The rule **ask_questions** has to count through the questions recursively, asking them and collecting answers, and at the same time keeping the points total. **ask_questions** ends when its counter has counted up to the total number of questions, contained in the boundary rule. The final points total at the end comes back into the rule **go** as **Total**. Having found the total, the decide_loan rules decide on an appropriate reply to write on the screen. Let us write the rule **ask_question**:

```
ask_question(10,0).
ask_questions(Q,Total):-
    NextQ is Q + 1,
    write_question(NextQ),
    write('Answer here: '),
    read(Answer),nl,
    data(NextQ,Answer,Points),
    ask_questions(NextQ,SmallTotal),
    Total is SmallTotal + Points.
```

This rule writes out each question, counting through the questions recursively. It gets the points for a given answer from the data fact and goes on to the next question, then totals the points as it unwinds out of the recursion, using the technique described in Chapter 15.

This rule is rather accident prone as it stands, as someone may type in something that is not an answer in the database, so we can add a 'catch-all rule' which will succeed when such an error causes the recursive rule to fail:

```
ask_questions(Q,Total):-
    write('Please try again!'),nl,
    ask_questions(Q,Total).
```

16.3 Complete bank manager program

We now have a complete program, an expert system to make a decision for a bank manager, and the complete listing is shown below. You can type it in and try it if you want to be a bank manager for a day.

```
/* BANK MANAGER EXPERT SYSTEM */
/* =========================== */

/* INFERENCE ENGINE */

/* Main program rule */

go:- put(12),write('** BANK MANAGER **'),nl,nl,
    ask_questions(0,Total),
    decide(Total).
```

```
/* Rule to ask the questions */

ask_questions(10,0).

ask_questions(Q,Total):-
    NextQ is Q + 1,
    write_question(NextQ),
    write('Answer here: '),
    read(Answer),nl,
    data(NextQ,Answer,Points),
    ask_questions(NextQ,SmallTotal),
    Total is SmallTotal + Points.

ask_questions(Q,Total):-write('Please try again!'),nl,
    ask_questions(Q,Total).

/* INTERFACE */

/* Rule to write out a question */

write_question(Q):-text(Q,Text),write(Text),nl,fail.
write_question(_):-nl.

/* KNOWLEDGE BASE */

/* Facts to make loan decision */

decide(Total):- Total > 35,
    write('You get your loan.'),nl.
decide(Total):- Total < 25,
    write('Sorry, no loan.'),nl.
decide(_):-write('You might get a loan.'),nl.

/* Text for questions */

text(1,'1.  Are you single, married, widowed, divorced,').
text(1,'    or separated? (Answer s, m, w, d or p.)').

text(2,'2.  What is your age?').

text(3,'3.  Would you describe the area where you live as').
text(3,'    run-down inner city, average or high class?').
text(3,'    (Answer r, a or h.)').

text(4,'4.  How many years (to the nearest year) have you').
text(4,'    been at your present address? (Answer 0.5 if').
text(4,'    six months or less.)').

text(5,'5.  Is your present address occupied as owner (o),').
text(5,'    tenant (t), unfurnished or council tenant (u),').
text(5,'    with parents or relatives (r), free with job').
text(5,'    (f), or lodger (l) ?').

text(6,'6.  Is your job office worker (o), skilled manual').
text(6,'    (s), part-time (pt), unemployed (u),').
text(6,'    supervisor (s), manager or director (md),').
text(6,'    professional (p), or self-employed (se) ?').
```

```
text(7,'7.   Can you supply employers name and address?').
text(7,'    (y/n)').

text(8,'8.   Credit cards: none (n), Access (a), Visa (v),').
text(8,'    Access and Visa (av), Amex (x), Diners (d).').

text(9,'9.   How many loans do you have outstanding? ').

text(10,'10.  Have you had previous credit with this bank?').
text(10,'    (Answer n for none, one for one successful').
text(10,'    loan, two for two or more successful loans,').
text(10,'    or term for a loan that was terminated.)').

/* Data facts for the answers given */
data(1,s,2).
data(1,m,5).
data(1,w,3).
data(1,d,1).
data(1,p,1).

data(2,X,1):-X < 25.
data(2,X,5):-X > 24, X < 30.
data(2,X,3):-X > 29, X < 50.
data(2,X,5):-X > 49, X < 60.
data(2,X,3):-X > 59.

data(3,r,2).
data(3,a,5).
data(3,h,9).

data(4,0.5,1).
data(4,Ans,3):-Ans > 0, Ans < 4.
data(4,Ans,4):-Ans > 3, Ans < 8.
data(4,Ans,6):-Ans > 7, Ans < 13.
data(4,Ans,7):-Ans > 12.

data(5,o,9).
data(5,t,4).
data(5,u,7).
data(5,r,1).
data(5,f,3).
data(5,l,2).

data(6,o,3).
data(6,s,3).
data(6,pt,2).
data(6,u,1).
data(6,s,4).
data(6,md,7).
data(6,p,9).
data(6,se,3).

data(7,y,4).
data(7,n,0).
```

```
data(8,n,1).
data(8,a,4).
data(8,v,4).
data(8,x,5).
data(8,d,5).

data(9,0,4).
data(9,1,6).
data(9,2,2).
data(9,Ans,1):-Ans > 2.

data(10,n,4).
data(10,one,7).
data(10,two,10).
data(10,term,-20).

/* END */
```

16.4 Estate agent expert system

An important part of an estate agent's job is valuing houses, ie. putting a value on them and deciding what price they can be advertised for. Suppose we have the following questionnaire which is used for house valuation, and want to use it as the basis for an expert system to do this part of the estate agent's job.

Questionnaire

1. Which part of the country do you live in? Answer n for North, s for South or m for Midlands.

    [Thousands of pounds: 30 for n, 40 for m, 50 for s.]

2. Are you in a good residential area (g), a down at heel area (d), or an average area (a)?

    [+ 10 for g, -10 for d, 0 for a.]

3. Is the house terraced, semidetached or detached? (t, s, or d.)

    [+ 10 for d, 0 for s, -5 for t.]

4. How many bedrooms has the house?

    [-3 for 2, 0 for 3, + 3 for 4, -5 for 1, + 10 for > 4.]

5. Is your garden large (l), average (a) or non-existent (n)?

    [+ 5 for l, − 5 for n, 0 for a.]

6. Do you have an extension? (y/n)

    [+ 5 for y, 0 for n.]

7. Do you have a garage, parking space only, or neither? (g, p or n)?

    [+ 5 for g, + 2 for p, 0 for n.]

8. Is the condition of the house good, average or poor? (g, a or p.)

    [+ 2 for g, 0 for a, -3 for p.]

LONG Question 16.2 *(answer on p.142)*

Put the following above data into an ESTATE AGENT expert system which values your house for you. Base your program directly on the bank manager program.

Notice that in this program you do not need to make a decision, simply to return the points score as the value of the house in thousands of pounds. This means that only one decision rule is needed:

**decide(Total):-write('House is worth £'),
write(Total),write(',000.'),nl,nl.**

You will also need:

   a different title
   a different number of questions
   question facts for the text
   data facts for the question, answer and score

Apart from this, the main inference engine and interface rules can be the same.

16.5 Converting to a shell

You will have found with the last question that the ESTATE AGENT system could be treated in a very similar way to the BANK MANAGER system. In fact we can separate the inference engine and interface part from the database as in Chapter 13, and produce a shell for this type of system.

The result has to be a general program, with no mention of estate agents or bank managers. It needs to get its title and number of questions from the knowledge base, and it needs to read in the knowledge base it is going to use from a separate file. This means it must also clear the database at the end of the program ready for another run, which it can do using **reconsult**. It looks as follows:

```
/* QUANTITATIVE EXPERT SYSTEM SHELL */

/* INFERENCE ENGINE */

go:- cls,
     write('Enter name of expert system file to use: '),
     read(File),reconsult(File),cls,
     title(Title),write(Title),nl,nl,
     ask_questions(0,Total),
     decide(Total).
```

```
/* Rule to ask the questions */

ask_question(N,0):-no_of_questions(N).

ask_questions(Q,Total):-
    NextQ is Q + 1,
    write_question(NextQ),
    write('Answer here: '),
    read(Answer),nl,
    data(NextQ,Answer,Points),
    ask_questions(NextQ,SmallTotal),
    Total is SmallTotal + Points.

ask_questions(Q,Total):-write('Please try again!'),nl,
    ask_questions(Q,Total).

/* INTERFACE */

/* Rule to write out a question */

write_question(Q):-text(Q,Text),write(Text),nl,fail.
write_question(_):-nl.

cls:- put(12).

/* END */
```

The knowledge base must now contain two extra facts, which for the BANK MANAGER system will be:

```
title('* BANK MANAGER *').

no_of_questions(10).
```

It will also contain, as before, **text** facts with the text for the questions, **data** facts with the data for the scores for the answers, and **decision** rules to determine the reply from the score.

A shell of this kind can be used as the basis for building a much more complex expert system to perform one of a number of tasks. The advantage of using Prolog to program an expert system, rather than using a commercial shell, is that it can be modified to do whatever a particular expert domain requires, while commercial shells tend to be restricted in some way or another.

16.6 Summary

There is a type of expert system which assesses the numerical likelihood of a single factor being true. Such an expert system program is described here, and developed into a shell.

The shells developed in this chapter and in Chapter 13 can be used as the basis for a number of simple expert system shells, for example in student projects.

Answers to questions

Answer 16.1

In a procedural language a systematic, structured, top-down approach is usually recommended, but this is not necessarily the most efficient in Prolog.

As Prolog is a language built around a database, it makes sense to start by constructing the database of information relating to the problem (or knowledge base). We can then formulate questions to draw out the information we require, making up the program.

Answer 16.2

```
/* ESTATE AGENT EXPERT SYSTEM */
/* ============================ */

/* INFERENCE ENGINE */

/* Main program rule */

go:- put(12),write('** ESTATE AGENT **'),nl,nl,
     ask_questions(1,Total),
     decide(Total).

/* Rule to ask the questions */

ask_questions(8,0).

ask_questions(Q,Total):-write_question(Q),
     write('Answer here: '),
     read(Answer),nl,
     data(Q,Answer,Points),
     NextQ is Q + 1,
     ask_questions(NextQ,SmallTotal),
     Total is SmallTotal + Points.

ask_questions(Q,Total):-write('Please try again!'),nl,
     ask_questions(Q,Total).

/* INTERFACE */

/* Rule to write out a question */

write_question(Q):-text(Q,Text),write(Text),nl,fail.
write_question(_):-nl.

/* KNOWLEDGE BASE */

/* Rule to decide on reply */

decide(Total):-write('House is worth £'),
     write(Total),write(',000.'),nl,nl.
```

```
/* Text for questions */

text(1,'1. Which part of the country do you live in?').
text(1,' (n for North, s for South, m for Midlands.)').

text(2,'2. Are you in a good residential area (g), a').
text(2,'2. down at heel area (d), or an average area (a)?').

text(3,'3. Is the house terraced, semidetached or ').
text(3,' detached? (t, s or d)').

text(4,'4. How many bedrooms has the house?').

text(5,'5. is your garden large (l), average (a), or').
text(5,' non-existent (n)?').

text(6,'6. Do you have an extension (y/n) ?').

text(7,'7. Do you have a garage, parking space only, or').
text(7,' neither ? (g, p or n)').

text(8,'8. Is the condition of the house good, average or').
text(8,' poor ? (g, a or p)').

/* Data facts for the answers given */

data(1,n,30).
data(1,m,40).
data(1,s,50).

data(2,g,10).
data(2,d,-10).
data(2,a,0).

data(3,d,10).
data(3,s,0).
data(3,t,-5).

data(4,1,-5).
data(4,2,-3).
data(4,3,0).
data(4,4,3).
data(4,X,10):-X > 10.

data(5,l,5).
data(5,n,-5).
data(5,a,0).

data(6,y,5).
data(6,n,0).

data(7,g,5).
data(7p,2).
```

```
        data(7,n,0).

        data(8,g,2).
        data(8,a,0).
        data(8,p,-3).
        /* END */
```

Programming practice: psychopath

Put the following information into a PSYCHO knowledge base file for the shell developed above, which simulates a psychoanalyst, and tells the user how psychopathic he or she is. This is rather easier than the first example above, because all the answers are a, b or c, and there is just one point for each psychopathic answer, but it can be along the same lines.

Are you a psychopath?

[Taken from *The Sunday Times*, 4th July 1993.]

1. Your memories of your early childhood are:

    a. A time of vivid fantasy.
    b. Non-existent.
    c. Some good times, some bad.

2. You stop fancying your lover and start a new affair. How do you explain the loss of desire?

    a. I have converted to a religion which demands celibacy.
    b. It's just one of those things.
    c. Probably something to do with my relations with my parents.

3. The boss expresses vehement disapproval of a plan you and a colleague cooked up together. Do you:

    a. Defend the bits you advocated, but criticise your colleague's ideas.
    b. Keep as silent as possible and leave your colleague to do all the talking.
    c. Recognise that nothing will change the boss and jettison the plan.

4. You see the boss taking a competitor for a job you want out to lunch. Do you:
    a. Have no feelings about it.
    b. Fear that the boss favours the competitor.
    c. Suspect the boss is plotting with your competitor by advising on the interview.

5. A series of calamities hits you over a six month period. Do you:

   a. Feel angry but powerless.
   b. Contemplate revenge on various adversaries.
   c. Wonder what you did to deserve it and get mildly depressed.

6. Your basic view of people is that they are:

   a. Animals with souls but largely driven by instinct.
   b. Totally different from an animal and far superior.
   c. More like machines than people, motivated by pursuit of wealth, status, sex and power.

7. As a driver you:

   a. Have been had up for a large number of offences.
   b. Bend the rules, but only if you're sure you won't get caught.
   c. Have an obsession about having to drive large cars.

8. In a war you would be best suited as:

   a. An entertainer of the troops.
   b. A spy.
   c. A frontline fighter.

9. Your attitude to stimulants is:

   a. A drink? yes. Drugs? yes. Can't get enough because neither seems to affect me much.
   b. A drink helps me in social situations.
   c. I love them but they make me act peculiarly.

10. Your attitude to sex is:

    a. It's a way of getting love.
    b. The more the merrier.
    c. The more partners the merrier.

Points scoring:

One point for each psychopathic answer. The psychopath's choices would be: 1b, 2a, 3c, 4c, 5b, 6c, 7a, 8b, 9a, 10c.

Decision making:

0-3 points – you have the normal tendency to self-preservation which is healthy.

4-6 points – You are unusually assertive and put yourself before others in ways that cause great distress. You are successful in what you do.

7-10 points – You are a psychopath.

Test yourself

A stock market expert system project

Write an expert system to analyse shares on the stock market. You will find some relevant information inside the back page of the Financial Times under 'London Share Service'.

The essential data you need to record is the name of a share ('Woolworths', 'BT' etc.), the current share price in pence, and the date. Other data which might be useful is the number of each share owned, the highest and lowest values for the year, etc.

Assume that you enter new data at regular intervals, such as each week. An obvious structure for the program is for it to be operated from a menu which offers such things as entering, deleting, updating and displaying a particular share. The most recent shares could be listed out, or displayed on a graph as explained in Chapter 15.

You should extend the program to analyse the share records in some way. Include a set of rules which analyses the share prices as a type of expert system.

As a hint, if you retrieve the last three weeks' prices from the database, and call them **Week1**, **Week2**, and **Week3** in order, then if **Week3 > Week1**, the shares are going up. **If Week3 – Week2** is greater than **Week2 -Week1**, the shares are going up more and more rapidly – go and buy some!

Note that if you retrieve all the shares of a particular company from your database as a list **List** in date order, perhaps by using **findall**, you can easily obtain the last three weeks' values by reversing the list, as follows:

... reverse(List,[Week3,Week2,Week1 | Rest]), ...

There is of course no end to the possible complexity of such a program! Only include what you can comfortably accomplish!

17 Natural language

17.1 Introduction

Using normal sentences to converse with computers, rather than command words and keypresses, is known in Artificial Intelligence as natural language. Prolog is particularly adept at handling words and sentences, by treating them as lists.

Before we can look at how to manipulate sentences to produce some interesting programs, we have two problems: how to convert input typed at the keyboard as a sentence into a list, and how to write out a list as a sentence on the screen. As the output problem is comparatively easy to solve, we will deal with it first.

17.2 Outputting lists of atoms as sentences

The following will write out a list of words with spaces. This is just the usual **writelist** rule we have used before.

> **eg. [the,cat,sat,on,the,mat] —> the cat sat on the mat**

> **writelist([]).**
> **writelist([L | Lt]):-write(L),write(' '),writelist(Lt).**

This can be improved upon as follows in a rule **writesent**, defined below, by adding a fullstop at the end and a capital letter at the beginning.

> **eg.   [the,cat,sat,on,the,mat] —> The cat sat on the mat.**

> **/* WRITING OUT A SENTENCE WITH CAPITAL AND FULLSTOP */**

> **writesent([L | Lt]):-name(L,[Z | Zt]),Y is Z-32,name(X,[Y | Zt]),**
> **   write(X),writesent2(Lt).**

> **writesent2([]):-write('.').**

> **writesent2([L | Lt]):-write(' '),write(L),writesent2(Lt).**

> **/* END */**

writesent uses **name** to convert the first word into a list of its ASCII codes. The first element of this list is converted to upper case by subtracting 32, then the ASCII codes are converted back to a word or atom. A subrule **writesent2** then

147

writes out the rest of the list of words representing the sentence, putting a full-stop when it ends.

17.3 Inputting sentences as lists of atoms

You might think that reading in a sentence as a list of words is really just a matter of extending our rule **getlist** to do the job, breaking the input up into a list of words instead of requiring them to be entered as words. This is true, but it turns out to be a tricky programming exercise. Fortunately the Prolog experts have worked on the problem before us.

The following rule **getsent** will read in a normal English sentence and convert it to a list of atoms, and is based on the version in the book by Clocksin and Mellish.

> e.g.   The cat sat on the mat. —> [the,cat,sat,on,the,mat]

```
/* READING IN A NORMAL SENTENCE AS A LIST */

getsent([W|Ws]):-get0(C),readword(C,W,C1),
    restsent(W,C1,Ws).

restsent(W,_,[]):-lastword(W),!.
restsent(W,C,[W1|Ws]):-readword(C,W1,C1),
    restsent(W1,C1,Ws).

readword(C,W,C1):-single_character(C),
    !,name(W,[C]),get0(C1).
readword(C,W,C2):-in_word(C,NewC),!,get0(C1),
    restword(C1,Cs,C2),name(W,[NewC|Cs]).
readword(C,W,C2):-get0(C1),readword(C1,W,C2).

restword(C,[NewC|Cs],C2):-in_word(C,NewC),!,
    get0(C1),restword(C1,Cs,C2).
restword(C,[],C).

single_character(44).      single_character(59).
single_character(58).      single_character(63).
single_character(33).      single_character(46).

in_word(C,C):-C>96,C<123.  in_word(C,C):-C>47,C<58.
in_word(39,39).            in_word(45,45).
in_word(C,L):-C>64,C<91,L is C+32.

lastword('.').  lastword('!').  lastword('?').

/* END */
```

This intricate piece of recursive code reads in text entered at the keyboard one character at a time, using **get0** rather than **read**. It can be looked on as a considerably expanded version of **getlist**, given in Chapter 14.

getsent gets the first character entered, reads the first word using **readword**, then deals with the rest of the sentence using **restsent**. **restsent** uses **readword** repeatedly to read in more words as long as they keep coming, ending the input when it encounters a **lastword**, one of **? !** .

readword gets the first character of a word, then gets the rest of the word using **restword**, converting the word, a list of ASCII codes, to an atom using **name**. It uses **single_character** to treat certain characters as words in themselves, **! , . : ; ?**

getword and **restword** test that the characters are alphanumeric using **in_word** as they come in, converting uppercase to lowercase and allowing through ' (39) and – (45).

This is a classic piece of Prolog code, and you will probably feel that it will be a long time before you can produce things like this! Not least because there are several examples of the cut (!) in it, which we have not covered yet. However, the main thing is to grasp what **getsent** does, so as to be able to use it in your programs.

We can try the rule **getsent** in the interpreter, having consulted it in, with something like:

```
?-   getsent(SentList).
The bat hit the ball.
SentList = [the,bat,hit,the,ball,'.']
```

Alternatively we can use a short test program:

```
go:- write('Enter a sentence: '),getsent(X),nl,
     write('This is now: '),write(X),nl.
```

17.4 Manipulating text to simulate conversation

This was first done by Joseph Weisenbaum in a program called ELIZA. A simple form of 'intelligent' program can consist of a dialogue between the computer and the user, using a simple loop:

> **Read input sentence from user.**
> **Test it in some way.**
> **Construct an output sentence in some way.**
> **Write an output sentence as an answer.**
> **Repeat.**

There are several ways such a conversational program can be written. One way is to make it respond to keywords with certain general, standard responses. For example, if the user types in a sentence containing the word 'computer', the program can respond with 'Do you know about computers?' This is easily done in Prolog using **member**.

```
/* KEYWORDS CONVERSATION PROGRAM */

/* Main program */

    go:-write('Ask me something.'),nl,chat([]).

    chat('Goodbye.'):-nl.
    chat(_):-getsent(Sent),data(Keylist,Reply),
        member(X,Sent),member(X,Keylist),
        write(Reply),nl,chat(Reply).

    member(X,[X|_]).
    member(X,[_|Lt]):-member(X,Lt).

/* Database for keywords */

    data([computer],'Do you know about computers?').
    data([i,me],'You are obsessed with yourself').
    data([you],'Dont be personal.').
    data([football,soccer],'I feel sick as a parrot.').
    data([and,but],'Too complicated for me.').
    data([what,why,how,who,where],'Sorry, no questions.').
    data([exit,stop,halt,end],'Goodbye.').
    data([_],'Sorry, I dont understand.').

/* Note: The rules for getsent are required as well */

/* END */
```

The program rule **go** says 'Ask me something' then goes to the program loop **chat**, which uses **getsent** to input a sentence as a list. **chat** then calls up one of the **data** facts, and uses its first argument, a list of keywords, to see whether there is any word **X** which is a member of the sentence list and also a member of the keyword list. If not, and **member** fails, it will backtrack and call up another **data** fact and check that also, working through all the **data** facts if necessary.

If **chat** finds a keyword, it takes the second argument of the **data** fact which is a response string, and writes it out as a reply. **chat** then loops back and repeats the process. If no keyword is found in any of the keyword lists, a standard response at the bottom of the database, 'Sorry I dont understand' is written out. The program terminates when **exit**, **stop**, **halt** or **end** occurs in an input sentence.

?

Question 17.1 (answer on p.154)

The rule **writesent** *above will write out all words except the first word of a sentence without a capital letter. It can be modified to do a check on each word and, if it occurs in a database of proper nouns, write it out with a capital. Try to make it do this, e.g.*

proper_noun(bill).
proper_noun(hull).
proper_noun(i).

[sailor,bill,lives,in,hull] —> Sailor Bill lives in Hull.
[fred,and,i,are,friends] —> Fred and I are friends.

17.5 Substituting words in a sentence

Another technique we can use to simulate conversation is to substitute for certain words in a sentence. For example, we might make up a database of words which can be changed into other words as follows:

substitute(i,you).
substitute(am,are).
substitute(yes,no).
substitute(no,yes).
substitute(silly,clever).

The program strategy is rather different here. The input from the user is checked for substitute words, and where they are found, words are substituted. The user's own sentence is then given back. So we can get an exchange like this:

[you,are,silly] —> [i,am,clever]
[yes,silly] —> [no,clever]
[no,silly] —> [yes,clever]

Of course, unless the program is extended much further, most exchanges will become gibberish! The Prolog implementation of this strategy is very easy.

/* SUBSTITUTION CONVERSATION PROGRAM */

/* Main program */

```
go:-write('Speak to me.'),nl,talk([]).

talk([goodbye,'.']):-write('Goodbye!'),nl.
talk(_):-getsent(Sent),change(Sent,ReplySent),
    write(' ')writesent(ReplySent),nl,talk(Sent).

change([],[]).
change([L | Lt],[X | Xt]):-substitute(L,X),change(Lt,Xt).
```

```
/* Substitution database */

    substitute(i,you).
    substitute(am,are).
    substitute(yes,no).
    substitute(no,yes).
    substitute(silly,clever).
    substitute(X,X).

/* Note: The rules for getsent and writesent are required as well */

/* END */
```

17.6 A French translation exercise

The word substitution program in Section 17.5 can readily be modified into a translation program. Let us approach this as a student exercise, starting with the following database of English words and their French translations:

```
trans(i,je).                    trans(you,vous).
trans(he,il).                   trans(she,elle).
trans(cat,chat).                trans(pen,plume).
trans(a,une).                   trans(me,moi).
trans(yes,oui).                 trans(no,non).
trans(who,qui).                 trans(have,avez).
trans(today,aujourdhui).        trans(the,le).
trans(X,X).
```

LONG Question 17.2 *(answer on p.154)*

Write a rule **translate(L1,L2)** *which translates a list L1 of English words into a list L2 of corresponding French words, using the* **trans** *database above. Words with no French equivalent in the database will be left as they are, because of the trans(X,X) fact at the bottom of the database.*

eg. ?- translate([give,me,the,pencil],French).
French = [give,moi,le,pencil]

Next put **translate** *into a short program* **franglay** *to read in normal English sentences repeatedly and convert them into 'franglais'. Use* **getsent** *and* **writesent** *above, e.g.*

The cat gave me a pen. —> Le chat gave moi une plume.

17.7 Some comments

Keywords are limited in conversational programs, but they are useful in searching through data stored in databases, for example library or research data. It is impossible to catalogue titles of research papers in every possible way, but a keyword search through titles will often find unusual papers required. There is an example in the labwork for this chapter later.

Substitution programs are similarly hard to implement for conversation, but they are more useful in translation programs.

Both the conversational programs above could be combined together into one. The combined program could first use a rule to test for substitution words, and if there are none, this rule could fail, and the program would go on to a second rule which tested for keywords. Such things are easy to do in Prolog. See if you can combine the programs together to work in this way.

The limitations of conversational programs are fairly obvious, but when several techniques of the kind shown are combined, a program can be quite convincing. In fact it can be quite illuminating about the way people carry on conversations – for example, if they cannot think of anything new to say, people will sometimes do what the program above does, simply repeat what the other person has said in a different way. Alternatively, people can be triggered by a certain word someone else says to come out with a routine comment.

When Weisenbaum had written ELIZA, the story goes that he left his secretary using the program, and came back to find her in tears because it was so sympathetic to her problems. This alarmed Weisenbaum, and for a while turned him against computers, thinking that they could very soon develop true intelligence! In fact, real intelligence in computers, rather than the simulated variety, is taking longer to arrive than some people expected.

17.8 Summary

One of the things Prolog does well is to handle 'natural language', which involves input and output in the form of words and sentences. This chapter provides rules which will read a normal sentence into a program and convert it into a list, and others which will output a list as a sentence. Two basic conversational programs are explained which operate using keywords and word substitution.

Note that in addition to this treatment of natural language based on lists, there is a special grammar notation in Prolog to extend its use for natural language. This is dealt with in Chapter 22.

Answers to questions

Answer 17.1

```
writesent([L | Lt]):-name(L,[Z | Zt]),Y is Z-32,name(X,[Y | Zt]),
    write(X),writesent2(Lt).

writesent2([]):-write('.').
writesent2([L | Lt]):-write(' '),
    check(L,X),write(X),writesent2(Lt).

check(L,X):-proper_noun(L),name(L,[Z | Zt]),Y is Z-32,
    name(X,[Y | Zt]).
check(L,L).

proper_noun(bill).
proper_noun(hull).
proper_noun(i).
```

Answer 17.2

```
/* 'FRANGLAY' TRANSLATION PROGRAM */

/* Main program */

    go:- say([]).

    say([goodbye,'.']):-write('Au revoir!'),nl.
    say(_):-
        write('Type in an English sentence: '),nl,nl,
        getsent(English),nl,translate(English,French),
        writesent(French),nl,say(English).

    translate([],[]).
    translate([L | Lt],[X | Xt]):-
        trans(L,X),translate(Lt,Xt).

/* Translation database */

    trans(i,je).              trans(you,vous).
    trans(he,il).             trans(she,elle).
    trans(cat,chat).          trans(pen,plume).
    trans(a,une).             trans(me,moi).
    trans(yes,oui).           trans(no,non).
    trans(who,qui).           trans(have,avez).
    trans(today,aujourdhui).  trans(the,le).
    trans(X,X).

/* Note: The rules for getsent and writesent are required as well */

/* END */
```

Programming practice:: A library program

Test the program **chat** described in the chapter which reads in sentences from a user using **getsent** and replies with standard responses after detecting certain keywords. Extend it with your own responses.

Write a program along the same lines which has a database of titles of library books saved as lists. The program can find a title that is required by searching for keywords, entered at the keyboard. Use **getsent** to read in the keywords, and **member** to carry out the tests.

18 The cut

18.1 Introduction

Prolog is a language based on logic, but it has to be implemented on conventional, procedural computers, and this causes problems.

Each time a rule is used in Prolog, markers are kept at the position of each of its subgoals in the database. These markers are stored on the computer stack, an area of computer memory. Recursion, as it involves rules calling themselves, uses the stack heavily in this way, and it is possible in large programs for it to become overloaded, causing a program to 'crash', or stop the computer.

Modern implementations of Prolog minimise this problem in various ways, and modern computers have large stack spaces anyway, so this is not a problem students often come up against. However, it is a consideration that has to be taken seriously in commercial programs, which need to be crash-proof.

In particular, if recursion is used for the main, 'top-level' program loop in a large commercial program, there will be danger of the program failing. The way to solve the problem completely is to use the cut.

18.2 The searching problem

As you will have realised, Prolog relies heavily on sequential searching of the database. In fact for every new subgoal, a new search from top to bottom of the database is initiated. Although computers are fast, this searching of the database takes time, and Prolog can be inefficient.

Early versions of Prolog were so slow as to be impractical, but with modern fast computers, and efficient modern implementations of Prolog interpreters, the problem is only noticeable with certain types of program. In the future, parallel processing offers the possibility of searching a Prolog database in blocks which are searched in parallel, at the same time. This would be very fast, but such implementations are not with us at the time of writing.

Such problems can be circumvented by use of the cut. The stack failure problem can be solved completely, and the searching problem can be drastically reduced. In addition, the cut enables some programs and rules to be written in ways that are better than would otherwise be possible.

18.3 What the cut is

*The **cut** is a mechanism to enable the programmer to control the execution of programs, so as to make them more efficient in terms of both time and storage.*

It is an exclamation mark written in a rule as a subgoal:

... ,!, ...

The **cut** does two things during execution of the rule.

First, as the **cut** is encountered, it always succeeds, and appears to have no effect. What happens behind the scenes is that all markers and other data for subgoals which have already succeeded are removed from the stack, clearing it and removing any immediate possibility of stack failure. So one reason for putting a **cut** into a program might be that you are getting worried at this point about overloading the stack.

Second, if there is backtracking at a later stage, and backtracking comes back to the **cut**, it is prevented from passing it. This has to be the case, because all the data concerning subgoals to the left of the **cut**, which would be needed for backtracking, has been thrown away. By stopping backtracking, the **cut** saves time. So another reason for putting a **cut** into a program might be to stop backtracking which the programmer knows will not serve any purpose, and thereby make the program run faster.

The **cut** thus acts as a sort of 'valve' which appears to have no effect on normal forward execution from left to right, but prevents backtracking from right to left.

What we have to answer now is – if there is backtracking, and it reaches the **cut**, and cannot pass it, what happens?

18.4 The mechanism of the cut

When a cut is encountered during backtracking it causes a return to the rule where the rule was called from, and backtracking continues from there.

To see what happens, suppose we have a rule which has, among others, subgoals p, q, r, and s. Subgoal r has subgoals a to f, and has a **cut** placed between c and d. This is shown below.

... p,q,r,s, ...

r :- a,b,c,!,d,e,f.

- Suppose this succeeds as far as f, which fails.

- There is backtracking among d,e,f until they all fail.

- Backtracking cannot pass the **cut**, but the rule r has not yet failed, so the execution cannot move on down to the next r.

- Unable to pass the **cut**, Prolog backtracks to the original subgoal r in the parent rule, then to q.

- If q succeeds a second time, execution moves forward again, and r is tried afresh, as though not tried before, i.e. the search for r is from the top of the database. This means the first r is tried again.

It might be thought that execution would now get trapped, with r being repeated over and over again. This is what happens, as long as q keeps succeeding, and d, e and f keep failing. However, the cycle can be broken if q eventually fails, or if d, e and f eventually succeed.

18.5 Repetition in Prolog using the cut

We can make use of the cut to construct loops. The following will loop forever:

> **... repeat,loop, ...**
>
> **loop:-write('Looping.'),nl,!,fail.**

This is a variation on a construction mentioned earlier, with a program health warning. Using **repeat** followed by **fail** is bound to result in a closed loop that cannot be broken.

The following will loop until X=end:

> **... repeat,loop, ...**
>
> **loop:-read(X),write('You typed '),write(X),nl,**
> **!,X=end.**

This type of loop has the advantage that it is guaranteed to go on all day without causing stack problems, unlike recursive loops. However, note that arguments cannot be passed from one execution of the loop to another by this method.

Question 18.1 (answer on p.161)

Write a program or rule started by **go** *to read in names, asserting the names into the database in the form* **person(emma)**, *until* **stop** *is entered. It then writes out all the names. The program uses cut but no recursion or lists.*

18.6 Counted repetition using assert/retract

It is possible to pass data from one cut loop to another, but only by asserting counters and flags in the database. Just to show how laborious this is, the following will loop X times:

> loop(X):-asserta(counter(0)),
>   repeat,subloop(X),
>   retract(counter(_)).
>
> subloop(X):-counter(N),M is N+1,
>   asserta(counter(M)),
>   retract(counter(N)),
>   !,M=X.

This is an excessively long-winded method of achieving counted repetition and would not normally be used. Use recursion instead.

?

Question 18.2 *(answer on p.162)*

*Write a rule **cls**, with subrule(s), which clears the screen by calling nl 25 times, and which uses the **cut**.*

18.7 Mutually exclusive rules

If cuts are placed at the end of each of a set of rules, the rule can only succeed once, because when it does no pointer is saved and all data is thrown away. Thus only one rule can succeed, and the rules are made 'mutually exclusive'.

```
e.g. a(1):- ... ,!.
     a(2):- ... ,!.
     a(3):- ... .
```

With long sets of large rules, this can improve efficiency enormously. Whenever you know that only one of a collection of rules is required to succeed, it is good practice to put cuts at the end of each of them (except the last, which does not matter).

18.8 Using the cut for new solutions to problems

In some cases the cut is useful in providing a different version of a rule. For example, a common rule which we have used several times is **member**, which tests whether an object is a member of a list.

```
member(X,[X|L]).
member(X,[Y|L]):-member(X,L).
```

We used **member** in the last chapter in a natural language program to find keywords, checking for an atom which was a member of an input list, and also a member of a list of keywords. The program took an atom that was a member of one list, checked it for membership of the other list, and if it failed, backtracked for the next member of the first list. It was possible for an atom to be a member of one list, but not the other. In this case, the successful solution of **member** had to be discarded and another found, until a member of both lists was found. We thus needed a **member** rule which could succeed more than once, and the version used (the one above) did this.

In different circumstances we might want to test whether an atom was a member of a list, and if so, stop searching for other solutions and wasting time. There is another version of **member** which does this, and only succeeds once, shown below:

```
member(X,[X|L]):-!.
member(X,[Y|L]):-member(X,L).
```

This differs only in having a **cut** at the end of the first rule, and it will find just one solution, even though X may occur in the list several times. Removing the **cut** enables **member** to go through all solutions.

If you go back and try the keywords program with this version of **member**, you will find it will not work properly.

Question 18.3 *(answer on p.162)*

*Re-write the following program non-recursively, using the **cut**, to be simpler and to avoid the possibility of stack failure:*

```
go:-go1(not_end).

go1(end).
go1(_):-do_things,read(X),go1(X).
```

18.9 Menu structures using the cut

When looking at recursion, we mentioned that main program loops using recursion were not good practice. After the comments in this chapter, you can probably see why.

If a whole large program is made recursive, during use it will be building up more and more data on the stack, and eventually will fail. This is not inevitable with all programs. As we also mentioned, there are various tricks in the inter-preter to prevent this happening where possible, but the larger the program, the more likely it is.

We can get round this using the cut. Generally speaking, with small self-contained rules recursion gives no trouble, but the main outer program loop is one place where you should try to use a cut method instead, to clear the stack each time round. The following menu-type program structure, which does a similar job to the recursive one given before, but in a totally different way, will do this.

```
/* A GENERAL PURPOSE PROGRAM STRUCTURE
USING THE CUT

The following program is a useful structure which
can be modified and used for Prolog programs, and
will not cause stack problems. */

go:-write('CUT MENU'),nl,nl,
    repeat,
    menu.

menu:-write('Enter a,b, or e to end: '),
    read(X),choice(X),nl,
    !,X=e.
```

```
choice(a):-write('Choice a.').
choice(b):-write('Choice b.').
choice(e):-write('Goodbye!').
choice(_):-write('Please try again.').
```

/* END */

This program is as simple as possible to illustrate a point, but it can be extended into a very large program by the addition of subrules. Note that any data which needs to be saved, or passed from one loop to another, needs to be asserted into the database.

The main rule **go** first writes a message on the screen, which is not repeated. It then passes **repeat**, and goes to **menu**, which puts a menu message on the screen, reads in the menu choice, and goes to subrule **choice**. One of the **choice** subrules is executed, then on returning to the menu rule the **cut** is passed, and the original input choice is tested. If this is not e, the test fails, causing backtracking. The cut sends the backtracking back to rule **go**, where **repeat** sends the execution forward again. The loop is repeated until choice e is entered, causing the **X=e** test to succeed, so that **menu** finally succeeds, making **go** succeed and end the program.

18.10 Summary

The cut, **!**, is used in Prolog to prevent program failures and also to make programs more efficient. As execution passes the cut, markers to subgoals saved so far in the rule are discarded. If there is backtracking subsequently, it cannot pass the cut, and execution returns to the parent rule where the rule with the cut was called from.

The cut can be used to form repetitive loops, including main program structures, which have the advantage that they are immune to program failures due to memory overload. It is extremely clumsy, however, for repetitive constructions which pass values from one loop to the next. The cut can also be used to make rules mutually exclusive, and to design different versions of rules for different purposes.

Answers to questions

Answer 18.1

```
go:-repeat,loop,nl,writenames.

loop:-write('Enter a name: '),read(Name),
    assertz(person(Name)),
    !,Name=stop.

writenames:-person(Name),write(Name),nl,fail.
writenames.
```

Answer 18.2

```
cls:-asserta(counter(0)),
    repeat,subloop,
    retract(counter(_)).

subloop:-counter(N),M is N+1,nl,
    asserta(counter(M)),
    retract(counter(N)),
    !,M=25.
```

Answer 18.3

The program can be written:

```
go:-repeat,go1.

go1:-do_things,read(X),!,X=end.
```

Programming practice: The periodic table

The following table shows data for the first five elements in the periodic table of the elements.

Element	Symbol	Atomic Number	Atomic Weight
hydrogen	H	1	1.008
helium	He	2	4.003
lithium	Li	3	6.941
beryllium	Be	4	9.012
boron	B	5	10.810

Make up a suitable database of facts called **element** to contain this data, and write a menu program to operate on the data and offer repeated options as follows:

a.   List all the element names

b.   Give all the data for a named element

c.   Give all data for an element by At.No.

d.   End program

The menu structure must use the **cut**.

Test yourself
Recursion and lists

1. The 'respectable' logical method of achieving repetition in a Prolog program is _____

2. It is stopped by placing a rule above the rule which repeats, which is called a _____

3. Write a rule which keeps saying 'Try again!' until the atom 'stop' is read in, in two ways:

   (a) using 'repeat':

   _____

   _____

   _____

   (b) using recursion:

   _____

   _____

   _____

   _____

4. For a database of people, which of the following would be most suitable?

   A. bill(smith,25,person).
   B. person([bill,smith],25).
   C. person(Bill,Smith,25).
   D. person(['Smith','Bill'],25).
   E. person(bill,smith,25).

5. Which of the following would be the least convenient data structure if it was required to list people with red hair?

   A. hair(mary,red).
   B. mary(hair,red).
   C. has(mary,[red,hair]).
   D. has(mary,red_hair).
   E. has(mary,hair(red)).

6. How are values normally passed from one rule to another in Prolog?

   A. As lists.
   B. As asserted facts.
   C. As variables.
   D. As global variables.
   E. As arguments.

7. Which of the following cannot be a valid list?

   A. [L | [X | Xt]]
   B. [a | [a, b, c]]
   C. [a, b | [b, c, d]]
   D. [M | Mt [ ]]
   E. Joe.

8. What does the following code do?

   ```
   enigma([]):- write('.'),nl.
   enigma([L|Lt]):- write(' '),name(L,[Z|Zt]),Y is Z-32,
       name(X,[Y|Zt]),write(X),enigma (Lt).
   ```

   A. Writes out a list vertically.
   B. Writes out a list, converting any capitals to lowercase.
   C. Writes out a list with capitals for all atoms.
   D. Writes out a list with capitals for all atoms and a full stop at the end.
   E. Writes out a list as a sentence, with a capital at the start and a full stop.

9. If a database contains facts of the type person ('Sherlock Holmes', 'Baker Street', 42) which of the following would produce a list of streets?

   A. findall(person(_,Address, _)).
   B. findall(Address, person(_, _,Address), List).
   C. findall(X, person(_, X, _),Address).
   D. findall(X, person(_, _, X),Address).
   E. person(_, Address, _),fail.

10. Look at the following rule:

    ```
    splitlist ([ ], [ ], [ ]).
    splitlist ([L,X|Xt], L1, L2):-
        L1 = [L|Yt], L2 = [X|Zt],
        splitlist (Xt, Yt, Zt).
    ```

    This rule splits a list into two others, using recursion. It does this by:

    A. Counting the terms in the list, dividing by two and separating off this number of terms.
    B. Repeatedly taking the head of the list until the first half is separated.
    C. Repeatedly taking the last term in the list until the last half is separated.

D. Repeatedly taking the last two terms and putting each into a different new list.
E. Repeatedly taking the first two terms and putting each into a different new list.

11. Study the following simple but complete program in Prolog.

```
go:- read(In),
     not In = [end],
     goto(In,Out),
     write(Out),nl,
     go.

go.

goto([],[]).
goto([H|T],[L|M]):-
     do(H,L),goto(T,M).

do(are,no).
do(you,'I am').
do(man,woman).
do(computer,person).
do(no,yes).
do(end,start).
do(X,X).
```

Which would you best describe this program as?

A. An expert system.
B. An artificial intelligence program.
C. A natural language program.
D. An Eliza type program.
E. A problem-solving program.

12. What does the input to the program in A11 need to be?

A. A single word.
B. A sentence.
C. A list of words.
D. A list containing one word.
E. A list of words that are in the 'do' facts.

13. How will the program in A11 respond to the following input assuming that it is entered in a correct manner according to your answer to A12:

are you a computer

A. no.
B. no I am a computer
C. no I am a person
D. no I am person
E. (with an error message).

14. The following is a very simple expert system:

```
go:- get_feature(start),
     animal_is(Animal),
     write('It is a '),
     write(Animal),nl.

get_feature(end).
get_feature(_):-
     write('What does the animal have?'),read(Feature),
     assert(feature(Feature)),get_feature(Feature).

animal_is(tiger):-it_is(mammal),feature(stripes),
     feature(carnivore).
animal_is(penguin):-it_is(bird),feature(swim),
     feature(cannot_fly).
animal_is(unknown).
```

A problem with this is

A. It will crash if the animal is not in the database.
B. It tests for several features but only reads in one.
C. It will crash if the animal is spelt wrongly.
D. It does not tell the user which features will be recognised.
E. It will not work if more than two features are entered.

15. In question 6, which of the following entries will be recognised?

A. bird swims
B. mammal stripes swims
C. bird stripes cannot_fly swims
D. mammal stripes swims carnivore
E. bird swims cannot_fly stripes

16. In question 6, which of the following would not improve this program?

A. Adding many more rules.
B. Ensuring that all rules have just two features.
C. Offering features in a menu to choose from.
D. Including negative features in the rules.
E. Enabling the system to learn new rules.

17. Consider the following rule which counts the elements in a list.

    count([ ],0).
    count([_ | Lt],N):- count(Lt,M),
        N is 1 + M.

    Now consider Prolog's response to a query as follows:

    A. **? − count([a,b,c],N).**
    B. **count([a | [b,c],N):- count([b,c],M), N is 1 + M.**
    C. **count([b | [c],N):- count([c],M), N is 1 + M.**
    D. **count([c | [ ]],N):- count([ ],M), N is 1 + M.**
    E. **count([ ],0).**

    Which is the first line in which all the variables become instantiated?

18. Which of the following can not be used as a basis for repetition?

    A. backtracking.
    B. instantiation.
    C. recursion.
    D. fail.
    E. !, fail.

19. Which of the following is not one of the reasons for the existence of '!' in Prolog? (When it is used correctly.)

    A. It makes programs more efficient.
    B. It makes programs more readable.
    C. It prevents stack failures.
    D. It can be used for iterative constructions.
    E. It sometimes provides a short solution to an otherwise difficult problem.

20. Which of the following reserved words from procedural languages has no equivalent in Prolog?

    A. IF.
    B. GOTO.
    C. AND.
    D. OR.
    E. END.

19 Route finding

19.1 Introduction

Problems which involve searching for best routes are another category of problem which seem to involve human intelligence, and seem beyond the ability of computers. As such they are a preoccupation for the field of Artificial Intelligence.

For example, if a person has to find the way from Piccadilly Circus to Euston Station on the London Tube, he or she will look at a map of the system and quickly search out the lines and stations which make up the best route. To devise a computer program to do this and suggest the best route may seem possible, but it is by no means obvious how to go about it. Such a problem can be quite complex, depending on the configuration of the system.

There is an extra dimension to searching problems. Apart from finding physical routes for actual travelling, it is possible to represent some problems in a mathematical 'problem space', and the solution to the problem becomes one of finding the best route through this problem space to get from the starting point to the required destination or solution. In general, such problems are ones where there are many possible solutions and the problem is to find the best one, or one fitting certain conditions.

We will not deal with such problem solving methods here, but will look at some more straight-forward physical situations. We will try to show how Prolog is especially well suited to route-finding, as might be expected, since route-finding involves searching and Prolog has a built-in searching mechanism.

19.2 Calculating distances by road

Suppose we have to drive between two major cities in the UK, Bristol and Edinburgh, and want to find the distance we will have to travel, so as to calculate the approximate time it will take, cost in petrol and so on. But suppose we only have the distances between certain combinations of cities as follows.

```
/* CITIES DATABASE 1 */

between(london,birmingham,110).
between(birmingham,manchester,80).
between(edinburgh,manchester,210).
between(manchester,glasgow,210).
between(london,bristol,115).
between(bristol,birmingham,90).
between(edinburgh,glasgow,45).
```

We could query this database as follows:

?- between(bristol,edinburgh,Distance).

… but the reply would be no, as there is no such fact in the database. We can try entering a rule as follows:

distance(C1,C2,Dist):-
between(C1,City,D1),between(City,C2,D2),
Dist is D1+D2.

This will go further, and will for example find the distance between London and Manchester, ie. cities not adjacent in the database but with just one other city between them. But it will still not find the distance between Bristol and Edinburgh, with two cities between. For longer distances we need to be smart and define a recursive rule, as follows:

distance(C1,C2,Dist):-between(C1,C2,Dist).
distance(C1,C2,Dist):-
between(C1,C,D1),distance(C,C2,D2),
Dist is D1+D2.

This will find any number of pairs of cities in the database, adding together the distances between them as it unwinds out of the recursion. Before we look at a worked example of how this rule operates, there is another slight problem.

The distance between Bristol and Birmingham is of course the same as the distance between Birmingham and Bristol, but the database facts do not express this. One way round it would be to double up all the facts, so that we have pairs like this:

between(bristol,birmingham,90).
between(birmingham,bristol,90).

This is untidy and will make the database twice as long. Instead we can rewrite the rules:

distance(C1,C2,Dist):-
(between(C1,C2,Dist) ; between(C2,C1,Dist)).
distance(C1,C2,Dist):-
(between(C1,C,D1) ; between(C,C1,D1)),
distance(C,C2,D2),Dist is D1+D2.

This gets round the problem, but let us rewrite the rules yet again as follows, with doubled-up rules, which is more usual in Prolog. It's longer, but clearer:

distance(C1,C2,Dist):-between(C1,C2,Dist).
distance(C1,C2,Dist):-between(C2,C1,Dist).
distance(C1,C2,Dist):-
between(C1,C,D1),distance(C,C2,D2),Dist is D1+D2.
distance(C2,C1,Dist):-
between(C1,C,D1),distance(C,C2,D2),Dist is D1+D2.

19.3 Worked example of finding distances

Now let us look in detail at how Prolog uses these rules to find the solution for the problem we originally looked at.

?- distance(bristol,edinburgh,Distance).

Prolog tries the first and second distance rules but fails to find a between rule giving the distance between Bristol and Edinburgh directly, so it goes on to the third distance rule, and searches for the first subgoal which provides a city adjacent to Bristol, which is Birmingham:

distance(bristol,edinburgh,Dist):-
between(bristol,birmingham,90),
distance(birmingham,edinburgh,D2),Dist is 90+D2.   {A}

Prolog now tries to find the distance between Birmingham and Edinburgh. This is not to be found directly either, so it finds a city adjacent to Birmingham, which is Manchester:

distance(birmingham,edinburgh,Dist):-
between(birmingham,manchester,80),
distance(manchester,edinburgh,D2),Dist is 80+D2.   {B}

Prolog now looks for the distance from Manchester to Edinburgh, and this can be found directly using the second distance rule, which provides the distance as 210 miles:

distance(manchester,edinburgh,210):-
between(edinburgh,manchester,210).   {C}

This rule is fully instantiated, so the recursion can now unwind, adding up all the distances as follows:

distance(birmingham,edinburgh,290):-
between(birmingham,manchester,80),
distance(manchester,edinburgh,210),290 is 80+210.   {B}

distance(bristol,edinburgh,380):-
between(bristol,birmingham,90),
distance(birmingham,edinburgh,290),380 is 90+290.   {A}

The distance required is written out by the interpreter:

?- distance(bristol,edinburgh,Distance).
Distance = 380

This set of rules now finds a distance for us, but it is not necessarily the shortest one, just the first thrown up by the ordering of the database. We can, however, tell Prolog to keep finding more solutions and see what the others look like.

19.4 Route finding

We may have found the distance from Bristol to Edinburgh, but we have not found a route, which would be a list of the cities along the way. Let us forget about distances for the moment, and rewrite our database as follows.

/* CITIES DATABASE 2 */

adjacent(london,birmingham).
adjacent(birmingham,manchester).
adjacent(edinburgh,manchester).

```
adjacent(manchester,glasgow).
adjacent(london,bristol).
adjacent(bristol,birmingham).
adjacent(edinburgh,glasgow).
```

We can now write rules which again follow a recursive sequence from a starting city to an end city, this time building up a list of cities along the way, something like the following:

getroute(Start,End,Route):- ...

This is a rule which takes a specified city **Start** to start from, and a specified city **End** to end at, and returns as the third argument **Route**, a list of the cities en route. Before writing the body of this rule, let us work out a strategy.

We want to start at one of the cities, find a city adjacent to it, and keep doing this until we come to the other city. Let us be clever at this point, and instead of starting with the **Start** city, let us start with the **End** city, and work backwards to the **Start** city. This is because it is easier to add something to the front of a list than to the end, and the list will also be built up in the correct order if we do this.

Let us take the **End** city, then, and add cities to it to build up a list. When we encounter the **Start** city, the list in its current state will be taken as the **Route** list, the third argument. Now, as we are starting with the **End** city, and adding to it to build up a list, it makes sense to put **End** as the first item in a list when we first call the rule, and call it as follows:

?- getroute(Start,[End],Route).

Let us now write the rule. For a start, let us try:

```
getroute(Start,[City | Rest],Route):-
    adjacent(Next,City),
    getroute(Start,[Next,City | Rest],Route).
```

The second argument of this rule is the important one. We take the head of this list, **City**, and find an **adjacent** fact which provides a city **Next** which is next to it. Having found such a city, we put **Next** on the front of the list. As the list was **[City | Rest]**, it now becomes **[Next,City | Rest]**. We recurse back into the rule with this new list, keeping **Start** and **Route** the same, and find more adjacent cities, building up the list.

We want to stop when we have come back to **Start**, as the head of the list. At this point we want to make the final list **Route** the same as the list we have been building up. We need to add a boundary rule as follows:

```
getroute(Start,Route,Route):-Route = [Start | _].
getroute(Start,[City | Rest],Route):-
    adjacent(Next,City),
    getroute(Start,[Next,City | Rest],Route).
```

These rules are now looking promising, but there are a few alterations to make. One is that the rule is liable to keep finding the same **adjacent** facts, and work round in a loop instead of going from one place to another. We need to do a check that the new city found is not already a **member** of the list of cities making up the current route. If it is, the rule needs to fail and backtrack to find another city. We can use the exclusive version of **member** for this, with a cut in it.

Also, we have the problem we had in the last program, that cities may be in the **adjacent** facts but in the wrong order. To fix this, we need to double up the second rule. Putting these changes into effect, and rewriting the boundary rule more concisely, we have:

> **getroute(Start,[Start | Rest],[Start | Rest]).**

> **getroute(Start,[City | Rest],Route):-**
> **adjacent(Next,City),not member(Next,Rest),**
> **getroute(Start,[Next,City | Rest],Route).**

> **getroute(Start,[City | Rest],Route):-**
> **adjacent(City,Next),not member(Next,Rest),**
> **getroute(Start,[Next,City | Rest],Route).**

> **member(X,[X | L]):-!.**
> **member(X,[Y | L]):-member(X,L).**

If you haven't quite followed the argument so far, see if a detailed example makes it clearer.

19.5 Worked example of route finding

Let us find a route again from Bristol to Edinburgh based on the **adjacent** database given, using the **getroute** rule, called thus:

> **?- getroute(bristol,[edinburgh],Route).**

Instantiating variables as early as possible, and just showing the rules which succeed as lettered rules, we have:

getroute(bristol,[edinburgh | []],Route):-
    adjacent(edinburgh,manchester),
    not member(manchester,[]),
    getroute(bristol,[manchester,edinburgh | []],Route).   {A}

getroute(bristol,[manchester | [edinburgh]],Route):-
    adjacent(birmingham,manchester),
    not member(birmingham,[edinburgh]),
    getroute(bristol,[birmingham,manchester | [edinburgh]],Route).   {B}

getroute(bristol,[birmingham | [manchester,edinburgh]],Route):-
    adjacent(bristol,birmingham),
    not member(bristol,[manchester,edinburgh]),
    getroute(bristol,[bristol,birmingham | [manchester,edinburgh]],Route). {C}

getroute(bristol,[bristol | [birmingham,manchester,edinburgh]],
    [bristol | [birmingham,manchester,edinburgh]]).   {D}

Rule D, the boundary rule, is the first rule to be fully instantiated. The recursion now unwinds, from D to C to B to A. The only variable not instantiated in C, B and A is **Route**, which now has the same value of the final list in all these rules. The original query can now be replied to:

?- getroute(bristol,[edinburgh],Route).
Route = [bristol,birmingham,manchester,edinburgh]

You will see a process similar to this if you type the rules in and use **trace** to step through the route-finding process.

This is not the only route, or necessarily the best. Prolog will backtrack and continue to search for more if told to.

19.6 A pub crawl exercise

The following table shows the time it takes to walk between pubs in a mythical locality, disregarding the state of inebriation of the walker.

Pub	Time between pubs in mins
Gravedigger's Arms to Sailor's Rest	10
Sailor's Rest to Bat and Ball	15
Bat and Ball to Bricklayer's Arms	6
Bricklayer's Arms to George and Dragon	25
George and Dragon to Nelson's Tavern	10
Nelson's Tavern to Hare and Hounds	30
Nelson's Tavern to Stag's Head	40
Hare and Hounds to Fighting Cock	20
Fighting Cock to Green Dragon	15
Green Dragon to Jolly Sailor	15
Jolly Sailor to Lively Lady	12
Jolly Sailor to Robin Hood	35
Lively Lady to Jubilee Tavern	35
Jubilee Tavern to Stag's Head	10
Stag's Head to Star and Garter	5
Star and Garter to Sailor's Rest	20
Star and Garter to Unicorn	10
Unicorn to Robin Hood	8
Robin Hood to Gravedigger's Arms	45

LONG Question 19.1 (answer on p.178)

Write a program to plan a pub crawl, which can be used to find all the different routes between any two pubs listed in the table above. (The best route might not be the shortest but might be the one with most pubs on it.) The total time spent walking between pubs is also required (there's a limit to how far you will be able to stagger in the circumstances). **getroute** *and* **distance** *need to be combined into one rule.*

19.7 Best routes

So far we have written programs which have found one route between cities, not necessarily the best, or have just continued finding more solutions. As we saw in the exercise above, we can force the program to keep finding more solutions by making it fail.

If we want the best solution, we need to save all these possible solutions. The simplest way to save all the route lists is to assert them into the database. We can do it like this:

```
go:- write('Enter place to start from: '),read(Start),
     write('Enter place to end at : '),read(End),
     getroute(Start,[End],Route),
     assert(route(Route)),nl,fail.
go.
```

Having saved all the possible routes, we can go through them using some criterion to pick out the best. For example, we can count the number of cities in each list, and take the shortest. A rule which will do this is:

```
rule:-route(Route),
      count(Route,Length),
      otherlength(OtherLength),
      not OtherLength < Length,
      write('Best Route is:'),nl,
      writelist(Route).

otherlength(Otherlength):-route(Other),
      count(Other,OtherLength).
```

What this rule does is to retrieve one of the routes from the database, count its length, then use a subrule to find another length of another route. This **OtherLength** is tested against the **Length** of the original route. Backtracking checks all the **OtherLengths** to ensure there is not one less than **Length**. If not, then Length is the shortest, and it is written out as the best solution.

If an **OtherLength** is found that is less than **Length**, Prolog backtracks to the route being considered, and gets the next one. This is tested, and so are all the others, until one is found which has no others shorter than it. This is the best route and it is written out.

We can modify this a little. Instead of using a new rule called **rule**, we can put this code into the second **go** above, which succeeds when the first **go** has found all the possible routes and has finally failed. A more concise way to write this rule is to put the subrule into a complex **not** expression as follows:

```
go:- route(Route),
     count(Route,Length),
     not (route(Other),
          count(Other,OtherLength),
          OtherLength < Length ),
     write('Best Route is:'),nl,
     writelist(Route).
```

The complete listing for the best route program, to work on the database of **adjacent** city facts, is now:

```
/* BEST ROUTE FINDING PROGRAM */

/* Uses smallest number of places en route. Needs CITIES
DATABASE 2 */

go:- write('Enter place to start from: '),read(Start),
     write('Enter place to end at : '),read(End),
     getroute(Start,[End],Route),
     assert(route(Route)),nl,fail.

go:- route(Route),
     count(Route,Length),
     not (route(Other),
         count(Other,OtherLength),
         OtherLength < Length ),
     write('Best Route is:'),nl,
     writelist(Route),retractall(route(_)).

/* Finds routes */

getroute(Start,[Start | Rest],[Start | Rest]).

getroute(Start,[City | Rest],Route):-
     adjacent(Next,City),not member(Next,Rest),
     getroute(Start,[Next,City | Rest],Route).

getroute(Start,[City | Rest],Route):-
     adjacent(City,Next),not member(Next,Rest),
     getroute(Start,[Next,City | Rest],Route).

/* Auxiliary rules */

member(X,[X | L]):-!.
member(X,[Y | L]):-member(X,L).

count([],0).
count([_ | Lt],N):-count(Lt,M),N is M+1.
writelist([]).
writelist([L | Lt]):-write(L),write(' '),nl,writelist(Lt).

/* END */
```

Another criterion we can use to pick out the best route, if we have found the length of routes, is to take the one with the shortest length.

We can use the version of **getroute** given in the solution to one of the exercises above, which finds a route and also its length. We save all the routes found in **route** facts, this time with an extra argument which is the length of the route. After finding all routes, the first **go** rule fails, anf the second one uses **findall** to collect a list of lengths of routes. We use **min** to find the minimum length in this list, then retrieve the route with this length.

The program is changed as follows.

/* BEST ROUTE FINDING PROGRAM */

/* Uses shortest distance. Needs CITIES DATABASE 1 */

```
go:- write('Enter place to start from: '),read(Start),
      write('Enter place to end at : '),read(End),
      getroute(Start,[End],Route,Dist),
      assert(route(Route,Dist)),nl,fail.

go:- findall(Dist,route(_,Dist),DistList),
      min(DistList,Min),route(Route,Min),
      write('Best Route is:'),nl,
      writelist(Route),retractall(route(_,_)).
```

/* Finds routes */

```
getroute(Start,[Start | Rest],[Start | Rest],0).

getroute(Start,[City | Rest],Route,Dist):-
      between(Next,City,D1),not member(Next,Rest),
      getroute(Start,[Next,City | Rest],Route,D2),
      Dist is D1 + D2.

getroute(Start,[City | Rest],Route,Dist):-
      between(City,Next,D1),not member(Next,Rest),
      getroute(Start,[Next,City | Rest],Route,D2),
      Dist is D1 + D2.
```

/* Auxiliary rules */

```
member(X,[X | L]):-!.
member(X,[Y | L]):-member(X,L).

min[Last],Last).
min([L | Lt],Min):-min(Lt,SubMin),
      ((L<SubMin,Min=L);Min=SubMin.

writelist([]).
writelist([L | Lt]):-write(L),nl,writelist(Lt).
```

/* END */

19.8 Cities of the world route-finding exercise

The table below shows very approximate distances between some major cities of the world.

Cities	Distance Between in thousands of miles
London to New York	3.2
London to Cape Town	5.8
London to Rome	0.8
London to Panama	4.5
Panama to Sydney	7.7
New York to San Francisco	2.5
New York to Panama	1.9
San Francisco Sydney	6.2
San Francisco to Tokyo	4.5
Tokyo to Calcutta	2.5
Tokyo to Sydney	4.1
Sydney to Calcutta	4.4
Sydney to Cape Town	6.0
Cape Town to Rome	5.1
Calcutta to Cairo	2.2
Cairo to Rome	0.9

LONG Question 19.2 *(answer on p.179)*

Use the above data of distances between major cities in the world to write a program to find best routes, using both numbers of cities en route and shortest distances. (The distances are very approximate.) You need to combine the two best route programs above.

19.9 Other route-finding strategies

There are various other ways of finding routes around physical systems and problem spaces.

The strategies used in this chapter have all been depth first, using Prolog's built-in **depth first** searching method in the simplest way. In finding a route among cities, for example, this involves finding a city next to the first, then a city next to that, and so on until the final city is encountered. The first route found is not necessarily the best. To find the best, all the routes have to be found and stored, then searched through.

An alternative strategy is **breadth first**, which involves finding all the cities next to the first, then all the cities next to those, and so on until the final city is encountered. When it is, the route has been found without any failures, and is automatically the one with the smallest number of cities en route, but it has involved finding a lot more cities at the same time.

There are others as well, such as **best-first** and **hill-climbing**. You can look these up in thicker Prolog textbooks than this one.

19.10 Summary

Prolog is well suited to problems involving route-finding, with its built-in searching mechanism.

Two types of route-finding program are explained in this chapter, one to find the shortest distance between two points, and one to find a route between two points which is extended to find the best route.

The treatment here uses only depth first searching methods. Other methods are mentioned but not explained in detail. We will not go any further with this introduction to the subject here, but several other books on Prolog do.

Answers to questions

Answer 19.1

The program, modified from the one explained in Sections 19.4 and 19.5, can be as follows.

```
/* PUB CRAWL PROGRAM */

go:- write('Enter pub to start at: '),read(Pub1),
      write('Enter pub to end at: '),read(Pub2),nl,
      write('The possible routes are as follows: '),nl,
      getroute(Pub1,[Pub2],Route,Dist),
      writelist(Route),nl,write(Dist),nl,
      write('<ENTER> to continue.'),get0(_),fail.

go.

/* Rule to find route lists AND total distances */

getroute(Start,[Start | Rest],[Start | Rest],0).

getroute(Start,[Pub | Rest],Route,Dist):-
      pubs(Next,Pub,D1),not member(Next,Rest),
      getroute(Start,[Next,Pub | Rest],Route,D2),
      Dist is D1 + D2.

getroute(Start,[Pub | Rest],Route,Dist):-
      pubs(Pub,Next,D1),not member(Next,Rest),
      getroute(Start,[Next,Pub | Rest],Route,D2),
      Dist is D1 + D2.

member(X,[X | L]):-!.
member(X,[Y | L]):-member(X,L).

writelist([]).
writelist([L | Lt]):-write(L),nl,writelist(Lt).

/* Pubs database */

pubs(gravediggers_arms,sailors_rest,10).
pubs(sailors_rest,bat_and_ball,15).
```

```
pubs(bat_and_ball,bricklayers_arms,6).
pubs(bricklayers_arms,george_and_dragon,25).
pubs(george_and_dragon,nelsons_tavern,10).
pubs(nelsons_tavern,hare_and_hounds,30).
pubs(nelsons_tavern,stags_head,40).
pubs(hare_and_hounds,fighting_cock,20).
pubs(fighting_cock,green_dragon,15).
pubs(green_dragon,jolly_sailor,15).
pubs(jolly_sailor,lively_lady,12).
pubs(jolly_sailor,robin_hood,35).
pubs(lively_lady,jubilee_tavern,35).
pubs(jubilee_tavern,stags_head,10).
pubs(stags_head,star_and_garter,5).
pubs(star_and_garter,sailors_Rest,20).
pubs(star_and_garter,unicorn,10).
pubs(unicorn,robin_hood,8).
pubs(robin_hood,gravediggers_arms,45).

/* END */
```

Notice the device in this program to make the rule go fail when it has produced a solution list, so that it is forced to backtrack and find another. Thus it will carry on until it finds all the possible solutions.

Answer 19.2

```
/* WORLD TRAVEL ROUTE FINDING PROGRAM */

go:- write('Enter city to start from: '),read(Start),
     write('Enter city to end at : '),read(End),
     getroute(Start,[End],Route,Dist),
     assert(route(Route,Dist)),fail.

go:- nl,best1,best2,retractall(route(_,_)).

/* Least cities rule */

best1:-route(Route,_),count(Route,Length),
     not (route(Other),
          count(Other,OtherLength),
          OtherLength < Length ),
     write('Best Route using least cities is:'),nl,
     writelist(Route),nl.

/* Shortest distance rule */

best2:-findall(Dist,route(_,Dist),DistList),
     min(DistList,Min),route(Route,Min),
     write('Best Route using shortest distance is:'),nl,
     writelist(Route),nl,write('Distance is'),
     write(Min),write('thousand miles.'),nl,nl.
```

```
/* Finds routes */

getroute(Start,[Start | Rest],[Start | Rest],0).

getroute(Start,[City | Rest],Route,Dist):-
    travel(Next,City,D1),not member(Next,Rest),
    getroute(Start,[Next,City | Rest],Route,D2),
    Dist is D1 + D2.

getroute(Start,[City | Rest],Route,Dist):-
    travel(City,Next,D1),not member(Next,Rest),
    getroute(Start,[Next,City | Rest],Route,D2),
    Dist is D1 + D2.

/* Auxiliary rules */

member(X,[X | L]):-!.
member(X,[Y | L]):-member(X,L).

min([Last],Last).
min([L | Lt],Min):-min(Lt,SubMin),
    ((L<SubMin,Min=L);(Min=SubMin)).

count([],0).
count([_ | Lt],N):-count(Lt,M),N is M+1.

writelist([]).
writelist([L | Lt]):-write(L),write(' '),nl,writelist(Lt).

/* Database */

travel(london,new_york,3.2).
travel(london,cape_town,5.8).
travel(london,rome,0.8).
travel(london,panama,4.5).
travel(panama,sydney,7.7).
travel(new_york,san_francisco,2.5).
travel(new_york,panama,1.9).
travel(san_francisco,sydney,6.2).
travel(san_francisco,tokyo,4.5).
travel(tokyo,calcutta,2.5).
travel(tokyo,sydney,4.1).
travel(sydney,calcutta,4.4).
travel(sydney,cape_town,6.0).
travel(cape_town,rome,5.1).
travel(calcutta,cairo,2.2).
travel(cairo,rome,0.9).

/* END */
```

Programming practice: navigating a maze

Write a program started by **go** which will find routes through the maze shown below. It is organised in the form of rooms, which are labelled. You start from point **a** outside and have to get to room **e**, but write the program so that the start and destination room can be changed.

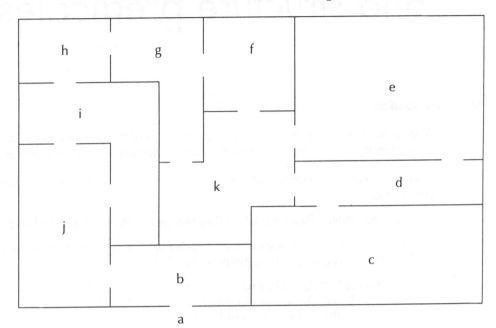

20 Structures and structure predicates

20.1 Introduction

A **structure** in Prolog is a single object made up of components which are other objects, such as atoms, constants, integers, variables or other structures.

A structure can be a simple fact, or a compound fact made up of complex objects, eg.

> ?- located('Public Library',book('The Carpetbaggers',author('Harold','Robbins'))).

It is better to set out complex structures in such a way as to make them easier to read, especially as they are, by definition, usually long:

> located('Public Library',
>   book('The Carpetbaggers',
>   author('Harold','Robbins'))).

We can find the names of authors using the anonymous variable:

> ?- located(_,book(_,author(X,Y))).
>   X = 'Harold'
>   Y = 'Robbins'

We can also retrieve a whole structure with a variable:

> ?- located(_,book(_,X)).
>   X = author('Harold','Robbins').

Note that a variable or the anonymous variable can be used to stand for a complete structure, but not for a predicate name:

> ?- located(_,book(X,_))

We could of course use separate facts for the above data:

> book('The Carpetbaggers').
> located('Public Library','The Carpetbaggers').
> author('The Carpetbaggers','Harold','Robbins').

This is more cumbersome, through having to repeat the title of the book several times to link the facts together. It is also likely to be a less convenient representation, as we cannot now manipulate the whole data as a single object, if we should need to, but only as three separate objects.

20.2 Small firm personnel example of structures

Let us write a short program of a type which is usually done with structures in other languages, one which stores and manipulates information concerning the employees of a small firm.

This is a collection of different types of data, unified into a single object through representing one person. To represent data of this type other languages usually have a type of built-in structure called a record (in fact called a structure in the language C). Prolog, as we have mentioned, does not have many special built-in structures, apart from the single basic clause, a fact or a rule, and the list.

For simplicity we will confine the data to surname, first names, date of birth, and address, entered as the lines to be written on an envelope, the last being the post code. This could of course be extended indefinitely to include things like National Insurance Number, current salary and others as well.

We can represent the data thus:

employee(names(Surname,Firstnames),Age,address(Lines)).

In this structure **Firstnames** and **Lines** are lists of strings. Let us suppose we have the data entered as the following database, and we want to retrieve data and display it in different ways.

```
/* Personnel database */

employee(names('Prendergast',['Martin','James']),
    33,
    address(['10, High Street',
        'Wimbleton',
        'Sheffield',
        'BU3 4SJ'])).

employee(names('Kennedy',['June','Alice','Diana']),
    27,
    address(['100, Castle Street',
        'Snodbury',
        'Leeds',
        'LJ5 6YF'])).

employee(names('Wallace',['Jonathan','Martin']),
    27,
    address(['The Grange',
        'Hassleton',
        'Leeds',
        'RF7 8GB'])).
```

This database uses a lot of data entered as strings. This can be entered using quotes when **read** is used, or as mentioned in Chapter 9, some versions of Prolog have a means of entering strings without the quotes. Let us assume that the data has been entered, and we just want our program to retrieve it in different ways. Using a menu program of the type described in Chapter 18, we can write the program like this:

```
                    /* SMALL FIRM PERSONNEL PROGRAM */

go:- repeat,
    menu.

menu:-put(12),nl,nl,write('SMALL FIRM DATABASE'),nl,nl,
    write('Do you want to display'),nl,
    write(' a.    A person by surname'),nl,
    write(' b.    People of the same age'),nl,
    write(' c.    People with a common first name'),nl,
    write(' d.    People who live in the same city'),nl,
    write(' e.    Exit'),nl,nl,
    read(Choice),choice(Choice),nl,
    write('Press enter to continue'),get0(_),
    !,Choice=e.

choice(a):-write('Enter the surname (use quotes): '),
    read(Surname),nl,writedetails(Surname).

choice(b):-write('Enter the age to search: '),
    read(Age),nl,
    findall(Surname,
        employee(names(Surname,_),Age,_),
        NameList),
    writepeople(Namelist),nl.

choice(c):-write('Enter the name to search: '),
    read(Name),nl,
    findall(Surname,
        (employee(names(Surname,Firstnames),_,_),
        member(Name,Firstnames)),
        NameList),
    writepeople(NameList),nl.

choice(d):-write('Enter the city to search: '),
    read(City),nl,
    findall(Surname,
        (employee(names(Surname,_),_,address(Address)),
        member(City,Address)),
        NameList),
    writepeople(NameList),nl.

choice(e).

choice(_):-write('Please try again.'),nl.

writepeople([]).

writepeople([P | Pt]):-writedetails(P),writepeople(Pt).

writedetails(Surname):-
    employee(names(Surname,Firstnames),
        Age,nl,address(Address)),
    write(Surname),write(', '),writelist(Firstnames),nl,
    write(Age),writelist2(Address),nl.
```

```
writelist([]).
writelist(L | Lt):-write(L),write(' '),writelist(Lt).

writelist2([]).
writelist2(L | Lt):-write(L),nl,writelist2(Lt).

member(X,[X | _]):-!
member(X,[_ | Lt]):-member(X,Lt).

/* END */
```

This program extracts data in some rather intricate ways, and if you have written this sort of program in procedural languages, handling a lot of complex data, you might agree that Prolog does it quite efficiently and elegantly.

The first **choice**, to retrieve a person's details using a specific surname, is straightforward if we assume that there is only one person with a particular surname in the database. Let us come back to this later. This rule inputs the surname required, then sends it to a rule **writedetails**, which writes out all the details for a person of a given surname. This makes use of two versions of **writelist**, which write out the list of first names horizontally, and the list of address lines vertically.

The second **choice**, to find people with the same age, uses **findall** to collect a list of the surnames of such people from the employee facts. It then sends this list of names to a rule **writepeople**, which writes out the details of all those in the list using **writedetails**.

The third **choice**, which finds people with the same first name, does the same sort of thing but this time shows a complex use of **findall**, with several specifying conditions bracketed together. The conditions for a **Surname** to be included in the **Namelist** are that a list of **Firstnames** exists for that **Surname**, and also that the first Name read in is a member of this list. Having found the list of surnames for people of this first name, it is sent to **writepeople** to write out their details.

The fourth **choice** is similar to the third, using a complex **findall** to collect a list of surnames with corresponding address lists, such that the city which has been read in is a member of the address list. The fifth **choice** simply ends the program.

Having seen how the other choices work, we can see how the first rule could be rewritten using **findall** to write out details in such a way that if several people happen to have the same surname, it will write out all their details:

```
choice(97):-write('Enter the surname (use quotes): '),
       read(Surname),nl,
       findall(Surname,
           employee(names(Surname,_),_,_),
           Namelist),
       writepeople(Namelist).
```

It is clear from this example that it is much better to use a single complex data structure for the details of one employee than to put them into a collection of different facts.

Question 20.1 *(answer on p.190)*

In the light of the example above, what would be a good structure to use for storing details for an electronic address book like the one in the project earlier, between Chapters 7 and 8 ? Assume that you need to store each person's first name, surname, telephone number, address, and date of birth.

20.3 Special structure predicates

To handle facts and structures in more unusual ways, there are some special built-in predicates, which we will explain individually first, then look at their use in a program.

functor(T,F,N)

The word **functor** is used to mean a predicate name or operator. Operators can usually be written alternatively in predicate form, though not the other way round. The term functor refers to either.

The predicate **functor** is a standard predicate which has three arguments. **T** is a structure with functor **F** and arity (number of arguments) **N**. Either **T** has to be instantiated, to return **F** and **N**, or both the others need to be instantiated, to construct a structure to match them.

> ?- functor(fun(a,b,next(c)),F,N).
>   F=fun, N=3

> ?- functor(X,person,3).
>   X=person(_40A3,_40BE,_40D9).

Note that operators such as + and – are also functors and can be used with the predicate **functor**:

> ?- functor(a+b,F,N).

This is really functor(+(a,b),F,N), and returns:

> F=+,N=2

It is important to note that a list is a structure which has the functor '.', with two arguments, the head and tail of the list:

> ?- functor([a,b,c],F,N).

This is the same as functor(.(a,[b,c]),F,N), and returns:

> F=.,N=2

arg(N,T,A)

This is used to access a particular argument of a structure. A is the Nth argument of structure T. The first two arguments must always be instantiated.

```
?- arg(2,person(john,bill,joe),X).
   X=bill

?- arg(2,[p,q,r],Z).
   Z=[q,r]
```

univ or X=..L

This is written as an operator **=..** and spoken as **univ**, a name that has persisted from the original French implementation of Prolog.

Structure **X** is converted to a list L, with the functor as its head.

```
?- X=..[likes,paul,prolog].
   X=likes(paul,prolog).

?- person(jane,female,20)=..L.
   L=[person,jane,female,20).

?- likes(john,jane)=..[X|Y].
   X=likes,Y=[john,jane].
```

call(Clause)

This succeeds by simply finding the clause **Clause** in the database. In most cases it is equivalent to stating the clause as a subgoal, but sometimes when **Clause** is represented by a variable some Prolog interpreters require the use of **call.** There is an example of the use of **call** in the spreadsheet example, which follows later in this chapter.

Question 20.2 *(answer on p.191)*

What will be the reply to the following queries at the prompt?

(a) ?- functor(details(names(smith,[mary,ann]),
            telephone(223344),
            address(['1, High Street','Wombledon','Bunden']),
            birthday(12,5,86)),
            F,N).

(b) ?- arg(4,details(names(smith,[mary,ann]),telephone(223344),
            address(['1, High Street','Wombledon','Bunden']),
            birthday(12,5,86)),
            N).

(c) ?- details(names(smith,[mary,ann]),telephone(223344),
            address(['1, High Street','Wombledon','Bunden']),
            birthday(12,5,86)) =..L.

20.4 A spreadsheet example using functor, arg, univ and call

The following program writes out a spreadsheet matrix, ten places by six, on the screen. It writes it out with stars or asterisks in the cells to begin with, so that you can see where it is, and subsequently allows anything in any of the cells to be replaced. It does not in its present state allow any operations on numbers which have been entered, such as adding up a column. (Nor does it let you use the mouse or cursor keys, which is a severe disadvantage if you are used to using commercial spreadsheets!)

To place things on the screen, the program uses the predicate **curs**, which we explained in Chapter 15 and which places the cursor on the screen as specified by its arguments. To repeat what was said there, this is not standard Prolog, and you will need to add this extra rule which makes use of the cursor-handling facilities of your version. If you are using LPA Prolog you will have to add:

curs(X,Y):-cursor('&:',X,Y).

Or if you are using Public Domain Prolog add:

curs(X,Y):-cursor(X,Y,0).

We will not explain the spreadsheet program in detail, except for the bits which make use of the structure predicates, but the program is annotated and you can probably deduce how the rest works.

```
/* A SIMPLE SPREADSHEET USING FUNCTOR, ARG AND UNIV */

/* Main rule writes out the spreadsheet from the spread facts, takes
   the details of a change to make, saves the change in the appro-
   priate spread fact, then repeats. */

go:- repeat,spreadsheet.

spreadsheet:- put(12),
     write_nums(1),write_rows(1),nl,nl,
     write('Type end to end at any point.'),nl,
     write('Which row to change? '),
     read(R),not R=end,
     write('Which column to change? '),
     read(C),not C=end,
     write('Enter new value: '),
     read(Val),enter_val(R,C,Val),
     !,Val=end.

spreadsheet.

/* These rules write out the spreadsheet from the spread facts.
   write_nums writes numbers along the top of the screen,
   write_rows uses write_cols to write out the columns, as many
   times as there are rows */

write_nums(11):-nl,nl,!.
write_nums(N):-C is (N+1)*6,curs(0,C),
     write(N),M is N+1,write_nums(M).

write_rows(7):-!.
write_rows(N):-M is N+1,write_cols(N,1),
     write_rows(M).
```

```
write_cols(_,12):-!.
write_cols(Row,Col):-functor(X,spread,11),
    X=..[spread,Row|_],call(X),arg(Col,X,Val),
    Newrow is (Row*2),Newcol is Col*6,
    curs(Newrow,Newcol),write(Val),
    C is Col+1,write_cols(Row,C).
```

/* These change a value in the spread data */

```
enter_val(Row,Col,Val):-functor(X,spread,11),
    X=..[spread,Row|Xt],call(X),List=[spread,Row|Xt],
    Z is Col+2,putval(Z,1,Val,List,NewList),
    Y=..NewList,retract(X),assert(Y).
```

/* This places a new Val (3rd argument) into the list
(4th argument) at position C (1st argument) creating
a new list (5th argument). The 2nd argument is a
counter */

```
putval(_,_,_,[],[]).
putval(C,C,Val,[L|Lt],[Val|Zt]):-M is
    C+1,putval(C,M,Val,Lt,Zt),!.
putval(C,N,Val,[L|Lt],[L|Zt]):-M is N+1,
    putval(C,M,Val,Lt,Zt).
```

```
curs(X,Y):-cursor('&:',X,Y).
curs(X,Y):-cursor(X,Y,0).
```

/* Facts to hold spreadsheet */
```
spread(1,*,*,*,*,*,*,*,*,*,*).
spread(2,*,*,*,*,*,*,*,*,*,*).
spread(3,*,*,*,*,*,*,*,*,*,*).
spread(4,*,*,*,*,*,*,*,*,*,*).
spread(5,*,*,*,*,*,*,*,*,*,*).
spread(6,*,*,*,*,*,*,*,*,*,*).
```

/* END */

Let us look at the parts of this program which use the special structure predicates. Look at the second rule **write_cols**. This rule needs to find and write on the screen the value **Val** of argument **Col** of a **spread** fact with **Row** as its first argument. We want to do this without having to specify all the arguments and count through to **Col**. We can do this as follows:

Use functor to create a spread fact X containing variables as arguments

Specify the first argument Row using univ:
    X=..[spread,Row|_]

Instantiate the spread fact using call(X)

Use arg to get argument C of X as Val

curs is then used to write out Val in the right position.

Now look at **enter_val**. This needs to put a new value **Val** which has been read in from the keyboard into the **spread** fact with first argument **Row**, substituting it for argument **Col+1**. Again we want to do this without writing out the whole long fact.

We use **functor** to create a **spread** fact **X**. We specify the first argument as **Row** with **X=..[spread,Row|Xt]**, then instantiate the variables of **X** using **call(X)**. We now have a fully instantiated list **List** provided by **univ**, and can send this to the rule **putval** which substitutes **Val** at the right point. The new list **NewList** returns containing **Val**, and is converted back to a **spread** fact using **univ** again. The new fact is inserted into the database.

Question 20.3 *(answer on p.191)*

*Devise a rule **extend** to add an extra argument to a fact. The first argument is the original fact, the second is the extra argument to be added to the fact, and the third argument is the new fact with its extra argument added. You need to use **univ**.*

> eg. ?- extend(person(julia,woman),25,Fact).
> Fact = person(julia,woman,25)

20.5 Summary

Data can be grouped together in Prolog to form complex facts, where it is convenient to do this. These structures are equivalent to records in some procedural languages. To assist in handling structures there are special Prolog predicates **functor**, **arg**, **univ** and **call**.

Answers to questions

Answer 20.1

There are numerous possible ways of doing this, of course, but generally speaking it is a good idea to use a single structure, and to group things with separate parts together within the structure. This leaves it open when programming to group things conveniently together.

For example:

```
details( names(Surname,Firstnames),
     telephone(Number),
     address(Lines),
     birthday(Day,Month,Year) ).
```

Firstnames can be a list of names as in the example above, and the **address** a list of lines entered as strings. If the **birthday** is stored as three separate variables it will be easy to search for all the people with birthdays in a particular month, for example, as follows:

```
        birthdays_in_month(Month):-
            details(names(Surname,_),_,_,birthday(_,Month,_)),
            write(Surname),nl,fail.
        birthdays_in_month(_).
```

Answer 20.2

(a) F = details, N = 4

(b) N = birthday(12,5,86)

(c) L = [details,smith([mary,ann]),telephone(223344),
         address(['1, High Street','Wombledon','Bunden']),
         birthday(12,5,86)].

Answer 20.3

```
        /* Rule to add an extra argument to a fact */

        extend(Fact,Extra,Fact2):-
            Fact=..List,
            append(List,[Extra],Newlist),
            Fact2=..Newlist.
```

For append, see Chapter 15.

Programming practice: structure predicates

Write a rule **total_column** to add a column of numbers entered into the spreadsheet given in the example above. You will probably need **functor**, **arg**, **univ** and **call**.

21 Operator definitions

21.1 Introduction

Operators are special identifiers, equivalent to predicates, which can be positioned in the program code in a specified way.

For example, the symbol or keyboard character **+** is predefined as an operator, so that we can write **X + Y**. However, **+** is really a built-in predicate, and **X + Y** is the same as **+(X,Y)**. As **+** is defined as an operator, we can write the expression either way. Try this in the Prolog interpreter with:

> **?- X is 2+3.**
> **X=5**

> **?- X is +(2,3).**
> **X=5**

> **?- X=3,Y=4,Z is X+Y.**
> **X=3,Y=4,Z=7**

> **?- X=3,Y=4,Z is +(X,Y).**
> **X=3,Y=4,Z=7**

You can define your own operators in Prolog, using a special predicate for defining operators, ie. for writing predicate names in operator form.

Why should you want to do this? Usually, the reason is readability. Clearly, we do not want to write all our arithmetic in the form **+(X,Y)**, as we are used to writing it in a different way. Similarly, it can be useful to write some facts in a form resembling English sentences. We will show this later.

21.2 op (Precedence,Position,Operator)

The predicate **op**, which succeeds by defining an operator, has three arguments.

The *first argument* is an integer which gives the precedence of the operator in relation to other declared operators, if the use of brackets does not make this clear. These integers are conventionally in units of 100.

The *second argument* signifies the position of the operator in relation to its arguments and is one of the following

fx	fy			prefix operator or functor
xf	yf			postfix operator or functor
xfx	xfy	yfx	yfy	infix operator or functor

The significance of the **x** and **y** is to denote associativity. For example, **yfx** means the operator **f** is left associative, **xfy** means it is right associative.

a + b + c is left associative, interpreted   (a + b) + c
a + b + c is right associative, interpreted   a + (b + c)

A **y** means that the argument can contain operators of equal precedence to the operator defined, an **x** means it cannot, and must contain operators of lower precedence.

eg.   If **not** is defined as **fy**, we can have **not not X**, but if it is defined as **fx** this is incorrect syntax and will cause an error.

The third argument is the definition of the operator itself.

It is usual to use **op** in the form **:-op(...).**, and put it at the beginning of a program. This means that it is called at the time the program is consulted into the database, and the operators to be used in the program are predefined so that the subsequent program code makes sense to the interpreter, and syntax errors do not occur while consulting in.

This is similar to putting **:-go.** at the end of a program, so that **go** is called at the end of consulting in, and the program is run immediately and automatically. Whereas **go** has to be put at the end of the program, so that the interpreter consults in the clauses it calls on first, **:-op** needs to go at the beginning, before the operators it defines occur in the program.

21.3 An example

We can define

:-op(600,xfx,then).

This defines **then** as an infix operator which can only occur once in an expression. (The **x** on either side has to be of lower precedence, so it cannot contain **then** itself.)

We can now have:

temperature then sick.

If we also define:

:-op(800,fx,if).

This defines **if** as a prefix operator which can be followed by an argument of lower precedence.

So we can now have:

if temperature then sick.

Notice that strings of characters defined as operators have to have spaces (or brackets) at either side of them, so that they are not confused with other identifiers.

This could also be written:

> if(then(temperature,sick)).

It is obvious which is the clearer way of writing it, and why defining operators can be useful!

21.4 Giving operators a meaning

Defining an operator simply defines a way it can be positioned in the program code, without giving it any meaning. For example, suppose we define an operator **greater_than** as follows:

> :-op(1000,xfx,greater_than).

We can then include in the program a fact **5 greater_than 3**, but we can also have **3 greater_than 5**. If we want the operator to have the conventional arithmetic meaning, we can enter a rule into the database which defines **greater_than** as follows:

> greater_than(X,Y) :- X > Y.

> or: (X greater_than Y) :- X > Y.

We can now try things like **7 greater_than 6**, which gives **yes**, and **6 greater_than 7**, which gives **no**, at the interpreter prompt. However, we can also still enter specific instances like **3 greater_than 5** as facts, and this will then be found and will succeed when entered at the prompt.

In other words, defining **greater_than** as an operator does nothing more than allow it to be placed in a certain way relative to other objects in the program, and to make use of it we still need to define it in terms of facts and rules in the database before it has any meaning in the program, just like any other predicate we choose to define.

21.5 A simple animals expert system example

It is often very useful, as an aid to readability, to define common English words, usually conjunctions, as operators, for example **if**, **and**, **or** and **then**.

The following program shows the use of some of these definitions in a simple expert system. The program reads in just two supposed features of an animal, and checks its animal database to try to identify the animal. It cannot cope with more than two features, it does not give the user any guidance on features that are allowed, it does not explain itself, and it only has four animals in its database, so it is not much of an expert system, but it has one advantage. The data can be entered as an English sentence, using **and**, **if** and **or**.

```
/* EXPERT SYSTEM WITH DEFINED OPERATORS */

/* Uses rules with declared english operators */

:-op(1100,xfx,if).
:-op(1000,xfy,or).
:-op(900,xfy,and).

go:-write('Enter a feature: '),read(F1),
    write('Enter another feature (n if none): '),read(F2),
    findanimal(Animal,F1,F2),
    write('Animal is a '),write(Animal),nl,nl.
go:-write('Animal is unknown.'),nl,nl.

/* Following allow for different phrasing */

findanimal(X,F1,_):-X if F1.
findanimal(X,_,F2):-X if F2.
findanimal(X,F1,_):-X if F1 or _.
findanimal(X,_,F2):-X if F2 or _.
findanimal(X,F1,_):-X if _ or F1.
findanimal(X,_,F2):-X if _ or F2.
findanimal(X,F1,F2):-X if F1 and F2.
findanimal(X,F1,F2):-X if F2 and F1.

/* Facts */

tiger if yellow and striped.
lion if maned.
zebra if fat and striped.
fish if swims or scales.

/* END */
```

The working of the program requires little explanation, apart from the rule **find-animal**. This rule returns an animal as its first argument when given two features as its second and third arguments, if there is one in the database matching the features.

One of the first two **findanimal** rules will succeed if one of the features occurs in a fact as a single identifying feature. Thus **maned**, entered in any order as either **F1** or **F2**, is sufficient to identify a **lion**. One of the next four rules will succeed if either **F1** or **F2** occurs as either the first or second part of a **;** condition. Thus either **swims** or **scales**, in any order, will identify a **fish**. One of the last two rules will succeed with two features that are both required, but in any order. Thus both **striped** and **yellow**, in any order, are required to identify a **tiger**, and similarly both **striped** and **fat** to identify a **zebra**.

Question 21.1 *(answer on p.201)*

It is possible to define a grammar using operators, so that we can write a sentence as a fact, eg.

> **the cat sat on the mat.**
> **tom sat at the table.**

*Define **the**, **sat**, **on**, and **at** to make this possible.*

We could then query

> **?- the cat sat Where.**
> **?- Who sat at the table.**

What would these queries produce?

21.6 An expert system that learns new animals

The expert system described here uses less operator definitions than the previous one, for simplicity, but it is superior in that it can deal with any number of defining features in its facts, and it will take in a natural language sentence as input, containing as many features as the user thinks are necessary. It also repeats instead of ending after one run.

In addition this system has a very superior feature – if the animal searched for cannot be found, it will ask the user for a name then enter it into the database, using the defined operators to store the new animal in an English language fact. It is thus a very simple example of a 'machine learning' program.

The program achieves its greater versatility through using the structure predicates described in the last chapter.

```
/* ANIMALS EXPERT SYSTEM WITH DEFINED OPERATORS */

/* Note: This program requires getsent to be imported from
        Chapter 17, and member and append from Chapter 15. It uses
        the standard predicate 'atom' where necessary to test that
        variables are instantiated to atoms.
        Features of the program are:
            Uses rules with declared English operators
            Accepts a normal sentence
            Handles any number of features
            Learns new animals
*/

/* Operator definitions */

:-op(1100,xfx,if).
:-op(900,xfy,and).
```

```
/* Main program */

go:-repeat,put(12),nl,nl,
    write('Describe the animal in a sentence.'),nl,
    write('Type stop to end.'),nl,nl,
    write('Describe animal: '),
    getsent(Sentence),nl,get_animal(Sentence),
    decide(Sentence).
    decide(Sentence):-Sentence = [stop,'.'],
    write('Goodbye!'),nl,nl.
    decide(_):-write('Enter to continue.'),get0(_),fail.

/* Finds list of features, finds animal to fit if possible,
or adds it to the database */

get_animal([stop,'.']).

get_animal(Sent):-(X if A),get_list(A,List),
    check_animal(List,Sent),
    write('Your animal is: '),write(X),nl,nl,
    write('Reason: '),write((X if A)),write('.'),nl,nl,!.

get_animal(Sent):-
    write('The animal is not in the database.'),nl,
    write('Do you want to give it a name? [y/n] '),
    read(R),nl,nl,R=y,
    write('What is the name? '),getsent(Animal),nl,nl,
    append(Animal,Sent,L),clip(L,[X | Xt]),
    convert(Xt,Z),Y=..[if,X,Z],
    write('Entered: '),write(Y),write('.'),nl,nl,
    assert(Y),!.

get_animal(_).

/* Gets a list from atoms linked by and operators */

get_list(A,L):-atom(A),L=[A],!.
get_list(A,[X,Y]):-A=..[and,X,Y],atom(Y),!.
get_list(A,[L | Lt]):-A=..[and | [L,Q]],get_list(Q,Lt).

/* Succeeds if animal features fit an animal */

check_animal([],_).
check_animal([L | Lt],Sent):-
    member(L,Sent),check_animal(Lt,Sent).

/* Converts a list into atoms linked by and operators */

convert([X],Z):-atom(X),Z=..[X],!.
convert([X,Y | []],Z):-atom(X),atom(Y),Z=..[and,X,Y],!.
convert([X | Xt],Z):-Z=..[and,X,Y],convert(Xt,Y).
```

```
/* Clips out the non-essential atoms from a list
of features */

clip([],[]):-!.
clip([L|Lt],Mt):-rem(L),clip(Lt,Mt),!.
clip([L|Lt],[L|Mt]):-clip(Lt,Mt).
```

```
/* Words and characters to remove from sentence */
```

rem(it).	rem(is).	rem(are).	rem(a).
rem(an).	rem(and).	rem(they).	rem(this).
rem(animal).	rem('.').	rem(with).	rem(has).
rem(have).	rem(got).	rem(he).	rem(',').

```
/* Facts */

tiger if yellow and striped.
lion if big and maned.
zebra if fat and striped.
fish if swims.
eagle if big and flies.
rhino if big and horn and armoured.
snake if long and thin and slimy and horrible.

/* END */
```

The main program **go** reads in a complete sentence using **getsent** from Chapter 17, then sends it off to **get_animal** for analysis.

Having returned from **get_animal** to **go**, the program goes to the rule **decide** which either ends if **stop** has been entered or repeats the program.

The rule **get_animal** has four versions. The first just succeeds if **stop** has been entered. The second looks for an animal in the database, by retrieving one of the facts of the form **X if A**, where **A** can be complex, converting **A** to a list using **get_list**. This is a rule which converts the animal features, all connected by **and**, into a list by using **univ** recursively. **get_animal** then sends this list off along with the input sentence to **check_animal**, which works through the list of features one by one, checking that each one is a **member** of the list of atoms making up the sentence. If so, it succeeds. Otherwise it fails.

If **check_animal** fails, **get_animal** backtracks to find more animal facts, and if it succeeds it goes on to write out the animal found, along with the reason supplied by the fact.

If the second **check_animal** finally fails, having inspected all the animal facts, Prolog moves on to the third rule, which asks if the user wants to name the animal. If not, this rule fails and the fourth **check_animal** succeeds, returning execution to **go**.

If the user answers yes, this rule reads in an animal name, and adds it to the front of the original input sentence using **append**. It then uses a rule **clip** to clip out or remove from the list all common and unwanted words in the **rem** facts. The rule then uses a subrule **convert** to convert the list recursively into a fact consisting of atoms separated by **and** operators, using **univ**. There is then a final use of **univ** to put an **if** operator onto the front of the fact, and after a message telling the user what is happening, the fact is asserted into the database.

Question 21.2 *(answer on p.201)*

Show how we could replace the rule **member** *(see Chapter 15) using an operator* **belongs_to**, *so that we could write* **member(Element,List)** *as:*

Element belongs_to List

21.7 A logic theorem prover example

We can define the logic operators for equivalence, implication, disjunction, conjunction and negation as conventional symbols, with their usual order of precedence, as follows:

```
?-op(250,xfy,<=>)./* equivalence */
?-op(225,xfy,=>). /* implication */
?-op(200,xfy,or).  /* disjunction */
?-op(150,xfy,&).   /* conjunction */
?-op(100,fx,~).    /* negation */
```

We can give meaning to the symbols defined above using appropriate rules for their use, and use them to solve problems, or prove theorems, in predicate logic.

If you have never studied logic, there is no space here to attempt a crash course. Suffice to say that logic is an age-old subject, a branch of mathematics, which attempts to formulate universal rules for proving theorems from a set of axioms or starting facts. If you do know some formal predicate logic, you will appreciate the program more, but even if not you will be able to see how it works, without recognising the theorems built into it.

Because Prolog itself is rooted in logic, the construction of a theorem solver is particularly concise and impressive.

```
/* A SIMPLE PROPOSITIONAL LOGIC THEOREM PROVER */

/* These define the logic operators. */

?-op(250,xfy,<=>).        /* equivalence */
?-op(225,xfy,=>).         /* implication */
?-op(200,xfy,or).         /* disjunction */
?-op(150,xfy,&).          /* conjunction */
?-op(100,fx,~).           /* negation */

/* Program. */

go:-repeat,prove(start).

prove(stop).
prove(_):-nl,write('THEOREM PROVER'),nl,nl,
        write('Symbols: <=> => or & ~ true'),nl,nl,
```

```
                        write('Enter your theorem, separating operators from'),nl,
                        write('operands with spaces. Type stop to end.'),nl,nl,
                        write('Enter theorem here: '),nl,nl,
                        read(T),nl,deduce(T),prove(T).

                deduce(stop):-!.
                deduce(T):-theorem(T),write('Valid.'),nl,nl,!.
                deduce(T):-write('Not valid.'),nl,nl.

                /* Expression conversion formulae. */

                theorem(~ true):-!.
                theorem(P <=> Q):-theorem((P => Q) & (Q => P)).
                theorem(P => Q):-theorem(~ P or Q).
                theorem(P or Q):-(theorem(P) ; theorem(Q)).
                theorem(P & Q):-theorem(P),theorem(Q).
                theorem(~ (~ P)):-theorem(P).
                theorem(~ (P <=> Q)):-theorem(~ (P => Q) & ~ (Q => P)).
                theorem(P => Q):-theorem(~ (P & ~ Q)).
                theorem(~ (P or Q)):-theorem(~ P & ~ Q).
                theorem(~ (P & Q)):-theorem(~ P or ~ Q).

                /* END */
```

This can be tested with expressions in the logical format we have defined. For example, common logic theorems such as the following will test as valid, as we would expect as they have direct counterparts in the database:

```
~ (~ A) <=> A
~ (P or Q) <=> ~ P & ~ Q
~ (P & Q) <=> ~ P or ~ Q
```

Something which is not directly in the database but which seems reasonable is that if A and B are true and this implies C is true, then this in itself implies C is true.

```
((A & B) => C) => C
```

Sure enough this tests as valid. But something made up like:

```
A(~ A(~ B)) <=> (B => A)
```

... tests as not valid. Try these and some others for yourself.

21.8 Summary

It is possible to define your own operators in Prolog using the built-in predicate **op**. This is largely for convenience and readability. It means English words such as 'and' and 'if' can be defined as operators, and expressions can be written in the form of English sentences. Also, unusual operators such as those of logic notation can be defined and given meaning.

Answers to questions

Answer 21.1

The sentence is grouped around the verb, **sat**, so this needs the highest precedence. The definite article **the** has to be attached directly to an atom, so it needs to have the lowest precedence. The others are in between. **sat** is an infix operator, all the others are prefix, so we can define them:

```
:- op(1000,xfx,sat).
:- op(600,fx,on).
:- op(400,fx,at).
:- op(100,fx,the).
```

the cat sat on the mat.

... would effectively be the structure

sat((the(cat)),(on(the(mat)))).

The queries would give:

?- the cat sat Where.
    Where = on the mat

?- Who sat at the table.
    Who = tom

Answer 21.2

We would define **belongs_to** as an infix operator:

:- op(500,xfx,belongs_to).

We would then replace **member** with:

belongs_to(L,[L | _]).
belongs_to(X,[_ | Lt]):-belongs_to(X,Lt).

... or rewritten in operator form:

Element belongs_to [Element | _].
Element belongs_to [_ | Tail] :- Element belongs_to Tail.

Programming practice: Transport ES with defined operators

Write a program for a TRANSPORT expert system with the following operator definitions, basing it on the animal expert systems given in this chapter.

```
:-op(1200,xfx,then).
:-op(1100,xfx,if).
:-op(1100,fx,if).
:-op(1000,xfy,or).
:-op(900,xfy,and).
```

This expert system should accept data with operators **and**, **then** and **if**, and **if** is defined in two ways, so that it can come at the start or in the middle of a fact. The program should cope with the following data:

```
/* Transport facts */

if land and sea then hovercraft.
road_transport if wheels and land.
if wings then aeroplane.
ship if floats.
```

The expert system need not deal with more than two features.

22 Prolog grammar notation

22.1 Introduction

We have looked at the subject of natural language briefly, but without attempting to analyse the construction of sentences, beyond breaking them up into a list of words as atoms.

Natural language has preoccupied the Artificial Intelligence community to such an extent that Prolog contains a special notation to deal with parsing of sentences, sometimes called 'context free grammar' notation.

22.2 The Prolog grammar notation

The grammar notation makes use of a built-in operator definition, —> , which can be read as 'is made up of'. Its use is best shown by an example.

A sentence in English can be represented using the Prolog grammar notation as follows:

> **sentence —> noun_phrase, verb_phrase.**
>
> **noun_phrase —> determiner, noun.**
>
> **verb_phrase —> verb, noun_phrase.**
> **verb_phrase —> verb.**
>
> **determiner —> [the].**
>
> **noun —> [orange].**
> **noun —> [man].**
>
> **verb —> [eats].**
> **verb —> [writes].**

The sentences 'the man eats the orange' and 'the man writes' will satisfy this grammar. However, it is context free in the sense that it pays no regard to the meaning of words. The sentence 'the orange eats the man' will also satisfy it.

The relations defined in this way can be tested using a built-in predicate **phrase**.

> **phrase(sentence,List)**

… will succeed if **List** can be broken down or parsed so as to satisfy the relations defined for predicate **sentence**.

In other words, we can enter queries at the prompt such as:

> **?- phrase(sentence,[the,man,eats,the,orange]).**
>   **yes**

Question 22.1 *(answer on p.208)*

How could we extend the grammar above to include adverbs, words which describe a verb?

22.3 Extending the grammar with arguments

We can refine the grammar above to test for singular and plural nouns and verbs.

> **sentence —> noun_phrase(X), verb_phrase(X).**
>
> **noun_phrase(X) —> determiner, noun(X).**
>
> **verb_phrase(X) —> verb(X), noun_phrase(_).**
> **verb_phrase(X) —> verb(X).**
>
> **determiner —> [the].**
>
> **noun(plural) —> [men].**
> **noun(singular) —> [man].**
>
> **verb(plural) —> [eat].**
> **verb(plural) —> [write].**
> **verb(singular) —> [eats].**
> **verb(singular) —> [writes].**

By giving the terms arguments we are tying the plurality of the verbs to that of the nouns. This grammar will distinguish between 'the man writes' and 'the men write', confirming each as correct grammar but returning 'the men writes' as incorrect.

22.4 An example grammar parsing program

A more elaborate grammar using prepositions, participles and adjectives is shown below. If you are not too familiar with such things as prepositions and participles, or with grammar in general, this is not the place for a potted grammar tutorial! There are plenty of books on grammar if this subject interests you.

This grammar is not, of course, by any means infallible. You can try testing its limits, and perhaps extending it. What the program does is explained at the approprate points by the comments in the code.

It will only respond correctly, of course, to sentences made up of words which are in its vocabulary database, but this can be extended indefinitely.

/* PROGRAM WHICH CHECKS GRAMMAR OF A SENTENCE */

/* Main program. Note that this requires getsent from
    Chapter 17, whose code is not repeated here. */

```
go:-write('Enter one complete sentence:'),nl,nl,
    getsent(Sentence),
    test(Sentence).

test(Sentence):-phrase(sentence,Sentence),
    write('Sentence is correct.'),nl.
test(_):-write('Sentence is incorrect.'),nl.
```

/* Basic Sentence */

```
sentence —> noun_phrase(N),verb_prep_phrase(N),fullstop.
```

/* Noun phrases. Accepts phrases joined by a conjunction */

```
noun_phrase(plural) —> noun_group(_),
    conjunction(and),noun_group(_),!.
noun_phrase(N)—>noun_group(N).
```

/* Nouns grouped with other words. Accepts determiners
and adjectives and distinguishes between nouns, proper
nouns and pronouns */

```
noun_group(N)—>determiner(N),noun_adj_group(N),!.
noun_group(plural)—>noun_adj_group(plural),!.
noun_group(N)—>adjective,propernoun(N),!.
noun_group(N)—>propernoun(N),!.
noun_group(N)—>pronoun(N).
```

/* Deals with nouns grouped with up to two adjectives */

```
noun_adj_group(N)—>adjective,adjective,noun(N),!.
noun_adj_group(N)—>adjective,noun(N),!.
noun_adj_group(N)—>noun(N).
```

/* These take care of prepositional phrases */

```
verb_prep_phrase(N)—>verb_phrase(N),prepositional_phrase,
    prepositional_phrase,prepositional_phrase,!.
verb_prep_phrase(N)—>verb_phrase(N),
    prepositional_phrase,prepositional_phrase,!.
verb_prep_phrase(N)—>verb_phrase(N),
    prepositional_phrase,!.
verb_prep_phrase(N)—>verb_phrase(N).
```

/* Verb phrases. Deal with verbs grouped with up to two
noun phrases, eg. He gave (her)(the book). */

```
verb_phrase(N)—>
    verb_group(N),noun_phrase(_),noun_phrase(_),!.
verb_phrase(N)—>verb_group(N),noun_phrase(_),!.
verb_phrase(N)—>verb_group(N).
```

```
/* These cater for up to two participles, eg. He is going.
He is sitting reading. */

    verb_group(N)—>verb(N),participle,participle,!.
    verb_group(N)—>verb(N),participle,!.
    verb_group(N)—>verb(N).

/* Prepositional phrases. Deals with up to two prepositions,
e.g. He goes to bed. He goes in to dinner. */

    prepositional_phrase
        —>preposition,preposition,noun_phrase(_),!.
    prepositional_phrase —> preposition,noun_phrase(_).

/* General vocabulary */

    determiner(singular)—>[the].
    determiner(plural)—>[the].
    determiner(singular)—>[their].
    determiner(plural)—>[their].
    determiner(singular)—>[a].
    determiner(plural)—>[some].
    determiner(singular)—>[her].

    conjunction —> [and].
    fullstop —>[.].

/* Some vocabulary */

    propernoun(singular) —> [barbara].
    propernoun(singular) —> [david].

    pronoun(plural) —> [they].
    pronoun(singular) —> [he].
    pronoun(singular) —> [she].

    verb(plural) —> [are].
    verb(singular) —> [is].
    verb(plural) —> [go].
    verb(singular) —> [goes].

    participle —> [sitting].
    participle —> [reading].
    participle —> [going].

    preposition —> [in].
    preposition —> [at].
    preposition —> [on].
    preposition —> [to].

    adjective —> [useful].

    noun(singular) —> [student].
    noun(singular) —> [pupil].
    noun(singular) —> [paper].
    noun(singular) —> [book].
```

```
noun(singular) —> [journal].
noun(singular) —> [library].
noun(singular) —> [table].
noun(singular) —> [chair].
noun(singular) —> [bed].
noun(singular) —> [dinner].
noun(plural) —> [dinner].
noun(plural) —> [beds].
noun(plural) —> [students].
noun(plural) —> [pupils].
noun(plural) —> [papers].
noun(plural) —> [books].
noun(plural) —> [journals].
noun(plural) —> [chairs].
noun(plural) —> [tables].
noun(plural) —> [libraries].
```

/* END */

It is possible to extend this, as a project-sized program, into quite an effective language teaching aid, where a student of English answers questions on a small comprehension passage, and the program checks the answer, written as a complete sentence. Several different questions can be distinguished by an extra argument attached to all the predicates. It is necessary to define an allowed vocabulary for each answer, perhaps using the method indicated in the next section. The program will check the grammar of the sentence, but whether the answer is along the right lines is best checked by using keywords as well, in a separate test. (See Chapter 17.)

22.5 Combining with normal notation

If we need to insert bits of conventional Prolog into a program written in grammar notation, we can do it using curly brackets, { ... }. For example, we can define all the nouns as conventional Prolog facts if we prefer:

noun(Noun) —> [Noun], { noun_is(Noun) }.

noun_is(man).
noun_is(table).   ... etc

As another example, suppose the sentence we are testing is the answer to a particular question, one of several, and we want to tie the answer the user gives to a certain collection of nouns. We can specify that a sentence is valid as the answer to question **N** by giving **sentence** an argument **N**, and specify this value of **N** for all the nouns used in the answer as follows:

sentence(N) —> noun_phrase(N), verb_phrase(N).

noun_phrase(N) —> determiner, noun(N).

verb_phrase(N) —> verb, noun_phrase(N).
verb_phrase(_) —> verb.

noun(N) —> [Noun], { allowed_noun(N,Noun) }.

determiner —> [the].

verb —> [eats].
verb —> [eats].

We can now define all our nouns in a database of **allowed_noun** facts which says which of the nouns can be used in particular answers.

allowed_noun(5,man).
allowed_noun(5,peach).
allowed_noun(7,chair).

This means that only sentences containing the nouns man and peach will be accepted as answers to question 5. A sentence with nouns of mixed numbers will be rejected, ie.

The man eats the peach.   **... is correct.**
The man eats the chair.   **... is incorrect.**

We can test this grammar at the prompt as follows:

?- phrase(sentence(5),[the,man,eats,the,peach]).
   yes

?-phrase(sentence(5),[the,man,eats,the,chair]).
   no

Question 22.2 (answer on p.208)

Show how the example program above in Section 22.4 can be linked with normal Prolog so that all the nouns and verbs can be written as facts of the type:

noun_is(man,singular).
noun_is(chairs,plural).

verb_is(are,plural).
verb_is(is,singular).

22.6 Some additional points

It is often helpful to plan the sentence structure we are trying to represent in Prolog graphically, in the form of a tree. The grammar in Section 22.2, and the example sentence, can be written:

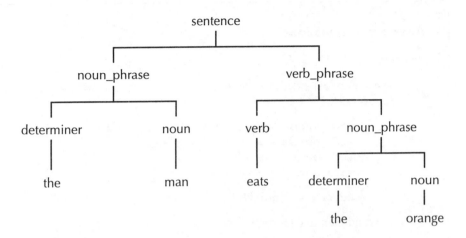

Notice that the grammar notation is just another, more efficient way of writing ordinary Prolog. We could say

sentence(X):-concat(Y,Z,X),noun_phrase(Y),verb_phrase(Z).

… instead of:

sentence —> noun_phrase, verb_phrase.

… and modify all the other relations in the same way. Obviously this is clumsy compared with the special notation.

We should point out that the treatment in this chapter is far from being the last word on natural language and grammar parsers, which is a large and well-researched subject. If it interests you (perhaps for a prospective project) a number of the books listed in the bibliography treat it more fully.

22.7 Summary

Prolog contains a special grammar notation consisting of the operator —>, the built-in predicate **phrase**, and the curly brackets {...}. This enables natural language programs which need to parse or analyse sentences to be written much more efficiently and clearly.

Answers to questions

Answer 22.1

We could extend the definitions of a verb_phrase in the grammar as follows:

> **verb_phrase —> adverb, verb, noun_phrase(_).**
> **verb_phrase —> verb, noun_phrase(_).**
> **verb_phrase —> adverb, verb.**
> **verb_phrase —> verb.**
>
> **adverb —> [quickly].**

It would then accept such things as:

> **the man quickly ate the orange.**
> **the man quickly writes.**

However, adverbs are the jokers in the pack of grammar parts, because they can go almost anywhere in a sentence. For example, all the following sound correct:

> **the man quickly ate the orange.**
> **quickly the man ate the orange.**
> **the man ate the orange quickly.**

In practice, a better strategy with adverbs might be simply to identify those present, using **member**, then remove them from the sentence list using **delete** before parsing the rest of the sentence.

Answer 22.2

We can write two rules for nouns and verbs as follows:

> **noun(N) —> [Noun], { noun_is(Noun,N) }.**
>
> **verb(N) —> [Verb], { verb_is(Verb,N) }.**

The rules of the type   noun(singular) —> [student].
        verb(plural) —> [go].

become facts like this   noun_is(student,singular).
        verb_is(go,plural).

Programming practice: **an alternative grammar notation**

Design an alternative grammar, dividing up a sentence not into **noun_phrase and verb_phrase**, but into **subject, verb and predicate**. A **predicate** can consist of just an **object**, or an **object**, a **preposition** and another **object**. A **subject** and an **object** are the same as what we called a **noun_phrase** before, eg.

The man eats the orange	**... is correct**
The man puts the book on the table	**... is correct**

Devise a way to define nouns as acceptable subjects for certain verbs, by using a type of fact

position(subject,man)
position(object,orange)

... so that

The man eats the orange.	**... is correct**
The orange eats the man.	**... is incorrect**

Keep the grammar simple – do not cater for plural and singular, for example (at least not at first).

Test yourself
Sample examination questions

These questions are of a type that might be set at the end of a one-year Prolog course.

Question 1

(a) (i) Write a Prolog rule circle(R), which takes the radius of a circle, R, as its argument and writes out its circumference and area.

[3 marks]

   (ii) Use the rule defined in (i) in a short program started by go which repeatedly asks for the radius of a circle and writes out the circumference and area of each circle, stopping when 0 is entered.

[5 marks]

(b) A grocer wants to keep a record of his stock, in such a way that he can easily check the current unit wholesale price, the current unit retail price which he sells the item for, and the number of units of each item he has in stock.

Devise a suitable simple fact stock to store this information, and a simple program, consisting of suitable rules, which offers a menu to do the following:

A. Enter a stock item.

B. Delete a stock item.

C. Give details of a named item.

D. List all items and their details.

E. Exit.

[Note: Do not use lists in this program.]   [12 marks]

Question 2

(a) A semantic net consists of nodes connected by links which represent relationships. Explain why Prolog is a natural choice for programming semantic nets.

[3 marks]

(b) *Read the following:*

There are a number of different bodies in the Solar System. At the centre is the **Sun**, a medium-sized **star**. Round it revolves nine **planets, Mercury, Venus, Earth, Mars, Jupiter, Saturn, Uranus, Neptune** and **Pluto**, in order of distance from the Sun. There are hundreds of **asteroids** revolving like minor planets mostly between Mars and Jupiter. A number of **comets** on long elliptical orbits spend most of their time out of sight and visit periodically. Round the planets rotate their **satellites**. The largest of Jupiter's are **Io, Europa, Ganymede** and **Callisto**.

Draw a semantic net showing the relationships between the bodies mentioned in the passage. To help you the bodies you need to include in your net are picked out in bold. Use isa (is a) links to show examples of objects (you need not show them all), and other links of your own devising.

[8 marks]

(c) *Convert your semantic net into an appropriate Prolog database.*

[4 marks]

(d) *Show how you could use your database to test whether Europa revolves round the Sun and what the result would be. If there is an anomaly here, suggest a rule or rules to resolve it.*

[5 marks]

Question 3

(a) *Describe the form the following take in Prolog and how they are used:*

(i) *facts*

(ii) *rules*

(iii) *lists.* [6 marks]

(b) *Consider the following Prolog database of facts. (It is incomplete and not necessarily mechanically accurate.)*

```
main_part(engine).
main_part(fuel_system).
main_part(exhaust_system).
main_part(steering).
main_part(transmission).
main_part(suspension).
main_part(ignition_system).
main_part(electrics).

part_of(fuel_system,carburettor).
part_of(fuel_system,petrol_tank).
part_of(engine,big_ends).
part_of(engine,head_gasket).

parts_concerned(no_petrol,[carburettor,petrol_tank]).
```

**parts_concerned(will_not_start,[engine,fuel_system,
ignition_system,electrics]).**

**parts_concerned(loss_of_power,[engine,fuel_system,
ignition_system]).**
**parts_concerned(runs_unevenly,[fuel_system,
ignition_system]).**

**symptom('Is the petrol gauge failing to register? y/n',
no_petrol).**
**symptom('Does the engine run unevenly? y/n',
runs_unevenly).**
**symptom('Does the engine refuse to start? y/n',
will_not_start).**

(i) *Write a rule* **find_parts(X)** *which lists all the parts of a named main
part of the car,*

e.g. ?-find_parts(engine).

. . . would list all parts of the engine. [3 marks]

(ii) *Write a rule* **need_help** *which asks a succession of questions and in
response lists which parts of the car to inspect for the cause.*

[6 marks]

(c) *Discuss the limitations of the above program and (without writing any
further code) how it would be possible to improve it using Prolog techniques you are familiar with.*

[5 marks]

Question 4

(a) *Define what is meant by the terms:*

backtracking
instantiation

and describe the effect of the cut (!) in a Prolog rule. [5 marks]

(b) *Here is a Prolog database:*

```
pred([],[]).
pred([H|[]],H).
pred([H|T],L):-pred(T,L).
```

Given the query:

?-pred([a,b,d] , X).

*With which of the clauses in the database will the query initially find a
match, and what will be the final value of X?*

[5 marks]

(c) Write a Prolog rule called **repeats** which has three arguments, the first being an object, the second a list, and the third being the number of occurrences of the object in the list. For example:

> **repeats(b , [a,b,c,b] , 2)**

is an instance of this relation which would succeed. [5 marks]

(d) In no more than 200 words, describe what you see as the main differences between programming in a declarative language such as Prolog compared with programming in a procedural language such as Pascal, ADA or C.

[5 marks]

Question 5

A simple medical diagnosis system contains a database of different medications and the symptoms they relieve, e.g.

> **relieves(aspirin,headache)**
> **relieves(penicillin,pneumonia).**

It also contains data showing what might be aggravated by the different medications.e.g.

> **aggravate(aspirin,peptic-ulcer).**
> **aggravate(penicillin,asthma).**

Write a small expert system which will query the user for the various symptoms and suggest the correct medication. Each predicate should have a brief description to explain its purpose.

For any low level predicate you are not coding, you must give a full description of its operation.

[20 marks]

Question 6

(a) The following is a rule which succeeds when <space> is entered, and waits until this happens.

```
getspace:-nl,write('Press space to continue.'),
     repeat, get0(Ch),getspace2(Ch), nl.

getspace2(32).
     getspace2(_):-!, fail.
```

Re-write this rule more simply without the subrule **getspace2**, and without using recursion.

[5 marks]

(b) Now re-write the rule **getspace** in part (a) using recursion, with no use of cut or fail.

[5 marks]

(c) The Prolog built-in predicate **get0(Key)** will instantiate **Key** to an ASCII number corresponding to a key pressed on the keyboard.

Using this, write an input rule

getkeypress(Atom,Char)

… which will return **Char** as an uppercase character (not an ASCII number) which is one of the characters making up the atom **Atom**. If a key is pressed which is not one of the characters of **Atom**, the rule will wait until one is pressed that is.

Your rule can call on subrules if required, and should be case independent. It should deal appropriately with characters which are entered but are not in the list. You can make use of standard predicates and commonly used standard rules, but identify the ones you are using.

[Note: Do not assume a standard rule to convert to uppercase. Uppercase letters are from ASCII 65 to 90, and lower case from 97 to 122.]

[10 marks]

Appendix 1
solutions to programming practice

Chapter 2

2. ?- assert(animal(lion)).
    ?- assert(animal(tiger)).
    ?- assert(animal(cow).

3. ?- animal(tiger).
    yes

4. ?- animal(cow),animal(lion).
    yes

5. ?-assert(carnivore(lion)).
    ?-assert(carnivore(tiger)).

6. ?- animal(lion),carnivore(lion).
    yes

    ?- animal(cow),carnivore(cow).
    no

Chapter 3

1. ?- aeroplane(hurricane).
        yes

    ?- aeroplane(jumbo).
        no

    ?- aeroplane(_).
        yes   (repeated solutions)

    ?- aeroplane(Plane).
        Plane= spitfire
        Plane = dakota etc.

2. ?- aeroplane(hurricane).
        yes

    ?- aeroplane(jumbo).
        yes

    ?- aeroplane(_).
        yes

    ?- aeroplane(Plane).
        yes

The variable **Plane** in the database acts as a wild card which can be instantiated to the argument in any query, so that a query always succeeds.

Chapter 4

(a) **?- animal(mammal,X,_,_).**

(b) **?- animal(mammal,X,carnivore,_).**

(c) **?- animal(mammal,X,_,stripes).**

(d) **?- animal(reptile,X,_,mane).**

Chapter 5

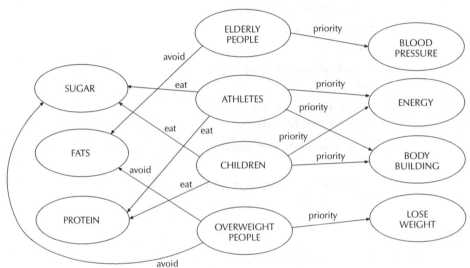

/* Database */

avoid(elderly_people,fats).
avoid(overweight_people,fats).
avoid(overweight_people,sugar).
eat(athletes,sugar).
eat(athletes,protein).
eat(children,sugar).
eat(children,protein).
priority(children,energy
priority(children,body_building).
priority(athletes,energy
priority(athletes,body_building).
priority(elderly_people,blood_pressure).
priority(overweight_people,lose_weight).

(a) **?- eat(Person,protein),priority(Person,body_building).**

(b) **?- eat(People,sugar),priority(People,Priority).**

Chapter 6

(a) Grandmother has to be the mother of the mother of X, or the mother of the father of X.

grandmother_of(Grandmother,X):-
mother_of(Mother,Grandmother),
mother_of(X,Mother).

grandmother_of(Grandmother,X):-
mother_of(Father,Grandmother),
father_of(X,Father).

(b) Brother has to be male, and Brother and X have to have the same father or the same mother (or both). Also we do not want Prolog to say someone is his own brother.

brother_of(Brother,X):-father_of(Brother,Father),
father_of(X,Father),male(Brother),not Brother=X.
brother_of(Brother,X):-mother_of(Brother,Mother),
mother_of(X,Mother),male(Brother),not Brother=X.

(c) We can make use of the brother_of rule for this. The uncle of X must be the brother of the mother of X, or the brother of the father of X. (We will deal only with blood relations, as the database does not tell us who everyone is married to.) He must also be male, but this is covered by the brother_of rule.

uncle_of(Uncle,X):-brother_of(Brother,Father),
father_of(X,Father).
uncle_of(Uncle,X):-brother_of(Brother,Mother),
father_of(X,Mother).

Chapter 7

The program is:

run:-write('What is your word? '),read(Word),
tran(Word,French),
write('The French is '),write(French),nl,nl.

For a catch-all, add the following at the bottom of the **tran** facts:

tran(_,'not known').

Chapter 8

1. (a) list all the capital cities in the database

    list_capitals:-capital(City),write(City),nl,fail.
    list_capitals.

    (b) list all the cities

    list_cities:-city_in(City,_),write(City),nl,fail.
    list_cities.

    (c)   list all the countries in the EC

```
list_countries:-belongs_to(Country,'EC'),
             write(Country),nl,fail.
list_countries.
```

2.   A rule to find the capital of a country:

```
capital_of(City,Country):-
       capital(City),city_in(City,Country).
```

3.   A rule to find capital cities in the EC:

```
capital_in_EC(City):-
       capital(City),city_in(City,Country),
       belongs_to(Country,'EC').
```

Chapter 9

```
/* TELEPHONE NUMBERS PROGRAM */

/* Program */

go:- reconsult('phone.dba'),
     write('TELEPHONE NUMBERS '),nl,nl,
     write('What would you like to do?'),nl,nl,
     write(' a. See the numbers.'),nl,
     write(' b. Add a new one.'),nl,
     write(' c. Change one.'),nl,
     write(' d. Delete one.'),nl,
     write(' e. Exit.'),nl,nl,
     write('Answer a, b, c, d or e: '),read(Choice),nl,
     choice(Choice),nl,nl.

/* Menu options */

choice(a):-telephone(Person,Number),write(Person),
     write(' '),write(Number),nl,fail.
choice(a).

choice(b):-getperson(Person,Number),
     assertz(telephone(Person,Number)),save_numbers.

choice(c):-getperson(Person,Number),
     retract(telephone(Person,_)),
     assertz(telephone(Person,Number)),save_numbers.

choice(d):-getperson(Person,Number),
     retract(telephone(Person,_)),save_numbers.

choice(e).

choice(_,_,_):-write('Wrong letter.').

/* Read in a persons new name and number */

getperson(Person,Number):-
     write('Enter the persons name: '),read(Person),
     write('Enter the number: '),read(Number),nl.
```

```
/* Save the file */
save_numbers:-del('phone.dba'),tell('phone.dba'),write_db,told.

write_db:-telephone(Person,Num),X=telephone(Person,Num),
    write(X),write('.'),nl,fail.
write_db.

/* END */
```

The file **phone.dba** is required, containing **telephone** facts, e.g. telephone ('**Police,999**').

Note that in LPA Prolog, **del** is required to delete the file before using **tell**. Some Prologs will not need this.

Chapter 10

```
/* JURASSIC */

/* Inference engine and interface */

go:- write('** DINOSAUR **'),nl,nl,
        write('Is it vegetarian or carnivorous? Choose,'),nl,
        write('from veg or carn: '),read(Eating),
        write('What is its habitat? Choose from land, sea,'),nl,
        write('air or swamp: '),read(Habitat),
        write('What size is it? Choose from '),nl,
        write('large or small: '),read(Size),
        write('How long is its neck? Choose from long, '),nl,
        write('short or none: '),read(Neck),nl,
        write('Describe its stance. Choose from quadruped,'),nl,
        write('biped, swimming or flying: '),read(Stance),
        write('Does it have any horns or crests? Choose'),nl,
        write('from three_horns, crest, domed_head, '),
        write('back_plates,beak or none: '),read(Horns),nl,
        assertz(size(Size)),assertz(habitat(Habitat)),
        assertz(neck(Neck)),assertz(stance(Stance)),
        assertz(horns(Horns)),assertz(eating(Eating)),
        rule(Rule,Dinosaur),
        write('The dinosaur is: '),write(Dinosaur),nl,nl,
        write('The rule used was Number '),write(Rule),nl,nl,
        retractall(size(_)),retractall(habtitat(_)),
        retractall(neck(_)),retractall(stance(_)),
        retractall(horns(_)),retractall(eating(_)).

/* Knowledge base */

rule(1,brachiosaurus):-horns(domed_head).
rule(2,protoceratops):-horns(beak).
rule(3,stegosaurus):-horns(back_plates).
rule(4,triceratops):-horns(three_horns).
rule(5,ichthyosaur):-habitat(sea),neck(none).
rule(6,plesiosaur):-habitat(sea),neck(long).
rule(7,pterodactyl):-habitat(air),horns(none).
```

221

```
rule(8,pteranodon):-habitat(air),horns(crest).
rule(9,corythoswaurus):-horns(crest),habitat(land).
rule(10,tyrannosaurus):-stance(biped),size(large),eating(carn).
rule(11,iguanodon):-stance(biped),size(large),eating(veg).
rule(12,velociraptor):-stance(biped),size(small),eating(carn).
rule(13,'brontosaurus or diplodocus'):-habitat(swamp).
rule(14,'not known.').

/* END */
```

Chapter 11

First version of display, to write shares out:

```
display:-share(Month,Price),write(Month),write(' '),
        write(Price),nl,fail.
display.
```

Second version, calling stars:

```
display:-share(Month,Price),write(Month),write(' '),
        stars(Price),nl,fail.
display.

stars(0).
stars(N):-write('*'),M is N-1,stars(M).
```

Chapter 12

The first solution uses a conventional boundary condition rule at the top. The second recursive loop reads in the marks and updates the total and counter. All three are passed as arguments. The first loop succeeds if the mark is < 0 and writes out the total and average. As the total and counter have been updated they have to be readjusted first.

```
go:-loop(0,0,0).

loop(Mark,Total,Count):-Mark<0,NewT is Total-Mark,
        NewC is Count-1,Average is NewT/NewC,
        write(NewT),nl,write(Average),nl.

loop(_,Total,Count):-write('Enter mark: '),read(Mark),
        NewT is Total+Mark,NewC is Count+1,
        loop(Mark,NewT,NewC).
```

The second solution uses a subsidiary rule, and does not involve readjustments. The first rule **loop** reads in the marks and passes the mark, the total and the counter to a subsidiary rule **test**. The first test succeeds if the mark is < 0 and writes out the total and average. If this fails, the second **test** updates the total and counter and recurses back to **loop**.

```
go:-loop(0,0).

loop(Total,Count):-write('Enter mark: '),read(Mark),
        test(Mark,Total,Count).
```

```
test(Mark,Total,Count):-Mark<0,Average is Total/Count,
    write(Total),nl,write(Average),nl.
```

```
test(Mark,Total,Count):-NewT is Total+Mark,
    NewC is Count+1,loop(NewT,NewC).
```

The last is probably the shortest and neatest solution. The first recursive loop reads in the marks and updates the total and counter. It fails if the mark is < 0. The second loop then succeeds and writes out the total and average.

```
go:-loop(0,0).
```

```
loop(Total,Count):-write('Enter mark: '),read(Mark),
    Mark>=0,NewT is Total+Mark,
    NewC is Count+1,loop(NewT,NewC).
```

```
loop(Total,Count):-Average is Total/Count,write(Total),nl,
    write(Average),nl.
```

Chapter 13

```
/* ZOO KNOWLEDGE BASE */
```

```
/* This is saved in a separate file and consulted in from
the shell */
```

```
/* Initial headers */
```

```
title('** ZOO QUEST **').
```

```
message('Please answer the following questions').
message('with y (yes) or n (no).').
```

```
/* Questions */
```

```
question('Does the animal have a mane?',mane).
question('Does it hunt other animals for food?',hunter).
question('Does it have a trunk?',trunk).
question('Does it have tusks?',tusks).
question('Is its normal way of life swimming?',swims).
question('Can it fly?',flies).
question('Is the animal small?',small).
question('Does it have stripes?,stripes).
```

```
/* Rules */
```

```
rule(1,lion):-observation(mane).
rule(2,tiger):-observation(stripes),observation(hunter).
rule(3,elephant):-observation(trunk).
rule(4,zebra):-observation(stripes),not observation(hunter).
rule(5,walrus):-observation(swims),observation(tusks).
rule(6,eagle):-observation(flies),observation(hunter).
rule(7,sparrow):-observation(flies),observation(small).
rule(8,shark):-observation(swims),observation(hunter).
rule(9,goldfish):-observation(swims).
rule(10,mouse):-observation(small).
```

/* Replies */

reply(lion,'It must be a lion.').
reply(tiger,'It has to be a tiger.').
reply(elephant,'The animal is an elephant.').
reply(zebra,'This is a zebra.').
reply(walrus,'That will be a walrus.').
reply(eagle,'It seems to be an eagle.').
reply(sparrow,'It will be a sparrow.').
reply(shark,'It will be a shark.').
reply(goldfish,'It must be a goldfish.').
reply(mouse,'The animal is probably a mouse.').

/* END */

Chapter 14

3. putlist([]).
    putlist([L | Lt]):-assert(element(L)),putlist(Lt).

4. caps(Lc,Uc):-name(Lc,[ASC]),ASC>64,ASC<91,NewASC is ASC+32,
    name(Uc,[NewASC]).
    caps(Ch,Ch).

Chapter 15

1. The rule to test a palindromic list is amazingly simple:

    palindrome(List):-reverse(List,List).

    We also need reverse from the chapter above:

    reverse (L1,L2):-rev(L1,[],L2).
    rev([],L,L).
    rev([X | L],L2,L3):-rev(L,[X | L2],L3).

2. pal:-write('Enter your word: '),read(Word),
    name(Word,List),palindrome(List).

    This will change Word into a list of its ASCII codes, List, then test this list of integers and answer yes if it is a palindrome.

3. convert([],[]).
    convert([L | Lt],[Q | Qt]):-L>64,L<92,Q is L+32,convert(Lt,Qt).
    convert([L | Lt],[L | Qt]):-convert(Lt,Qt).

4. The program becomes:

    pal:-write('Enter your word: '),read(Word),
    name(Word,List),convert(List,NewList),
    palindrome(NewList).

Chapter 16

```
/* KNOWLEDGE BASE (Read in as separate file) */

/* Title fact */

title('** ARE YOU A PSYCHOPATH ? **').

/* Total number of questions */

no_of_questions(10).

/* Facts to make loan decision */

decide_loan(Total):- Total < 4,
    write('You are fairly normal.'),nl.

decide_loan(Total):- Total < 7,
    write('You are unusually assertive.'),nl.

decide_loan(_):-write('You are a raving psychopath.'),nl.

/* Text for questions */
text(1,'1.    Your memories of your early childhood are:').
text(1,'      a.   A time of vivid fantasy').
text(1,'      b.   None existent').
text(1,'      c.   Some good times, some bad').

text(2,'2.    You stop fancying your lover and start a new ').
text(2,'      affair. How do you explain the loss of desire?').
text(2,'      a.   I have converted to a religion which').
text(2,'           demands celibacy').
text(2,'      b.   It''s just one of those things').
text(2,'      c.   Probably something to do with my relations').
text(2,'           with my parents').

text(3,'3.    The boss expresses vehement disapproval of a').
text(3,'      plan you and a colleague cooked up together.').
text(3,'      Do you:').
text(3,'      a.   Defend the bits you advocated, but').
text(3,'           criticise your colleague''s ideas').
text(3,'      b.   Keep as silent as possible and leave your').
text(3,'           colleague to do all the talking').
text(3,'      c.   Recognise that nothing will change the').
text(3,'           boss and jettison the plan').

text(4,'4.    You see the boss taking a competitor for a job').
text(4,'      you want out to lunch. Do you:').
text(4,'      a.   Have no feelings about it').
text(4,'      b.   fear that the boss favours the competitor').
text(4,'      c.   Suspect the boss is plotting with your').
text(4,'           competitor by advising on the interview').

text(5,'5.    A series of calamities hits you over a six').
text(5,'      month period. Do you:').
text(5,'      a.   Feel angry but powerless').
```

```
text(5,'      b.    Contemplate revenge on various adversaries').
text(5,'      c.    Wonder what you did to deserve it and get').
text(5,'            mildly depressed').

text(6,'6.    Your basic view of people is that they are:').
text(6,'      a.    Animals with souls but largely driven').
text(6,'            by instinct').
text(6,'      b.    Totally different from an animal and').
text(6,'            far superior').
text(6,'      c.    More machines than people, motivated by').
text(6,'            pursuit of wealth, status, sex and power').

text(7,'7.    As a driver you:').
text(7,'      a.    Have been had up for a large number').
text(7,'            of offences').
text(7,'      b.    Bend the rules, but only if you"re sure').
text(7,'            you won"t get caught').
text(7,'      c.    Have an obsession about having to drive').
text(7,'            large cars').

text(8,'8.    In a war you would be best suited as:').
text(8,'      a.    An entertainer of the troops').
text(8,'      b.    A spy').
text(8,'      c.    A frontline fighter').

text(9,'9.    Your attitude to stimulants is:').
text(9,'      a.    A drink? yes. Drugs? yes. Can"t get').
text(9,'            enough because').
text(9,'            neither seems to affect me much').
text(9,'      b.    A drink helps me in social situations').
text(9,'      c.    I love them but they make me act').
text(9,'            peculiarly.').

text(10,'10. Your attitude to sex is:').
text(10,'     a.    It"s a way of getting love').
text(10,'     b.    The more the merrier').
text(10,'     c.    The more partners the merrier').

/* Data facts for the answers given */

data(1,a,0).
data(1,b,1).
data(1,c,0).

data(2,a,1).
data(2,b,0).
data(2,c,0).

data(3,a,0).
data(3,b,0).
data(3,c,1).

data(4,a,0).
data(4,b,0).
data(4,c,1).
```

```
data(5,a,0).
data(5,b,1).
data(5,c,0).

data(6,a,0).
data(6,b,0).
data(6,c,1).

data(7,a,1).
data(7,b,0).
data(7,c,1).

data(8,a,0).
data(8,b,1).
data(8,c,0).

data(9,a,1).
data(9,b,0).
data(9,c,0).

data(10,a,0).
data(10,b,0).
data(10,c,1).

/* END */
```

Chapter 17

```
/* LIBRARY KEYWORD SEARCH PROGRAM */

/* Main program (ended with 'stop') */

go:-getword([]).

getword([stop,'.']):-write('Goodbye!'),nl,nl.
getword(_):-write('Enter some keywords: '),nl,nl,
    getsent(Key),test(Key),nl,nl,getword(Key).

test([stop,'.']).
test(Key):-book(Keywords),
    member(X,Keywords),member(X,Key),
    write('The book is: '),writesent(Keywords).
test(_):-write('Sorry, no book.')

/* Output rules – versions of 'writesent' which puts capital on every
word */

writesent([]).
writesent([L|Lt]):-name(L,[Z|Zt]),Y is Z–32,name(X,[Y|Zt]),
    write(X),write(' '),writesent(Lt).

/* Standard rules */

member(X,[X|_]).
member(X,[_|Lt]):-member(X,Lt).

delete(_,[],[]).
delete(X,[X|L],M):-!,delete(X,L,M).
```

```
delete(X,[Y|L1],[Y|L2]):-delete(X,L1,L2).
```

/* Database of keywords */

```
book([jane,eyre]).
book([the,bible]).
book([encyclopaedia,brittanica]).
book([jurassic,park]).
book([brighton,rock]).
```

/* Note: The rules for getsent are required as well */

/* END */

Chapter 18

/* PERIODIC TABLE */

```
go:- write('* PERIODIC TABLE *'),nl,nl,
    repeat,menu.
```

```
menu:-
    write('a. List all the element names'),nl,
    write('b. Give all the data for a named element'),nl,
    write('c. Give all data for an element by At.No.'),nl,
    write('d. End program'),nl,nl,
    read(X),choice(X),
    !,X=d.
```

```
choice(a):-element(Name,Symbol,Num,Wt),
    write(Name),nl,write(Symbol),nl,
    write(Num),nl,write(Wt),nl,nl,fail.
    choice(a).
```

```
choice(b):-write('Which element? '),read(Name),nl,
    element(Name,Symbol,Num,Wt),
    write(Name),nl,write(Symbol),nl,
    write(Num),nl,write(Wt),nl,nl.
```

```
choice(c):-write('Which number? '),read(Num),nl,
    element(Name,Symbol,Num,Wt),
    write(Name),nl,write(Symbol),nl,
    write(Num),nl,write(Wt),nl,nl.
```

```
choice(d):-write('Goodbye!'),nl.
choice(_):-write('Please try again.'),nl.
```

/* Database for elements */

```
element(hydrogen,'H',1,1.008).
element(helium,'He',2,4.003).
element(lithium,'Li',3,6.941).
element(beryllium,'Be',4,9.012).
element(boron,'B',5,10.810).
```

Chapter 19

The data for the problem can be written as follows:

```
connected(a,b).
connected(b,j).
connected(j,i).
connected(i,h).
connected(h,g).
connected(g,f).
connected(g,k).
connected(f,k).
connected(k,d).
connected(c,d).
connected(d,e).
connected(e,k).

start_room(a).
end_room(e).
```

We can use the **getroute** program, slightly modified so that it is run from a program rule rather than the interpreter.

```
/* ROUTE THROUGH A MAZE */

go:- start_room(S),end_room(E),
     getroute(S,[E],Route),writelist(Route),nl,fail.
go:-nl.

getroute(Start,[Start | Rest],[Start | Rest]).

getroute(Start,[Room | Rest],Route):-
     connected(Next,Room),not member(Next,Rest),
     getroute(Start,[Next,Room | Rest],Route).

getroute(Start,[Room | Rest],Route):-
     connected(Room,Next),not member(Next,Rest),
     getroute(Start,[Next,Room | Rest],Route).

member(X,[X | L]):-!.
member(X,[Y | L]):-member(X,L).

writelist([]).
writelist([L | Lt]):-write(L),write(' '),writelist(Lt).

/* END */
```

Notice the device used here to enable the start and end room to be changed easily, by putting them in the database as separate facts.

Chapter 20

A possible solution is as follows. To test, run the spreadsheet program, fill a column with numbers, end, then run 'total_column'.

```
/* Rule to total a spreadsheet column */

total_column:-
    write('Enter column to total: '),read(C),Col is C+1,
    total(Col,1,Total),write(Total),nl.

total(_,7,0).
total(Col,Row,Total):-NewRow is Row+1,
    total(Col,NewRow,SubTotal),
    functor(X,spread,11),
    X=..[spread,Row|_],
    call(X),
    arg(Col,X,Val),
    Total is SubTotal+Val.
```

Chapter 21

Here is a suggested solution:

```
/* TRANSPORT EXPERT SYSTEM WITH DEFINED OPERATORS */

/* Operator definitions */

:-op(1200,xfx,then).
:-op(1100,xfx,if).
:-op(1100,fx,if).
:-op(1000,xfy,or).
:-op(900,xfy,and).

/* Main program rule */

go:- write('Enter a feature: '),read(F1),
    write('Enter another feature (n if none): '),read(F2),
    findtransport(Transport,F1,F2),
    write('Transport is a '),write(Transport),nl,nl,nl.
go:- write('Transport is unknown.'),nl,nl.

/* Finds a type of transport for given features. These rules
define the cause and effect use of if and then */

findtransport(T,F1,F2):-(if X then T),check(X,F1,F2).
findtransport(T,F1,F2):-(T if X),check(X,F1,F2).

/* Following allow for different phrasing */

check(X,F1,F2):-X=(F1 and F2).
check(X,F1,F2):-X=(F2 and F1).
check(X,F1,_):-X=(F1 or _).
check(X,_,F2):-X=(F2 or _).
check(X,F1,_):-X=(_ or F1).
check(X,_,F2):-X=(_ or F2).
check(X,F1,_):-X=F1.
check(X,_,F2):-X=F2.
```

/* Transport facts */

if land and sea then hovercraft.
road_transport if wheels and land.
if wings then aeroplane.
ship if floats.

/* END */

Chapter 22

A possible solution is:

```
sentence —> subject, verb, predicate.
sentence —> subject, verb.

subject —> noun_phrase(subject).

predicate —> noun_phrase(object), preposition,
    noun_phrase(object).

predicate —> noun_phrase(object).

noun_phrase(Position) —> determiner, noun(Position).

noun(Position) —> [Noun], { position(Position,Noun) }.

determiner —> [the].

verb —> [eats].
verb —> [puts].

preposition —> [on].

position(subject,man).
position(object,orange).
position(object,book).
position(object,table).
```

Appendix 2
test yourself solutions

Test yourself: *Prolog basics*

(These solutions are not always the only ones.)

1. The name Prolog stands for **PROgramming in LOGic**.

2. Prolog is unlike the more usual procedural languages in being a **declarative** language.

3. Prolog consists of two main parts, an **interpreter** where queries are entered and a **database** of clauses.

4. There are two basic types of clause in Prolog, **facts** and **rules**.

5. Prolog answers a query entered at the ?- prompt by **matching** it with clauses in the database.

6. A fact in Prolog consists of a **predicate** and one or more **arguments** in brackets after it.

7. A rule in Prolog consists of a **head** and a **body** connected by a :- operator.

8. For a rule to succeed, all the subgoals must **succeed also**.

9. The process of giving a variable a value during a search is called **instantiation**.

10. Names of variables in Prolog are distinguished from atoms by **starting with a capital letter**.

11. The scope of a variable in Prolog, or the area within which its name is valid, is **just the rule it is used in**.

12. Values of variables are normally passed between rules as arguments.

13. The underscore in Prolog is called the anonymous variable and is used as a **variable which the interpreter does not instantiate**. (ie. Its value is unimportant.)

14. Prolog continues searching for solutions even after a sub-goal fails by a process called **backtracking**.

15. This results in a searching strategy called **depth first searching**.

16. Say briefly what the following predicates do when used in a Prolog program:

save(Filename)	**Saves the whole database**
tell(Filename)	**Opens Filename for output**
told	**Closes current output file**
see(Filename)	**Opend Filename for input**
seen	**Closes current input file**
get0(Ch)	**Gets ASCII code from keyboard**

17. The function of the predicate **fail** in Prolog is that it always fails and is used to **cause backtracking**.

18. The predicate **repeat** has a special use in Prolog, which is **to stop backtracking and send execution forward again**.

19. A semantic net can be converted to facts quite simply by writing the **links as predicates** and writing the **nodes as arguments**.

20. For the following database, write rules as follows:

    ```
    country(uk,london,europe,english).
    country(zaire,kinshasa,africa,swahili).
    country(kenya,nairobi,africa,swahili).
    country(usa,washington,north_america,english).
    ```

    (a) A rule **countries** (no arguments) which writes out a list of the names only of the countries in the database, then succeeds:

    ```
    countries:-country(Country,_,_,_),
        write(Country),nl,fail.
    countries.
    ```

    (b) A rule caps which writes out a list of the cities in Europe where English is spoken, then succeeds:

    ```
    caps:-country(_,City,europe,english),
        write(City),nl,fail.
    caps.
    ```

Test yourself: *Recursion and lists*

1. The 'respectable' logical method of achieving repetition in a Prolog program is **using recursion**.

2. It is stopped by placing a rule above the rule which repeats, which is called a **boundary rule or condition**.

3. Write a rule which keeps saying 'Try again!' until the atom 'stop' is read in, in two ways:

   (a) using 'repeat':

   ```
   go:-repeat,write('Try again! '),read(Atom),
       Atom = stop.
   ```

   (b) using recursion:

   ```
   go(stop).
   go(_):-write('Try again! '),read(Atom),
       go(Atom).
   ```

4. For a database of people, which of the following would be most suitable?

   A. bill(smith,25,person).
   B. person([bill,smith],25).
   C. person(Bill,Smith,25).
   D. person(['Smith','Bill'],25).
   E. person(bill,smith,25).

   … because it has names with capital letters and allows any number of names.

5. Which of the following would be the **least** convenient data structure if it was required to list people with red hair?

   A. hair(mary,red).
   B. mary(hair,red).
   C. has(mary,[red,hair]).
   D. has(mary,red_hair).
   E. has(mary,hair(red)).

   … because the database would need a different fact for each name, and it would be tricky to list them using either **fail** or **findall**.

6. How are values normally passed from one rule to another in Prolog?

    A. As lists.
    B. As asserted facts.
    C. As variables.
    D. As global variables.
    E. As arguments.

7. Which of the following cannot be a valid list?

    A. [L| [X| Xt]]
    B. [a| [a, b, c]]
    C. [a, b | [b, c, d]]
    D. [M|Mt [ ]]
    E. Joe.

    Incorrect syntax – it could be written [M|[Mt,[]]], for example.

8. What does the following code do?

    enigma([]):- write('.'),nl.
    enigma([L|Lt]):- write(' '),name(L,[Z|Zt]),Y is Z-32,
    name(X,[Y|Zt]),write(X),enigma(Lt).

    A. Writes out a list vertically.
    B. Writes out a list, converting any capitals to lowercase.
    C. Writes out a list with capitals for all atoms.
    D. Writes out a list with capitals for all atoms and a full stop at the end.
    E. Writes out a list as a sentence, with a capital at the start and a full stop.

9. If a database contains facts of the type

    person ('Sherlock Holmes', 'Baker Street', 42).

    … which of the following would produce a list of streets?

    A. findall(person(_,Address, _)).
    B. findall(Address, person(_, _,Address), List).
    C. findall(X, person(_, X, _),Address).
    D. findall(X, person(_, _, X),Address).
    E. person(_, Address, _),fail.

10. Look at the following rule:

    splitlist ([ ], [ ], [ ]).
    splitlist ([L,X|Xt], L1, L2):-
    L1 = [L|Yt], L2 = [X|Zt],
    splitlist (Xt, Yt, Zt).

This rule splits a list into two others, using recursion. It does this by:

A.   Counting the terms in the list, dividing by two and separating off this number of terms.

B.   Repeatedly taking the head of the list until the first half is separated.

C.   Repeatedly taking the last term in the list until the last half is separated.

D.   Repeatedly taking the last two terms and putting each into a different new list.

E.   **Repeatedly taking the first two terms and putting each into a different new list.**

11.   Study the following simple but complete program in Prolog.

```
go:- read(In),
     not In = [end],
     goto(In,Out),
     write(Out),nl,
     go.

go.

goto([],[]).
goto([H|T],[L|M]):-
     do(H,L),goto(T,M).

do(are,no).
do(you,'I am').
do(man,woman).
do(computer,person).
do(no,yes).
do(end,start).
do(X,X).
```

Which would you best describe this program as?

A.   An expert system.

B.   An artificial intelligence program.

C.   A natural language program.

D.   **An Eliza type program.**

E.   A problem-solving program.

12.   What does the input to the program in Question 11 need to be?

A.   A single word.

B.   A sentence.

C.   **A list of words.**

D.   A list containing one word.

E.   A list of words that are in the 'do' facts.

13. How will the program in Question 11 respond to the following input assuming that it is entered in a correct manner according to your answer to Question 12:

   are you a computer

   A. no.
   B. no I am a computer
   C. no I am a person
   D. no I am person
   E. (with an error message).

14. The following is a very simple expert system:

   ```
   go:- get_feature(start),
        animal_is(Animal),
        write('It is a '),
        write(Animal),nl.

   get_feature(end).
   get_feature(_):-
        write('What does the animal have?'),read(Feature),
           assert(feature(Feature)),get_feature(Feature).

   animal_is(tiger):-it_is(mammal),feature(stripes),
        feature(carnivore).
   animal_is(penguin):-it_is(bird),feature(swim),
        feature(cannot_fly).
   animal_is(unknown).
   ```

   A problem with this is

   A. It will crash if the animal is not in the database.
   B. It tests for several features but only reads in one.
   C. It will crash if the animal is spelt wrongly.
   D. It does not tell the user which features will be recognised.
   E. It will not work if more than two features are entered.

   … all the others are incorrect.

15. In Question 14, which of the following entries will be recognised?

   A. bird swims
   B. mammal stripes swims
   C. bird stripes cannot_fly swims
   D. mammal stripes swims carnivore
   E. bird swims cannot_fly stripes

   Note that swims will not be accepted – the rules use swim.

16. In Question 14, which of the following would not improve this program?

    A. Adding many more rules.
    B. Ensuring that all rules have just two features.
    C. Offering features in a menu to choose from.
    D. Including negative features in the rules.
    E. Enabling the system to learn new rules.

    At present the program will accept any number, a more flexible feature.

17. Consider the following rule which counts the elements in a list.

    count([],0).
    count([_ | Lt],N):- count(Lt,M),N is 1 + M.

    Now consider Prolog's response to a query as follows:

    A. ? – count([a,b,c],N).
    B. count([a| [b,c],N):- count([b,c],M), N is 1 + M.
    C. count([b| [c],N):- count([c],M), N is 1 + M.
    D. count([c| []],N):- count([],M), N is 1 + M.
    E. count([],0).

    Which is the first line in which all the variables become instantiated?

    E is the first instance of the rule which succeeds. The recursion then 'unwinds' through the rules in the order E, D, C, B, A, instantiating the variables, reaching D first. (In line D, M = 0, N = 1.)

18. Which of the following can not be used as a basis for repetition?

    A. backtracking.
    B. instantiation.
    C. recursion.
    D. fail.
    E. !, fail.

19. Which of the following is not one of the reasons for the existence of '!' in Prolog? (When it is used correctly.)

    A. It makes programs more efficient.
    B. It makes programs more readable.
    C. It prevents stack failures.
    D. It can be used for iterative constructions.
    E. It sometimes provides a short solution to an otherwise difficult problem.

20. Which of the following reserved words from procedural languages has no equivalent in Prolog?

    A. IF.   Equivalent :-
    B. GOTO.
    C. AND.   Equivalent ,
    D. OR.   Equivalent ;
    E. END.   Equivalent .

Test yourself: *Sample examination questions*

Question 1

(a)   circle(R):-Circumf is 2*3.142*R*R,
            write('Circumference is: '),write(Circumf),nl,
            Area is 3.142*R*R,
            write('Area is: '),write(Area),nl.   [3 marks]

(b)   go:-write('Enter radius: '),read(R),not R=0,
            circle(R),go.

        go.   [5 marks]

(c)   *The fact could be:*

                stock(Item,Wprice,Rprice,Number).
                eg. stock(potatoes_kg,45,65,125).

        A possible program solution:

                menu:-write('a. Enter item.'),nl,
                    write('b. Delete item.'),nl,
                    write('c. Details of an item.'),nl,
                    write('d. List all items.'),nl,
                    write('e. Exit.'),nl,nl,
                    read(Choice),option(Choice).

                option(a):-write('Name of item: '),read(Item),
                    write('Wholesale price: '),read(Wprice),
                    write('Retail price: '),read(Rprice),
                    write('Number in stock: '),read(Number),
                    assertz(stock(Item,Wprice,Rprice,Number)),menu.

                option(b):-write('Item to delete: '),read(Item),
                    retract(stock(Item,_,_,_)),menu.

                option(c):-write('Item required: '),read(Item),
                    stock(Item,Wprice,Rprice,Number),
                    write(Wprice),nl,write(Rprice),nl,
                    write(Number),nl,getreturn,menu.

```
option(d):-write(;Item required: '),read(Item),
    stock(Item,Wprice,Rprice,Number),
    write(Wprice),nl,write(Rprice),nl,
    write(Number),nl,fail.

option(d):-getreturn,menu.

option(e):-write('Goodbye!'),nl.

option(_):-write('Please try again.'),nl,getreturn,menu.

getreturn:-write('Press return to continue.'),nl,
    get0(_).
```

Alternatively this can be done using cut, for more marks.   [12 marks]

Question 2

(a) *Labelled links on the net can be written as predicate names, and nodes as arguments. The conversion of the net to Prolog code is thus almost mechanical.*

[3 marks]

(b)

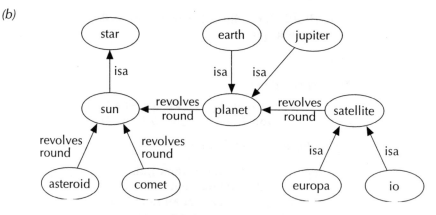

[8 marks]

(c)   isa(sun,star).

isa(mercury,planet).
isa(venus,planet).
isa(earth,planet).
isa(mars,planet).
isa(jupiter,planet).
isa(saturn,planet).
isa(neptune,planet).
isa(uranus,planet).
isa(pluto,planet).

isa(io,satellite).
isa(europa,satellite).
isa(ganymede,satellite).

isa(callisto,satellite).

revolves_round(sun,planet).
revolves_round(sun,comet).
revolves_round(sun,asteroid).
revolves_round(planet,satellite). [4 marks]

(d) ?- revolves_round(sun,europa)... *would give answer 'no'.*

This is anomalous as Europa actually revolves round Jupiter which revolves round the Sun, so Europa also revolves round the Sun. In fact even

?-revolves_round(sun,jupiter).

would give 'no'.

Rules are required in the database to correct this, e.g.

revolves_round(sun,X):-isa(X,Y),revolves_round(sun,Y).
revolves_round(sun,X):-isa(X,Y),revolves_round(Y,Z),
    revolves_round(sun,Z).

This would give 'yes' to both the above. [5 marks]

Question 3

(a) See the relevant chapters. Some points:

Fact – predicate name with arguments in parenthesis. Used to store data.
[2 marks]

Rule – a fact as its head with a body added consisting of subgoals which must all succeed for the rule to succeed. Expresses relationships between data.
[2 marks]

List – a collection of objects contained in square brackets [], following certain rules for their manipulation. The equivalent in Prolog of an array in other languages.
[2 marks]

(b) (i) find_parts(X):-part_of(X,Y),write(Y),nl,fail.
find_parts(_). [3 marks]

(ii) need_help:-symptom(Message,Symptom),
    write(Message),nl,
    read(Reply),Reply=y,
    write('The parts to look at are: '),nl,
    parts_concerned(Symptom,List),
    write_list(List).
need_help:-write('Sorry, cant help.'),nl.

write_list([]).
write_list([L|Lt]):-write(L),nl,writelist(Lt).

. . . or something similar. [6 marks]

(c) *Input could be improved – all symptoms will not fall into the 'y/n' category. Need a recursive loop to collect several symptoms. Main limitation is that the program only indicates parts concerned – it does not identify what is wrong. To expand the program to do this would require a different data structure, with rules to analyse a collection of symptoms.*

[5 marks]

Question 4

(a) **Backtracking** *is the mechanism in Prolog whereby when a subgoal fails, execution goes back to the previous subgoal and moves on to the next example of it in the database. Execution then moves forward again and tries again the subgoal which failed.*

Instantiation *is the process in Prolog whereby a variable is given a value so as to make a question and a clause in the database match. A variable can be unified with an integer, an atom, a structure, etc.*

The effect of the **cut (!)** *in a rule is to prevent backtracking. As no backtracking can take place past the cut, markers to previous subgoals are cleared from memory when the cut is passed. As execution cannot backtrack past the cut, it jumps back to the point where the rule was called from.*

[5 marks]

(b) *The first clause will not match because [a,b,d] is not an empty list [], the second because [H|[]] means a list of one term, and [a,b,d] has three terms. The third clause matches thus:*

    pred([a | [b,d]],X):-pred([b,d],X).

This calls pred again recursively:

    pred([b | [d]],X):-pred([d],X).   **(Third rule again)**
    pred([d | []],d).   **(Second rule)**

The final value of X will be d. This is a rule to get the last element in a list.

[5 marks]

(c) *The following is a solution:*

    repeats(Item,[],0).
    repeats(Item,[Item | Rest],N):-repeats(Item,Rest,N1),N is N1+1.
    repeats(Item,[_ | Rest],N):-repeats(Item,Rest,N).

This counts through the list (Arg2) recursively (third rule). If it finds an example of **Item** *it increments the counter when the recursion 'unwinds' (second rule). When it reaches the empty list [], N is 0 (first rule).*

[5 marks]

(d) *Among others:*

There are virtually no control structures in Prolog – no repeat loops, and no while or for...do loops. Repetition is by recursion. In Prolog the infor-

mation relating to a problem is expressed in a database, and the problem is then solved by querying the database. The language does much of the work of searching the database. A 'program' in Prolog consists of a database of facts and rules. There are no lists of instructions as such for the language to work through. Prolog is declarative rather than procedural, though it has procedural features.

[5 marks]

Question 5

```
/* Main rule to read in symptoms, check for a medication, and write it
out */

go:-getsymptoms(any),check(Medication),
    write('The medication is: '),write(Medication).

/* Reads in the symptoms and asserts them as symptom facts */

getsymptoms(end).
getsymptoms(_):-write('Enter symptom (end to end): '),
    read(Symptom),assert(symptom(Symptom)),
    getsymptoms(Symptom).

/* Makes a list of all symptoms recorded, and finds a
medication that does not aggravate another symptom */

check(Medication):-findall(S,symptom(S),SymptomList),
    relieves(Medication,Symptom),
    member(Symptom,SymptomList),
    not( aggravate(Medication,OtherSymptom),
        member(OtherSymptom,SymptomList) ).

check('None found.').
```

This solution uses **member**, a 'low-level predicate' which succeeds if its first argument is a member of a list, its second argument. It is used to check that **Symptom** and **OtherSymptom** are members of the list of symptoms.

[20 marks]

Question 6

(a)
```
getspace:-nl,write('Space to continue.'),
    repeat,get0(Ch),Ch=32.
```
[5 marks]

(b)
```
getspace:-nl,write('Space to continue.'),
    get0(Ch),getspace2(Ch).

getspace2(32).
getspace2(_):-getspace.
```

[5 marks]

(c) **getkeypress(Atom,Char):-name(Atom,List),**
   repeat,
   get0(ASC),convert(ASC,NewASC),
   (member(ASC,List) ; member(NewASC,List)),
   name(Char,[NewASC]).

convert(ASC,NewASC):-ASC>96,ASC<123,NewASC is ASC-32,!.
convert(ASC,ASC).

*The rule converts the atom **Atom** to a list of ASCII codes, then reads in an ASCII code **ASC**. It uses **convert** to convert this to upper case, **NewASC**, if it was lower case. It then tests whether either **ASC** or **NewASC** is a member of the list of ASCII codes, thus being case independent. If this test fails, it backtracks to read in another ASCII code. When a satisfactory ASCII code has been read in, the upper case ASCII code is converted to a character using name and returned as Char.*

***name** is a standard built-in predicate which converts anatom to a list of ASCII codes and vice versa.*

***repeat** always succeeds and stops backtracking. Here it will stop the rule ever failing, so that eventually it must get a character in the right range.*

***member** is a common predicate, the built-in predicate on in LPA Prolog, which tests whether an object is a member of a list.*

[10 marks]

Bibliography

Some introductory books on Prolog

W.F. Clocksin & C.S. Mellish, *Programming in Prolog*, Springer-Verlag, 1984

J.B. Rogers, *A Prolog Primer*, Addison Wesley, 1986

C. Marcus, *Prolog Programming*, Addison Wesley, 1986

A.G. Hamilton, *The Professional Programmer's Guide to Prolog*, Pitman, 1989

More advanced books

L. Sterling & E. Shapiro, *The Art of Prolog*, M.I.T., 1986

I. Bratko, *Prolog Programming for Artificial Intelligence*, Addison Wesley, 1986

K.A. Bowen, *Prolog and Expert Systems*, McGraw Hill, 1991

A. Gal, G. Lapalme, P. Saint-Dizier & H. Somers, *Prolog for Natural Language Processing*, John Wiley, 1991

There are many books on Prolog now, the above being just a selection. There are also many specialist books on Artificial Intelligence and Expert Systems.

Useful addresses

Association for Logic Programming (ALP)

to join ALP contact Dr Krysia Broda, Department of Computing, Imperial College, 180 Queen's Gate, London.)

LPA Prolog

can be obtained from Logic Programming Associates Ltd, Studio 4, Royal Victoria Patriotic Building, Trinity Road, London SW18 3SX, UK.

Public Domain or PD Prolog

free, and available through shareware or Automata & Design Associates, 1570 Arran Way, Dresher, Pennsylvania 19025, USA.

Index

In this index, the Prolog predicates which are part of the Edinburgh/Clocksin and Mellish standard, like **write** and **read**, are shown in bold. Page numbers which refer to the most substantial discussion of an item are shown in bold.